The Thatcher Revolution

The Thatcher Revolution

Margaret Thatcher, John Major, Tony Blair, and the Transformation of Modern Britain, 1979–2001

Earl A. Reitan

ROWMAN & LITTLEFIELD PUBLISHERS, INC.
Lanham • Boulder • New York • Oxford

ROWMAN & LITTLEFIELD PUBLISHERS, INC.

Published in the United States of America
by Rowman & Littlefield Publishers, Inc.
A Member of the Rowman & Littlefield Publishing Group
4720 Boston Way, Lanham, Maryland 20706
www.rowmanlittlefield.com

PO Box 317
Oxford
OX2 9RU, UK

British Library Cataloguing in Publication Information Available

Library of Congress Cataloging-in-Publication Data

Reitan, E. A. (Earl Aaron), 1925–
  The Thatcher revolution : Margaret Thatcher, John Major, Tony
Blair, and the Transformation of Modern Britain, 1979–2001 / Earl A. Reitan.
      p. cm.
Includes bibliographical references and index.
  ISBN 0-7425-2202-4 (alk. paper) — ISBN 0-7425-2203-2 (pbk. : alk.
paper)
  1. Great Britain—Politics and government—1979–1997. 2. Great
Britain—Politics and government—1997– 3. Thatcher, Margaret. 4.
Major, John Roy, 1943– 5. Blair, Tony, 1953– I. Title.
  DA589.7 .R45 2002
  941.085—dc21
                                                      2002008628
Printed in the United States of America

⊗™ The paper used in this publication meets the minimum requirements of
American National Standard for Information Sciences—Permanence of Paper for
Printed Library Materials, ANSI/NISO Z39.48-1992.

~

Contents

~

Preface

The word "revolution" is a slippery one, but if the word means anything, it means changes of a fundamental nature in a comparatively brief period of time. The word fits the American, French, and Russian Revolutions; maybe the Industrial Revolution, maybe not. The changes that took place in Britain from 1979, when Margaret Thatcher became prime minister, to 2001, when the first ministry of Tony Blair ended, certainly were revolutionary. The Thatcher Revolution broke down institutionalized barriers to development and opened a failing country to the forces of globalization. Britain became a leader, not a laggard, in the emerging world civilization of the late twentieth century.

This book is a revision, expansion, and extension of a book published in 1997 entitled *Tory Radicalism: Margaret Thatcher, John Major, and the Transformation of Modern Britain, 1979–1997*. It is more than a new edition; all chapters of the earlier book have been revised, some of them extensively, and three new chapters have been added. The book presents a fair-minded account of the ideas commonly called "Thatcherism" and the policies adopted by three prime ministers to implement them. It is not scholarly in the conventional sense, although it has been written by a professional historian. It is based on readily available sources. Special attention has been given to the rise of "New Labour," as led and defined by Neil Kinnock and Tony Blair. Three new chapters cover the first Blair ministry and consider the extent to which the objectives of New Labour were achieved. The book has been written by an American historian for North

American readers. For British readers it will provide an American point of view.

During my more than four decades as a professor of British history, my family and I have been well treated on our many visits to Britain. We have enjoyed Britain's splendid public facilities as well as the hospitality of individuals. Special thanks are due for the help and encouragement of British historians, who share with American scholars in the joint enterprise of learning, teaching, and writing about British history.

Earl A. Reitan
Normal, Illinois

~

Introduction

Britain Victorious, 1945

On May 8, 1945, Britain rejoiced at the end of the war in Europe. Britain was a victorious power—an integral part of the alliance, dominated by the United States and the Soviet Union, that had won the greatest and most complete victory of modern times.

When he became prime minister in the dark days of 1940, Winston Churchill formed a coalition government that included the leaders of all three political parties: Conservative, Labour, and Liberal. When the war in Europe ended, Churchill wanted to preserve the coalition government to complete the war against Japan, but the Labour members refused. Public opinion overwhelmingly favored an election, which would begin the process of putting Britain back on a peacetime footing.

During the war, parliamentary elections had been suspended. The election that took place in June 1945 was the first in ten years. Churchill had led Britain through its darkest hours and to its greatest victory, but the British people did not see him as the man who could fulfill their aspirations for the postwar world.

The leader of the Labour Party was Clement Attlee, who had served loyally and well in Churchill's wartime Cabinet. The Labour Party offered a specific platform: a planned economy, nationalization of major industries, full employment, extensive building of houses, a national health service, and a comprehensive system of social security.

Although the Conservative Party manifesto included similar items, Churchill campaigned poorly, railing against the dangers of socialism. The result was a landslide victory for Labour, which gained a strong majority of the seats in the House of Commons.

The Labour Revolution

The polity that turned to Margaret Thatcher in 1979 was shaped by the British Labour Party in the years following World War II. A new and vastly expanded role for government was justified by two vivid memories: World War II had shown the capacity of the state to organize and direct the resources of the nation to the achievement of national objectives; the Depression and mass unemployment of the 1930s had made clear, it seemed, the faults of capitalism and private enterprise. Furthermore, only the state could supply the leadership and capital needed for postwar reconstruction. Britain's factories had been inefficient and run-down before the war, and rebuilding or repairing them had been impossible under wartime conditions. Britain had lost many of its prewar markets. Much of its merchant marine was at the bottom of the sea. Overseas investments, which had been an important part of the national income before the war, had been liquidated to help pay for the war. Until the United States came to the aid of Britain and Western Europe with the Marshall Plan, Britain's condition was desperate.

The leadership of the Labour Party was comprised of two main groups: well-educated, middle-class socialists and the leaders of the trade unions. It was an unstable combination, because socialist ideology consorted uneasily with trade union pragmatism concerning jobs and wages. The economic policy of Labour was based on planning, which was regarded as superior to the capitalistic, market-oriented economy that had failed dramatically in the 1930s. Planning was expected to give coherence to Labour's plans to rebuild Britain, including nationalization of basic industries ("the commanding heights of the economy"), full employment, trade union power, and an expanded welfare state to provide security "from the cradle to the grave."

Labour's plans for reform were derailed by the challenges of postwar reconstruction. After six years of heroic effort and wartime stringency, the British people felt that they were entitled to a better life. Instead, they were asked to make additional sacrifices until exports revived and Britain could pay its way in the world. In 1947 declining productivity in the mines, a shortage of railroad cars to move the coal, and an exceptionally severe winter combined to create a fuel shortage. Factories were closed, idling millions of workers and undercutting the effort to increase exports. Rations of basic foods, such as bread, potatoes, meat, and sugar were tightened. Households were deprived of electricity, widely used for home heating, for five hours each day. Probably more than anything else, the fuel crisis of 1947 led to a loss of public confidence in the Labour government.

A special problem was the shortage of dollars. With much of the world in shambles, the United States was the only country that could provide capital goods, food, fiber, petroleum, and other products necessary for survival and reconstruction. Dollars were needed to purchase these goods, but Britain was unable to earn dollars through exports until the economy recovered. During the war, American Lend-Lease had maintained the British standard of living at an acceptable level, but that ended with the war and an American loan went quickly. A desperate effort ensued to obtain dollars and apply them to essential uses. Imports of American movies, for example, were restricted to save dollars for more important needs. Additional resources were obtained from the Commonwealth countries, which still used the British pound sterling.

With Britain as a world center of financial services, the strength and reliability of the pound had always been a major consideration of British governments. This priority did not change with Labour, which sacrificed many of its domestic goals to preserve the international value of sterling. When postwar inflation weakened the pound abroad, Sir Stafford Cripps, chancellor of the Exchequer, bit the bullet and devalued the pound by about 30 percent, which made exports cheaper and imports more expensive. Although this step was damaging to the City (the financial district of London), it was beneficial to manufacturing and the economy began to revive.

In the meantime, the Labour government pursued its agenda in a hit-and-miss fashion. Attempts at economic planning were devoted mainly to managing the postwar crisis, and long-term economic planning fell by the wayside. The socialist principles of the Labour Party were an embarrassment to busy ministers, and the implementation of socialism was halfhearted at best. Nationalization was expected to bring order and efficiency to Britain's unprogressive and run-down industries and avoid a postwar crisis of unemployment. In actuality, postwar reconstruction ended the threat of unemployment. Most nationalizations were improvised to meet immediate needs, either to support failing industries, like coal, or to rationalize public utilities.

Nationalization of the Bank of England, which had long served as a quasi-public institution, was intended to give the government better control of the supply of money and credit, but in practice little changed. Nationalization of the fragmented and inefficient coal industry was intended to improve the production of the most important source of energy. Other industries taken into public ownership were the railroads, electricity, gas, seaports, overseas cables, buses, and most long-distance trucking. Compensation for run-down factories, mines, and railroads was generous. The iron and steel industry was nationalized in 1951, just as the Labour government was coming to a close.

The nationalized industries were organized in corporations under the control of boards that were expected to run them as a business while performing a better public service. In reality, ministers often interfered for political reasons, and some of these industries required heavy subsidies.

Apart from the change of ownership, the nationalized industries continued to be operated much as before. Despite the Labour Party's commitment to socialism, most of Labour's planning and controls were devoted to making an orderly transition from wartime direction and regulation to a peacetime economy. Britain remained a free-enterprise country and approximately 80 percent of the economy was privately owned and operated.

Labour's plans for centralized economic management required the cooperation of organized labor, the bedrock of the Labour Party. The British labor movement was fragmented into hundreds of unions, loosely united under an umbrella organization called the Trades Union Congress (TUC). Given the needs of reconstruction, one of Labour's objectives, full employment, had been met. The government's main problem was to persuade the unions to accept wage controls to curb inflation, while the main concern of the unions was to preserve free collective bargaining. Despite the promise of an era of industrial cooperation, after the first several years, the adversarial character of British industrial relations resumed.

The welfare state was the major achievement of the Labour government. An improved National Insurance system, based on contributions from employers and employees, paid benefits for unemployment, sickness, retirement, maternity, widows, and death. Family Allowances were introduced to assist the working poor in raising children. There was also a means-tested program of National Assistance for those who needed help for other reasons. Benefits were low, with the expectation that workers would save for retirement or "a rainy day." With a wide range of low-cost or free public services, modest benefits were thought to be sufficient.

Labour had promised health care for everyone, and fulfilled its promise by establishing the National Health Service (NHS), which essentially took over the medical facilities of the country. The NHS provided free medical, dental, and hospital care as well as free drugs, eyeglasses, and dentures. Individuals and families registered with doctors (general practitioners), who provided primary medical services, referring them to specialists (consultants) if necessary. Doctors, usually organized in partnerships, received a basic payment to maintain their facilities and a flat amount for each patient, whether ill or not. Most specialists practiced in hospitals, treating patients referred to them by the doctors. To satisfy the British Medical Association, doctors and specialists were permitted to supplement their incomes by treating private patients for fees, and beds were set aside in the hospitals for patients willing to pay personally.

In the boldest move of all, the local-authority hospitals were nationalized and funded out of general revenue. Regional hospital boards managed them. The hospitals became the greatest problem for the National Health Service. Most were old and expensive to replace, and their staff worked long hours for low pay in poor working conditions. With a few noteworthy exceptions, the mental hospitals were wretched. In its early years, the National Health Service was swamped by a vast backlog of unmet medical needs, and there were great shortages of medical resources. Despite many shortcomings, the NHS gave the British people far better medical care than they had received under private medicine.

One of the most pressing needs of the postwar period was to provide housing. People had been badly housed in prewar Britain, and bombing had wreaked great destruction of homes. Returning veterans were ready to marry and settle down. The Labour government committed substantial sums to subsidize the building of houses by the local authorities. In the next five years, the Labour government built more than a million houses. Labour also introduced extensive planning procedures for land use, to devote this scarce resource to the public benefit and avoid ugly urban sprawl.

Under Labour, education did not receive a high priority. The Education Act of 1944, passed by the wartime coalition government, promised free primary and secondary education for all, with an eventual school-leaving age of sixteen. Progress in this direction was limited by the existing stock of school buildings, many of them old and run-down, and the more pressing need for construction of housing and hospitals.

Within the Labour Party, strong differences of opinion existed concerning the class orientation of most schools. Students were examined at age eleven and sent to separate schools on the basis of the results. This practice created pronounced differences in the curricula and quality of the schools and tended to separate middle-class and lower-class children. Many Labour leaders had risen through the system and wanted to preserve and extend it. Others advocated "comprehensive schools" in which all children would attend together, thus breaking down the class-consciousness of Britain. This dispute, in one form or another, has continued to agitate the Labour Party to the present time.

Foreign Policy

With the end of World War II, the United States and the Soviet Union emerged as superpowers. Britain had been an important factor in World War II, especially in the early years, but after the war British foreign policy faced an uncertain future, as the Cold War came to dominate world affairs.

Foreign Secretary Ernest Bevin was a dominant figure in the Labour Party. He was a strong opponent of domestic communists, whom he had long battled in the labor movement, and of the Soviet Union, their spiritual home. Bevin persuaded the United States to come forward as the leader of the West. Under the Marshall Plan, the United States provided extensive economic aid to the countries of Western Europe, including Britain. The United States led in the formation of the North Atlantic Treaty Organization (NATO), which maintained large forces in Europe to resist possible Soviet military aggression.

Like Churchill, Bevin believed that Britain could survive only as a major power with global political and economic interests. To support the role of a great power sitting at the diplomatic head table, Britain maintained more than a million troops, a large navy, and began to develop an atom bomb—drains on human and financial resources, including scarce dollars, that Britain could ill afford. The first British atom bomb was detonated in 1952.

Through NATO, Britain made a long-term commitment of ground forces to the defense of Europe. In 1951, Britain faced an important decision in its relations with Western Europe. France, Germany, the Netherlands, Belgium, Luxembourg, and Italy began a process of economic integration by forming the European Coal and Steel Community. Britain was invited to join but refused; the global role took precedence over close involvement with Europe.

The once-mighty British Empire had become the Commonwealth: an association of independent nations (Canada, Australia, New Zealand, and South Africa) and dependent colonies that were in various stages of self-government. The Commonwealth was thought to be essential to Britain's continuance as a world power. The members of the Commonwealth used the British pound in trade with Britain and among each other, and they provided Britain with important foodstuffs, raw materials, and markets. Reluctantly the Labour government was forced to recognize that Britain's imperial role was slipping away. India was the "crown jewel" of the empire, but Britain's postwar weakness and strong local independence movements made it necessary to grant independence to India, Pakistan, Burma (Myanmar), and Ceylon (Sri Lanka).

Britain's position in the volatile Middle East was also crumbling. In 1947, the United States took over British responsibilities for the defense of Greece and Turkey. At the end of World War II, a large Jewish immigration into Palestine led to clashes between Jews and Arabs, and British troops were unable to maintain order. In 1948, Britain pulled out of Palestine. War broke out between the Arabs and the Jewish settlers, which led to the establishment of the state of Israel.

Although British resources were greatly overstretched, Britain was determined to maintain a position of influence in the Middle East. Her principal base was the Suez Canal Zone, which she held from Egypt on a lease until 1956. A backup base was established on the island of Cyprus. Other British forces were stationed in the Persian Gulf to protect Britain's oil interests, which at that time were 30 percent of her overseas investments.

In 1948, the unity of the Commonwealth was further challenged when a white Nationalist government came to power in the Union of South Africa, an economic powerhouse with a strategic location. The Nationalists introduced rigid policies of racial segregation called *apartheid*. Black leaders emerged who challenged *apartheid* in South Africa and British authority in other African colonies.

A New Era Emerges

In Britain an election must be held within five years of the previous election, but the prime minister (with the formal consent of the king or queen) may call it sooner. Labour's five-year electoral mandate expired in 1950, and it was necessary to go again to the voters. By that time, most of Labour's agenda had been completed and some leaders were calling for a policy of consolidation. Labour won a narrow victory, but its modest manifesto indicated that the period of fundamental reform had ended.

In 1951, the crumbling ministry of Clement Attlee called an election in an effort to get a clear mandate to govern. Although Labour received a slim majority of votes, the Conservatives won more seats in the House of Commons. Winston Churchill returned to No. 10 Downing Street as the leader of a Conservative government.

In the 1950s, Britain's postwar problems began to disappear. There was a sense of optimism. King George VI, who had remained in Buckingham Palace with his family throughout the war, died and was succeeded by his eldest daughter, who became Queen Elizabeth II. Her coronation in 1953 seemed to inaugurate a new era. In 1955 Winston Churchill retired, laden with honors and the symbol of Britain's "finest hour."

CHAPTER ONE

~

The Rise of Margaret Thatcher

Growing Up

Margaret Roberts, the daughter of a grocer and local councillor, was born in 1925 in Grantham, a small city in eastern England. Her adolescence was shaped by six years of war in which Grantham had been directly involved. There were numerous Allied airbases in the area, including Bomber Command Group No. 5. She saw, on the streets and in her family shop, soldiers and airmen of many nations, including Americans. Grantham experienced air raids, and as a schoolgirl she learned how to take shelter when the warning sounded. In important ways, Margaret Thatcher's foreign policy views were shaped by her early experience of Anglo-American cooperation in World War II.

Margaret grew up in an apartment over her parents' grocery, where she developed the Victorian virtues of honesty, work, cleanliness, and Christian service. She and her sister helped in the shop, waiting on customers, shelving stock, and packaging bulk products. She enjoyed the general sociability of retailing. She saw the workings of the market first hand, because customers would go elsewhere if they could get better quality or price. Her father was an avid reader, and once a week Margaret brought home books from the public library.

The Methodist chapel was the center of their social life. In contrast to the elegant worship and social cachet of the established Church of England, Methodism offered ordinary working people a plain Gospel message, a firm

1

morality, and peppy hymns. Another important institution in Margaret's life was school. She was a scholarship student at the Kesteven and Grantham Girls' School, where she was consistently at the top of her class.

Despite their modest life, the Roberts family owned that totem of middle-class respectability—a piano. Margaret took lessons and won several local prizes. Her great uncle, a skilled builder of pianos and organs, made the piano on which she played.

She gained her interest in politics from her father, a respected citizen of Grantham, who was a member of the town council for twenty-five years and eventually became mayor—in Britain an honorary office. She described her father as an "old-fashioned liberal" and an advocate of "individual responsibility and sound finance." In national politics he was "a staunch Conservative." In the election of 1935 (the last until after the war), Margaret was given the task of carrying messages between the polling place and Conservative Party headquarters.

In 1943, Margaret entered Oxford, where she studied chemistry. She joined the John Wesley Society and participated with other students in religious activities. While Margaret was a student, she realized that her true interest was politics, but she had already embarked on her chemistry major and needed to complete it for future employment. Strong religious convictions often lead to strong political convictions. In her last year, she was elected president of the Oxford University Conservative Association, which enabled her to meet visiting Conservative politicians.

Getting into Politics

After her graduation, Margaret worked as a research chemist while continuing her involvement in Conservative politics. In the election of 1950, at the age of twenty-four, she was selected (nominated) to run for Parliament in Dartford, a Labour-dominated constituency, where she could gain experience, although she had no chance of winning. Her upbringing in the shop and the Methodist chapel had given her an understanding of ordinary people, and her feisty spirit and quick wit enabled her to hold her own in face-to-face campaigning. As a good-looking young woman, she received considerable attention. Her picture was published in *Life* magazine. A German magazine described her as "a young woman with charm."

At her nomination dinner, Denis Thatcher, a prosperous businessman who was a partner in a paint factory, volunteered to drive Margaret to London to catch her train home. During her campaign, he drove her around in his Jaguar, cheering her on. The attraction was mutual, and in 1951, after another unsuccessful campaign, Margaret and Denis were married. Denis gave Margaret the personal and financial support that she needed to pursue a new career. She studied law, and in 1953 she passed the bar exam and gave birth to twins. For the next few years she was occupied with the busy life of a mother and lawyer.

When Margaret entered politics, the Conservative Party was no longer the party of appeasement and depression. As prime minister, Churchill wished to preserve the national unity that had carried Britain through the war to victory, and he admired the efforts and sacrifices that had been made by ordinary people. He wanted to make good on the wartime promises of a better life for everyone. He accepted the Labour settlement of 1945–1951, with few changes. The iron and steel industry and long-distance trucking were sold back to private enterprise, but the other nationalized industries remained as before. The National Health Service (NHS) and other aspects of the welfare state were kept, and the Conservative ministry continued building council houses. A national consensus had been achieved that lasted for the next thirty years.

As prosperity returned, Labour's moment seemed to have passed. When Churchill retired in 1955, Anthony Eden, foreign secretary during World War II and again in Churchill's second ministry, succeeded him. In 1956, Eden faced a crisis, when Colonel Gamal Abdel Nasser, the charismatic leader of Egypt, nationalized the Suez Canal, Britain's vital link with the East. At that point Israel, in collusion with Britain and France, attacked Egypt. The Israelis routed the Egyptian army, while the British and French sent troops into the Canal Zone. When the United Nations and the United States denounced the attack on Egypt, the British withdrew in humiliation. Eden had a nervous breakdown and resigned. Clearly, Britain's attempt to maintain the role of a world power had crashed.

Eden's successor, Harold Macmillan, restored public confidence and the image of the Conservatives as "the natural party of government." In the 1930s, Macmillan had been one of a group of progressive young Conservatives who had advocated a "middle way" between laissez-faire capitalism and socialism. Now a poised and mature leader, Macmillan was the embodiment of the paternalistic "One Nation" Toryism of Disraeli, which saw the elite as responsible for the well-being of the country and especially for those at the lower end of the economic scale.

Macmillan was the first British political leader to make effective use of television, projecting a calm, confident, Edwardian image in interviews and on talk shows. In the general election of 1959, he skillfully used television and national prosperity in his campaign, remarking that "most of our people have never had it so good." The Conservatives won almost 50 percent of the popular vote and a majority in the House of Commons. Macmillan's popularity gave him the nickname "Supermac."

That year, Margaret Thatcher returned to politics. The twins were six, and she decided to run for Parliament again. The selection committee in her own constituency turned her down, saying that she should stay home and look after her children. She was then selected for Finchley, a suburb north of London. She benefited from the Macmillan landslide and took her seat in the House of Commons as Conservative member for Finchley, a seat that she held until 1992, when she was elevated to the House of Lords.

As a new Member of Parliament (MP), Thatcher had her first experience of office as a junior minister in the Ministry of Pensions. She worked hard at her job, where she learned how difficult it was to maintain a balance between helping people who needed help and avoiding welfare dependency by people capable of taking care of themselves.

After the Suez fiasco, Britain began a reappraisal of her place in the world. The failure of the United States to support Britain in the Suez crisis made a closer relationship with the European Economic Community (EEC) look more attractive. The EEC joined the Western European nations (France, West Germany, Italy, the Netherlands, Belgium, Luxembourg) into a single economic system, but the purpose of the EEC went beyond economics. Powerful idealism was also at work: with the devastating effects of World Wars I and II in mind, the peoples of Western Europe were determined to develop closer political relations and rid themselves of the national rivalries that had torn the continent apart.

Britain could not afford to be excluded from the European market, but she did not wish to give up her national sovereignty, "special relationship" with the United States, role as the center of the Commonwealth, and her global interests in finance and trade. The British were an insular people, conscious of their national identity, and they did not share the idealistic motivations that had contributed to the movement for European unity. To the British, membership in the EEC was not a mission, but a matter of practical economics.

By 1960, however, the growing strength of the EEC was evident, and Macmillan applied for membership. A rising young Conservative, Edward Heath, was put in charge of the negotiations. The British application was vetoed by President Charles de Gaulle of France, who believed (perhaps rightly) that the British could never be good Europeans.

Close relations with Europe were also important due to the declining importance of the Commonwealth and the movement for independence throughout the British colonies. In 1960, Macmillan warned white South Africans that "the wind of change is blowing through this continent, and, whether we like it or not, this growth of national consciousness is a political fact." Ghana became independent in 1957, followed by Nigeria and other African colonies, Jamaica and other Caribbean possessions, Singapore, and Malaysia.

In 1963, Kenya was given independence and a black-controlled government took over; white and Asian inhabitants left in large numbers. When black-majority governments came to power in Northern Rhodesia (Zambia) and Nyasaland (Malawi), a white-controlled government in Southern Rhodesia (Zimbabwe) rejected British authority and declared its independence from the Commonwealth.

Time ran out for Macmillan in 1963. Restlessness among younger Conservatives had led him to dismiss one-third of his Cabinet the previous year, giving him a new nickname "Mac the Knife." Later in the year, ill health convinced Macmillan that he must resign as prime minister and leader of the Conservative Party. From his hospital bed, Macmillan kept firm control of the choice of a successor, and Queen Elizabeth II came to the hospital to receive the verdict.

Macmillan informed the queen that the choice of the party leaders was the foreign secretary, the Earl of Home (pronounced Hume). A recent change in the law enabled Lord Home to renounce his peerage, which he did. As Sir Alec Douglas-Home, he was elected to the House of Commons in a by-election and became prime minister.

The choice of the party leader and new prime minister by a few insiders aroused so much criticism that the Conservative Party decided that in the future the leader would be chosen by the Conservative MPs. On the first ballot a winner would require a majority plus 15 percent. A second ballot, if necessary, would require only a simple majority.

Sir Alec was capable and likable, but a mature landed gentleman was not right for "the swinging sixties." Home called an election the next year, in which he faced a new leader of the Labour Party—forty-eight-year-old Harold Wilson.

Wilson realized that Labour had to move beyond its base of cloth-capped industrial workers. With growing prosperity, Britain was developing a lower middle class of people with steady jobs who were employed in new technical and service industries and raising families in the growing suburbs. Wilson appealed to them by promising to bring to Britain "the white heat of the technological revolution." A low turnout seemed to indicate that most voters did not see much difference between the two parties. Wilson won a narrow victory and organized a Labour government committed to new initiatives. Despite the Conservative defeat, Thatcher managed to carry her constituency of Finchley.

Harold Wilson, 1964–1970

Harold Wilson was one of the rising meritocracy of men and women who had climbed the scholarship route from grammar school to university rather than attending a prestigious private school. He was identified with Labour's left wing, but he was a pragmatic politician who attempted to modernize the policies of the Labour Party in a direction that eventually led to New Labour.

Wilson was much influenced by new ideas in the Labour Party that minimized the value of public ownership of basic industries. Some Labour intellectuals argued that Labour should concentrate its efforts on the private sector and use Keynesian methods of fiscal and monetary policy to manage the economy. Economic growth, it was argued, could be achieved through the restructuring of Britain's mainly capitalist economy and the development of new industries. Instead of a partnership with the trade unions, these thinkers recognized that in a dynamic economy many conflicts would arise between management and labor, in which public intervention should seek a balanced resolution.

Wilson shared these views, but as a political leader, he had to find ways to get them accepted by his party and the trade unions. He won the allegiance of Labour loyalists by renationalizing steel, but otherwise he left behind Labour's commitment to public ownership. He gave lip service to the idea of central planning by instituting a national plan, with "projections" and "targets" for industry and labor, but no means of implementation were provided. He abandoned Labour's preoccupation with the declining industries of the past and established a Ministry of Technology to encourage high-tech industries, such as engineering and aircraft. Wilson continued Labour's commitment to an active role for the state in modernizing the economy, by pouring public funds into private-sector firms in new industries, such as aluminum.

Wilson realized that a modern, high-tech economy would require improved education. British secondary schools were of three kinds: grammar schools for students bound for a university, secondary modern schools for the general student population, and technical schools providing training for students with specialized aptitudes or interests. In addition, a small number of elite boarding schools (oddly called public schools) produced most of Britain's leaders in government and business. Admission to grammar school was based on an examination taken at the age of eleven.

Labour's objective was to reduce the academic and social inequalities characteristic of British education. In 1951, Labour established the General Certificate of Education, giving students who had not passed the eleven-plus exam a second chance to show what they could do. Labour advocated "comprehensive schools" that would bring together students of all abilities and social backgrounds. These schools were expected to break down class barriers by providing opportunities for students from various social classes to interact. With a "baby boom" reaching school age, Labour's policy of spending only to build comprehensive schools ensured that comprehension became the norm in England.

An extension of higher education was also required by a dynamic, modern economy. The *Robbins Report* (1964), initiated by the Conservatives, called for increased public investment in higher education to provide places for all students who qualified. This was a proposal that both parties could accept, and a process of expansion began, including the establishment of many new universities. By the end of the decade, the number of university students had increased by 75 percent.

Wilson took pride in the growth of the polytechnics, institutions of higher education with career-oriented programs and broader admission standards than the universities. Another innovation was the Open University, which enabled employed people to obtain degrees through correspondence, radio, and television. The establishment of the Department of Education and Science institutionalized Wilson's commitment to high-level knowledge as the basis for a new kind of British economy.

The Wilson ministry was a forerunner of New Labour in that it tended to define socialism as a broad range of public services within a capitalist economy. Wilson fulfilled his election pledges to increase social security benefits and the state pension. Energetic but misguided efforts were made to provide modern housing by building tall blocks of flats that later became ghettos for the poor. An ambitious program of hospital building was undertaken. An investigation of mental hospitals and care of the handicapped, elderly, and infirm revealed appallingly low standards. Eventually the social services ("community care") were separated from the National Health Service. A new method of allocating funds to the NHS shifted additional resources to the north and other deprived areas.

Wilson's approach appealed to the growing number of white-collar and service workers. In 1966, he called an election to strengthen his support in Parliament. He was rewarded with a comfortable majority and 48 percent of the vote. Some began to think that Labour, given a veneer of modernity by Wilson, had established itself as the majority party.

Wilson discovered that his surprising electoral victory was the beginning of a sea of troubles. He regarded a stable exchange rate as a matter of international prestige and essential to the role of London as a financial center. Britain's inefficient economy, overloaded by the costs of an extended foreign policy and a comprehensive welfare state, led inevitably to foreign-exchange crises, as international money markets lost confidence that Britain could pay its bills. To stabilize the pound, Wilson needed to obtain emergency credits from the International Monetary Fund, which required deep spending cuts, the imposition of high interest rates and indirect taxes, and a freeze on wages and prices. These requirements prevented Wilson from taking Keynesian steps, such as tax cuts or deficit spending, to stimulate the economy.

In 1967, the British economy was hit hard by the Arab–Israeli Six-Day War, which closed the Suez Canal, interrupted the supply of oil from the Middle East, and led to another run on sterling. The chancellor of the Exchequer, James Callaghan, had no choice but to bite the bullet and devalue the pound from $2.80 to $2.40, a step followed by more tax increases and spending cuts. Although Wilson assured doubters that "the pound in our pockets" was the same as before, the public was not convinced. More tax increases followed in 1968. Under those blows, the economy stagnated and unemployment raised its ugly head. More than anything else, Wilson's devaluations and tax increases destroyed the prestige of his government.

Many of Britain's problems grew out of the low productivity of British industry, which was characterized by sluggish management, restrictive unions, overmanning, and badly designed products. Union power rested on the shop-room floor, where shop stewards contended with management and competed with each other in jurisdictional disputes. They called disruptive unofficial strikes ("wildcat strikes") that were not approved by the national union. *I'm All Right, Jack*, a popular comedy starring Peter Sellers, satirized absentee owners who lived in luxury, managers who did not manage, workers who did not work, and a testy shop steward (Sellers) alert for grievances and eager to call a strike. Other countries pitied the former workshop of the world, now debilitated by "the British disease."

In a publication entitled *In Place of Strife* (1969) the Wilson government proposed active involvement of the state in industrial relations. A Commission on Industrial Relations would be established to resolve differences before they led to strikes. The powers of national unions would be strengthened to reduce the number of wildcat strikes. A strike would require approval by the workers in a secret ballot. The assumption was that most workers did not want strikes, which reduced their income and might threaten their jobs. Wilson's proposal was opposed within the Cabinet by Callaghan, who maintained strong ties to the unions, and by most Labour MPs. Wilson dropped the proposal rather than face a party split. He had failed again, tied down by a party that would not accept change.

Like his Labour predecessors, Wilson was determined to continue Britain's high-cost role as a world power. He strengthened the British nuclear deterrent by adopting American Polaris (submarine-based) missiles. Britain stationed large forces in Western Europe, the Mediterranean, and scattered bases around the world. A major factor in Britain's balance of payments problems was foreign policy expenditures overseas, and eventually Wilson had to cut back. He decided that Britain would abandon the effort to maintain military forces "east of Suez." Small garrisons would remain in Gibraltar, Cyprus, Hong Kong, and the Falkland Islands, with a modest naval force in the Persian Gulf.

Wilson also attempted to maintain Britain's posture as an imperial power, but the decline of Britain's role as leader of the Commonwealth was dramatized by a crisis in Rhodesia. In 1965, the white minority government, led by Ian Smith, declared independence rather than yield to British insistence on granting political rights to the black majority. The Wilson government declared that this action was a rebellion and supported the United Nations economic sanctions. British weakness and popular sympathy with "kith and kin" in Rhodesia foreclosed any stronger steps.

The Commonwealth connection contributed to another issue, immigration. In the 1950s, full employment attracted many West Indians to Britain, where they filled low-paid jobs in London Transport, the National Health Service, and elsewhere. In the 1960s, large numbers of immigrants from India and Pakistan settled in Britain and were joined by Asian minorities fleeing despotic governments in Kenya and Uganda.

Labour's socialist leaders were idealistically sympathetic to racial minorities, but the union rank and file feared the threat of immigrants to jobs and the stability of their neighborhoods. From time to time racial disturbances broke out in cities in which immigrants had settled in large numbers. The right-wing National Front, which opposed "colored" immigration, was established in 1967 and began gaining adherents. In 1968, the Wilson government responded by restricting immigration from Commonwealth countries to persons with close connections to Britain by birth, descent, or naturalization.

Although public opinion favored limiting immigration from the non-white Commonwealth countries, there was also strong support for equal treatment of immigrants who had already arrived and settled in Britain. Two Race Relations Acts prohibited discrimination in jobs, housing, or commercial services. This pattern of restriction *cum* nondiscrimination was to characterize British immigration policy until nonwhite Commonwealth immigration was virtually shut down by Thatcher.

The breakdown of the Commonwealth and the decline of the world power role led some in the Labour Party to advocate joining the European Community. With the United States tied down in Vietnam, the "special relationship" looked less special. Another application was made for membership. Once again President De Gaulle imposed his veto.

In the meantime, the Conservative Party was also undergoing a change of leadership and direction. The party looked to the younger generation when it chose Edward Heath as its leader. Like Wilson and Thatcher, Heath came from a modest background. Son of a small builder of houses, he attended Oxford on a scholarship and supplemented his income by playing the organ. He served in the army in World War II, rising to the rank of colonel.

In Britain, the opposition parties in Parliament choose "shadow" ministers who are responsible for giving special attention to their counterparts in the Cabinet. Thatcher served her apprenticeship by holding several shadow offices: housing and land, Conservative spokesperson on taxes under the shadow chancellor of the Exchequer, and shadow minister of education.

Six years in opposition had given the Conservative Party the inducement and opportunity to reconsider its policies. Under Macmillan, the "One Nation" Conservatives had maintained and extended the welfare state, but a group of younger Conservatives expressed doubt that these commitments could be sustained without impairing economic growth. Geoffrey Howe, a successful lawyer, was one of them. He argued for a reduction of the role of the state and the size of the public services and criticized subsidizing inefficient industries with public money.

The Conservative election manifesto showed the influence of the new ideas by proposing lower taxes, elimination of many regulations (some of which went back to wartime), limitation of trade union power, a strong attack on crime and public disorders, and an end to large-scale immigration. These ideas foreshadowed the policies that Margaret Thatcher would adopt a decade later.

In 1970, Wilson sought a fresh mandate by calling an election that he expected to win. The economy was doing better, the standard of living was rising, and home ownership was increasing. But Wilson's grand plans for reform had floundered. The Conservatives promised to bring to government the fresh ideas of a new generation. Heath's campaign managers made good use of television, while Wilson was content to run on his reputation and look thoughtful while sucking his pipe.

Heath's message was attractive to the lower-middle-class workers who had provided Wilson's margins in 1964 and 1966, and they gave the Conservative Party an upset victory. Thatcher was reelected for Finchley and took a seat in the Heath Cabinet as minister for education and science.

The Ministry of Sir Edward Heath, 1970–1974

Like Wilson, Heath was seen as a vigorous leader from the new generation, who would implement the ideas that the Conservatives had developed in opposition. The prime minister made many important decisions himself, delegating secondary matters to Cabinet committees, and dominating Parliament and elections. Thatcher was content to follow the leader. She listened and learned, and many of the policies that she adopted when she became prime minister were first put forward under Heath.

Heath's first priority was British membership in the European Economic Community (EEC), to which he was strongly committed for idealistic as well as economic reasons. When President Charles de Gaulle of France retired in 1969, the way was open for Britain to join, the goal dearest to Heath's heart. The main advantage of joining the EEC was access to a large and growing European market for British products. In his eagerness to join, Heath paid a high price, agreeing to a British financial contribution that was out of line with the wealth of the British economy. The EEC intended to move from economic unity to political unity, but Heath minimized this aspect of membership.

Both political parties were divided on the issue, and on the crucial division, the treaty was ratified by only eight votes. Many Conservatives disliked the sacrifice of national sovereignty that membership entailed. Others emphasized the importance of relationships with the United States and the Commonwealth. Within the Labour Party, the socialists objected to joining a capitalistic economic entity, while trade unionists feared their cherished powers and work rules would be eroded.

The British people did not feel a strong sense of identity with continental Europe; polls showed no more than one-third of the voters in favor. Heath insisted, and the decision to join was accepted more as a practical matter of economics than as a full acceptance of the European ideal. Britain entered the European Community on New Year's Day, 1973.

When Heath came to office, he announced that his would be a government of change. He began his ministry with a commitment to free-market capitalism and reduction of the role and cost of government. He declared his opposition to central planning, control of prices and wages, and subsidies for floundering nationalized industries. He advocated limitation of trade union powers. To stimulate the economy, income tax rates were cut and the lowest-paid workers were exempted entirely. Interest rates were reduced and credit controls were removed.

Heath's commitment to competition meant that some "lame-duck" industries would go under. When the prestigious Rolls Royce Corporation, a high-tech maker of airplane engines, faced bankruptcy, Heath lost his nerve and bailed out the company with a national subsidy. A similar policy was adopted toward the declining shipbuilding industry of Scotland.

Heath's "dash for growth" soon foundered on the same problems of productivity and inflation that had stymied Wilson. Tax cuts poured money into the economy, and lower interest rates further stimulated consumer demand. The sluggish British economy could not supply the necessary goods and services, and the result was inflation. From 1970 to 1974 retail prices rose an average of 8 percent per year and wages 14 percent per year.

Much of the money released into the marketplace by Heath's tax and monetary policies did not go into productive investments but into real estate speculation. With money and credit easily available and wages rising, people bought houses, borrowing with low down payments to finance their purchases. House prices rose by 50 percent in eighteen months as more buyers entered the market, thinking that prices would continue to rise. Money also went into a consumption binge. Spending on foreign goods and holidays increased. Imports rose, the balance of payments turned unfavorable, and the pound again came under attack.

With the boom getting out of hand, Heath reverted to the former policies of state planning and control of the economy. As inflation mounted to 9 percent, he abandoned his faith in the free market and imposed statutory controls on prices and wages (the "U-Turn"). Public spending was cut and interest rates were raised to a record 13 percent.

The economic expansion came to a grinding halt; the brief boom in commercial real estate ended and housing prices plummeted, leaving many people with a mortgage greater than the value of their house. The middle class, the core of the Conservative Party, was hard hit by the "stop-go" policies that Heath had criticized so severely under Wilson.

The Arab–Israeli War of 1973 aggravated the twin problems of inflation and the balance of payments. The Arab oil-producing states imposed an embargo on oil shipments, which dramatically increased the price of oil. The embargo hit hard the economies of advanced and developing nations alike. Unemployment rose to more than a million and inflation reached 24 percent, which forced Heath, like Wilson before him, to devalue the pound. The immediate effect was to protect the balance of payments by making imports more expensive, although in the long run devaluation was expected to stimulate exports and create jobs.

Heath believed that modernization of the economy required fundamental reform of British industrial relations. Unlike many countries, Britain did not have a strong, centralized labor organization that could cut a deal and make it stick. It was generally agreed that irresponsible trade union power on the shop floor was an important factor in Britain's poor economic performance. When a crisis arose, the government had to intervene and compel organized labor to live up to its contracts. Strikes were especially damaging in industries with a direct impact on the public, such as the railroads or electrical power generation.

Shortly after taking office, the Heath government passed the Industrial Relations Act, which established in Britain a comprehensive code to regulate relations between employers and employees, with an industrial court to resolve disputes. The act included many of the provisions that Wilson had advocated in *In Place of Strife*. Unions were required to register and adhere to approved rules. The employment secretary was authorized to impose a "cooling-off period" in strikes that endangered the national interest and could require approval by the workers in a secret ballot before a strike could go into effect. The right to strike was not infringed, but when these procedures were violated, the employer could sue the union for damages.

At this point the Trades Union Congress (TUC) mounted its most energetic political effort. A rally of more than one hundred thousand people was held in Trafalgar Square, and member unions were advised not to cooperate with the terms of the act. The TUC's leadership role soon foundered on the independence and varying views of its member unions. Some of the largest unions decided to accept the act, while the more militant unions called for stronger action.

A rash of strikes followed, led in 1972 by the coal miners, whose wages had fallen behind inflation and who saw jobs disappearing because of closures of unprofitable pits. The miners organized bands of "flying pickets" to prevent coal from being transported to the power stations. Among the leaders was Arthur Scargill, who a decade later would attempt similar tactics against Thatcher.

The railway men and truckers, who refused to haul coal past the pickets, aided the miners. Soon it would be necessary to reduce power generation, and industry would come to a halt. Not for the last time, the principle of collective bargaining was pitted against public needs. Faced with disaster, the Heath ministry established a commission to report on the miners' grievances.

When the commission sided with the miners and recommended large wage increases, the ministry caved in. From her seat in the Cabinet, Thatcher looked on and learned.

As part of its commitment to modernizing Britain, the Heath ministry undertook a fundamental reform of local government, establishing a two-tier system. The upper tier consisted of forty-six counties, including the Greater London Council and six "metropolitan counties" created for areas of urban sprawl. The lower tier consisted of 296 rural and urban districts. Some of the latter were called boroughs and kept the honorary office of mayor. The Department of the Environment was created to coordinate the activities of local government units in respect to housing, transport, and public works. Local water systems were merged into ten regional water districts under the National Water Board.

These local government units had important and extensive functions for roads, transportation, sanitation, schools, and social services. They spent approximately 30 percent of all public money. Although most local government funding came from the Treasury, a considerable amount was based on "the rates," taxes on houses and commercial property. Homeowners, most of whom were Conservatives, had long complained about the rates. The Heath ministry considered a variety of reforms, but nothing came of it until Thatcher returned to that issue a decade later.

In Office

Thatcher had come to the attention of Conservative Party leaders by her obvious intelligence and energy and by her ability to win elections. She clearly deserved a ministerial post. She plunged eagerly into her job as secretary of state for education and science and gained valuable experience from it. Thatcher was determined to preserve the grammar schools that prepared the more able students for university admission.

Her first day in office, she abrogated Labour's commitment to comprehensive schools, leaving the matter to local education authorities. By that time the movement toward comprehension could not be stopped. More comprehensive schools were established during her time as minister of education than under any other minister. By 1979, more than 90 percent of the secondary schools were comprehensive. An important step during her term of office was a long-planned raising of the school-leaving age to sixteen.

Thatcher came to public attention as a result of the decision of the Heath ministry to cut spending, including spending on schools. Facing cuts, she decided to give priority to academic needs at the expense of school meals and free milk. She argued that families that were comfortably off could afford to pay for lunches and milk, while those who could not afford them should be helped by the Ministry of Health and Social Security.

When the Heath ministry introduced her bill to end free milk in the schools, a furor arose in the Labour Party and the press. Thatcher was called "Thatcher, the milk snatcher," and her reputation for hard-heartedness was established, never to be lost. In November 1971, the popular tabloid, *The Sun*, at that time a left-wing newspaper, described her as "the Most Unpopular Woman in Britain." In her autobiography she wrote: "I learned a valuable lesson. I had incurred the maximum of political odium for the minimum of political benefit."

Heath met his downfall in another confrontation with organized labor. In 1973, the National Union of Mineworkers took advantage of the energy crisis precipitated by the Arab oil embargo and demanded wage increases far beyond the guidelines. To enforce their claim they refused all overtime work. They were supported by the electrical workers and the railway men, who had pay claims of their own.

Heath was determined not to give in so easily this time. He proclaimed a state of emergency. To save electricity, business was limited to a three-day week; darkened shop fronts reminded people of wartime. Streetlights were turned off and television broadcasting was reduced. The miners responded with an all-out strike.

Early in 1974, Heath, driven to desperation, called for an election to determine "who governs Britain." Although the polls were favorable, public support of the government did not appear at the ballot box. Heath had not changed the direction of the economy, controlled inflation, or resolved his disputes with organized labor.

The British people, tired of confrontation and crisis, turned back to a somewhat surprised Wilson, who won a plurality of four seats, although Labour lacked a clear majority in the House of Commons. The two major parties each won 37 percent of the popular vote, to the benefit of the Liberals, who made a startling comeback with almost 20 percent. Nationalist parties in Scotland and Wales also made gains.

Later in the year, Wilson called another election, which gave him a slim majority of three seats, with Labour winning 39 percent of the vote and the Liberals holding their own with 18 percent. The Conservatives hit rock bottom, receiving only 36 percent of the votes.

In her autobiography Margaret Thatcher wrote: "I was upset at the result. We had finally squared up to the unions and the people had not supported us. . . . I knew in my heart that it was time not just for a change in government but for a change in the Conservative Party."

The Challenger

After two electoral defeats in 1974, Heath found himself vulnerable. He was aloof and authoritarian, and had offended many in his Cabinet and party. His "U-Turn" in 1972 and his failure to deal effectively with trade union power led many Conservatives to look elsewhere. Determined to change the direction of the Conservative Party, Thatcher stepped forward to wrest the leadership of the Conservative Party from Heath.

In her autobiography, she writes that she went to Heath's office, where she found him at his desk.

"I must tell you," she said, "that I have decided to stand for the leadership."

"He looked at me coldly," she continues, "turned his back, shrugged his shoulders, and said: 'If you must.' I slipped out of the room."

Her main support came from the Conservative 1922 Committee, a body of backbenchers (MPs who are not party leaders). They introduced a new rule for the choice of the Conservative leader, who was required to seek re-election every year. Other Conservative leaders had no desire to provoke a party fight by challenging Heath, but the new rule gave Thatcher—the maverick—the opportunity she needed.

As an outsider she promised a fresh start, and the backbenchers rallied behind her. She narrowly missed election on the first ballot. Heath, recognizing that he had lost the confidence of his party, stepped down, and Thatcher won comfortably on the second ballot. To the amazement of the press, the public, and many Conservatives, Margaret Thatcher was now leader of the Conservative Party and prime minister in waiting.

Next, she had to find Conservatives willing to follow her leadership in a party in which she had little standing. One of the first to join her shadow Cabinet was William Whitelaw, who had stood against her in the second ballot of the leadership contest. "Willie" was an astute politician noted for his ability to reconcile differences and smooth troubled waters. Another was Sir Geoffrey Howe, who shared her views on free-market economics. Michael Heseltine, a forceful and ambitious younger member, was made shadow minister for industry, where he focused on blocking Labour's proposals for further nationalizations. Heath refused her invitation to join the shadow Cabinet.

The Foundations of Thatcherism

When she became the Tory leader, Thatcher's political views were not well formed, and many who voted for her did not know what they were getting.

She was obviously intelligent and exhibited enormous intensity and determination. She claimed to have been influenced by the works of F. A. Hayek, whose *The Road to Serfdom* condemned intervention of government in the economy as harmful and leading to an authoritarian state.

Thatcher gave special credit to her friend and mentor, Sir Keith Joseph, whose Centre for Policy Studies prepared policy positions that advocated a reduced role for government and free-market economics. Joseph had served as secretary of state for social services in the Heath government. This experience led him to the view that government intervention in society and the economy, no matter how well intended, exacerbated the very problems that it was supposed to resolve or created new problems that would lead to further government intervention.

His objective was to restore to Britain the enterprise culture, weakened by Labour collectivism and Conservative paternalism. His solution was to cut taxes, spending, and borrowing and give more responsibility to businesses and individuals for their own well-being. He advocated selling off the nationalized industries, leaving them to sink or swim in a competitive environment. The commitment to full employment would have to be abandoned.

Joseph adopted the "monetarism" of Milton Friedman, an economist at the University of Chicago. Friedman identified inflation as the most crucial problem, for it aggravated all the others. He proposed to keep the money supply constant (with some allowance for underlying inflation) and let all economic adjustments be made by market forces. He held that monetary expansion could not be effective in reducing unemployment (except temporarily), for the resulting inflation would only make unemployment worse. For that reason, government should counter inflation by reducing its spending and borrowing and contracting the money supply. Friedman's ideas were especially relevant to the powerful inflation and economic stagnation ("stagflation") that swept the global economy in the 1970s.

With respect to individuals and families, Joseph was a compassionate man, realizing the enormous adjustments that a return to a free-market economy would cause. For that reason, he saw the need for a safety net in a period of economic change, but one that would not become a hammock. His main concern was to break "the cycle of deprivation" that kept families in poverty for generations. To break the cycle, he advocated improvements in education and an end to welfare dependency.

It was Thatcher's task to translate the theoretical ideas of Joseph and the Centre for Policy Studies into proposals that would be accepted by her party and resonate with the voters. The core support of the Conservative Party came from the middle class, and Thatcher appealed especially to them.

"I believe we should judge people on merit and not on background," she said. "I believe that person who is prepared to work hardest should get the greatest rewards and keep them after tax. That we should back the workers and not the shirkers: that it is not only permissible but praiseworthy to want to benefit your own family by your own efforts."

She also sounded another powerful refrain in British conservatism: law and order. In the 1960s and 1970s, crime increased dramatically; additional problems were the misbehavior of hooligans in public places and the activities of Irish terrorist groups. Thatcher believed that permissiveness in society and reluctance to impose strong penalties were responsible for the increase in crime. She offered a return to "traditional values" and "the smack of firm government."

Thatcher had a strong interest in foreign policy, and she was by no means willing to accept the view that Britain could no longer be a force in international affairs. As leader of the Conservative Party and a prospective prime minister, she had the opportunity to become acquainted with world leaders and problems. During the next four years she visited leaders in France, West Germany, Italy, Rumania, Yugoslavia, the Middle East, India, Singapore, China, Australia, New Zealand, and the United States.

In foreign affairs, her main concern was the Cold War, which had taken on new intensity as a result of technological advances in nuclear weapons. She recognized that the leadership of the United States was essential to European security and world peace. She believed that the Soviet Union had entered an aggressive phase that should be resisted. Her militant attitude led a Russian journalist to give her the name "The Iron Lady."

The Emergence of a Crisis

When Wilson returned to office in 1974, he was faced with the legacy of Heath's boom: inflation, rising unemployment, a budget deficit, a balance of payments crisis, and demands for pay increases from workers in the civil service and the nationalized industries. His main goal was to hold the Labour Party together, as left-wingers and the unions became more militant. He ended the coal strike with a settlement favorable to the miners. Heath's Industrial Relations Act and pay policy were repealed. Organized labor received legislation that strengthened the powers of the unions. Wilson attempted to reduce inflationary pressures by a "social contract" with the unions to restrain wage increases. The promise was an empty one; in the next year wage increases averaged 30 percent.

Wilson faced the task of making a declining mixed economy work at a time of worldwide inflation and recession. He was trapped by his own party. Over time, the responsible socialists and trade union leaders of the Attlee era had been replaced by left-wingers determined to undermine capitalism and create a socialist state. They argued that Wilson had failed because he had not been radical enough. They advocated more nationalizations, additional investments in public services, and expanded welfare benefits. They wanted to reduce Britain's foreign policy and defense commitments and withdraw from the European Economic Community. Wilson owed his leadership of the Labour Party to them, and he was on a tightrope trying to reconcile their views with the broad public support needed by the leader of the government.

The left-wingers insisted on traditional Labour solutions to the problems of a new age. Taxes and expenditures were increased to subsidize nationalized industries, provide for the growing number of the unemployed, and expand the welfare state. It was clear that many of Britain's problems were the result of a lack of investment and low productivity. Labour's answer was for the state to step in, and an "industrial strategy" was adopted. The National Enterprise Board (NEB) was established to invest in promising new industries, such as electronics and biotechnology. Instead, the NEB dissipated its resources in futile efforts to keep failing private sector companies afloat. Facing bankruptcy, Britain's largest automaker, British Leyland, was nationalized, as were British Aerospace (a defense contractor) and the shipyards.

Labour's commitment to the welfare state was again demonstrated by increases in the state pension and an earnings-based supplementary pension plan (SERPS) for workers who did not have private pension plans provided by their employers. The special needs of women were addressed by requiring paid maternity leave for pregnant women and the requirement of equal pay for equal work. Family Allowance was replaced by Child Benefit, which was paid to the mother regardless of income, giving many working-class mothers the first dependable income they had ever known. Legislation was passed banning job discrimination based on gender, protecting women suffering from domestic violence, and granting mothers equal rights with fathers in bringing up the children.

A long-standing Labour Party grievance was resolved when the remaining grammar schools lost their government grants; some became fee-paying day schools and others (mainly Catholic) joined the school systems maintained by the local authorities.

Wilson's ability to finesse controversial issues was seen on the issue of British membership in the European Economic Community. There were opponents of the EEC in both parties: in the Labour Party they were the left-wingers, whose primary concern was socialism at home; in the Conservative Party they were nationalists, who objected to the loss of British sovereignty. To settle the matter once and for all, Wilson proposed a referendum on the issue. Although the British people felt little commitment to European unity, they gave overwhelming approval to continuance in the EEC. The referendum marked the high point of British popular support for membership.

In 1976, Wilson announced his decision to resign. He had brought about the revival of the Labour Party, but it was clear that its prescriptions for the country had either been discredited (nationalization) or accomplished (the welfare state). The consensus that had been established after World War II was running out. The problems of the 1960s had ripened into a general crisis, a condition that the Labour Party was poorly equipped to handle.

Wilson's successor as prime minister was genial James Callaghan, a man of long and varied experience in Labour politics. Usually a defender of traditional Labour policies and the unions, Callaghan recognized that Britain could not be insulated from the great changes taking place in the world markets.

The decade of the 1970s was a time of economic turbulence throughout the industrialized world, aggravated by large increases in the price of oil in 1973 and 1979. Great masses of capital flowed through the emerging world economy as multinational companies transferred huge investments and cash balances from one place to another. Arab money generated by high oil prices flitted through the international money markets.

Fixed exchange rates based on the dollar disappeared, and currencies floated, subject to the vagaries of speculators with vast resources. The only way, in Britain and elsewhere, to prevent the flight of capital to more attractive sites was by high interest rates and by other anti-inflationary policies that stifled economic growth. Keynesian management of the national economy by fiscal and monetary policy was no longer feasible.

The British economy, depending as it did on finance and trade, was especially hard hit. Inflation remained higher than in most industrial countries, stimulated by rising levels of public spending and borrowing. Manufacturing industry continued its steady decline. Unemployment rose to over a million; the goal of full employment was no longer a reality. As confidence in the British economy declined, the balance of payments turned strongly against Britain, and the pound sterling fell to record lows.

Callaghan knew that the inflationary environment of the 1970s had ended the age of Keynesian economics. In 1976, he expressed monetarist views when he said to the Labour Party's annual conference: "We used to think you could spend your way out of a recession by cutting taxes and boosting spending. I tell you in all candour that this option no longer exists and that in so far as it ever did exist, it only worked by injecting a bigger dose of inflation into the system."

The other members of the EEC faced similar problems. They accepted the monetarist view that the primary consideration in economic policy must be control of inflation. In 1978, the EEC established the Exchange Rate Mechanism (ERM), which required the member countries to adopt budgets and interest rates that would keep their currencies in a close relationship with the strong German mark. The Callaghan government refused to join the ERM. Labour opposed external control of British monetary policy, for it would end Labour's vision of a socialist economy.

Callaghan and his chancellor of the Exchequer, Denis Healey, had no choice but to adopt the new economics. Britain was overloaded by the costs of inefficient nationalized industries, the comprehensive welfare state, and the great power role. Even within the Labour Party, the idea took root that it might be necessary to cut the cost of government to reduce inflation and to provide capital for productive investment. When the pound fell to $1.60, Callaghan, like Wilson before him, had to go hat in hand to the International Monetary Fund (IMF) for an emergency loan to support sterling in the world money markets.

To meet the standards of the IMF, Healey was required to increase taxation and cut spending on housing, health, and food subsidies. Nationalized industries were given cash budgets and were expected to adjust to inflation by cutting staff or by finding other ways to save. To slow the economy, the availability of credit was tightened and interest rates were raised.

Fortunately, Britain was becoming an oil producer, as oil fields were opened up in the North Sea. Some shares in British Petroleum, now becoming valuable because of North Sea oil, were sold to help balance the budget. Reluctantly, Callaghan and Healey had moved in the direction that Thatcher would follow. In that respect, they were precursors of New Labour.

As inflation soared to an average annual rate of 15 percent, workers' wage demands rose proportionately. Desperately, Callaghan attempted to stabilize the economy with an incomes policy that limited wage increases to 5 percent, despite the assumption of the social contract that organized labor would itself maintain restraint. At first the Trades Union Congress (TUC) declared its support, but by 1978 the real wages of the average worker had fallen by 7 percent, and the TUC was unable to check the pay demands of its member unions.

In 1978, the Labour Party conference rejected all restraints on pay. Strikes and slowdowns plagued industry. With no good way to fight back, managements agreed to wage demands that they passed on to consumers in higher prices, thus contributing to more inflation, which led to more demands for higher pay. Factories shut down, and in 1977, unemployment rose to 1.4 million, an unprecedented number. Labour's claim to a superior capacity to maintain industrial peace was shattered.

By 1979, Britain was slowly coming out of the recession. Inflation was falling, the growth rate was respectable, and Healey's rigorous spending cuts had brought the public finances under control. The main problem was unemployment, which was now at 1.3 million, but that could be expected to improve. Callaghan's great mistake was to insist on continuing the incomes policy another year, when it was palpably unfair to wageworkers, who lost confidence in Labour as the party that responded to their concerns.

For some time, immigration and race relations had been political issues. The immigration issue was intensified by the rise of the National Front, which was ostentatiously nationalistic and strongly anticommunist. It opposed British membership in the EEC and urged a crackdown on crime. Above all, it was openly racist and opposed nonwhite immigration, which it claimed took jobs away from trueborn Englishmen. It took its cause to the streets, winning attention by ostentatious marches that usually led to violent confrontations. The National Front showed growing strength among white voters in East London and in other cities where immigrants had settled in large numbers.

All the parties had attempted to reduce racial tensions by limiting immigration and passing legislation to prevent racial discrimination. In 1976, the Race Relations Act widened the definition of discrimination and established the Commission for Racial Equality to investigate complaints and support local authorities in enforcing the law on racial matters.

Thatcher made clear her firm opposition to racial discrimination against people who had already settled in Britain, but she also took a strong stand against further immigration from the nonwhite Commonwealth countries. In a television interview she stated: "People are really rather afraid that this country might be swamped by people with a different culture. We do have to hold out the prospect of an end to immigration except, of course, for compassionate cases." Almost immediately the Conservatives shot up 10 percent in the polls.

Devolution

Callaghan's problems were compounded by dissidence in "the Celtic fringe." The United Kingdom is comprised of four main nationalities: the English, the

Welsh, the Scots, and the Irish of Northern Ireland. The English have long been dominant, politically and economically, and the English language is used throughout the country. Nevertheless, the smaller nationalities have preserved some of their traditional culture, and as Britain floundered in the 1970s, they began to look to their past to imagine a different future for themselves.

In the middle 1970s, nationalist movements arose in Scotland and Wales seeking "devolution," meaning delegation of some powers of the central government to elected assemblies established for those regions. Devolution was weak in Wales, for Welsh nationalism centered on a language that few spoke and was located primarily in rural areas. The English-speaking majority feared that a devolved government for Wales would mean a government controlled by backwoodsmen who would be indifferent to the needs of the urbanized, industrialized parts of Wales.

Scotland was different. A long national history, separate administrative, legal, educational, and religious institutions, a different form of local government, and a national culture that included such distinctive elements as kilts and bagpipes strengthened Scottish nationalism. Furthermore, Scotland's economic prospects looked good with the development of North Sea oil and natural gas, most of which was landed on the Scottish coast. Meanwhile, the heavy industries that dominated the Scottish economy were declining steadily and required large government subsidies and unemployment benefits. Industrial Scotland was a stronghold of militant unions ready to defy any government in pursuit of their local concerns.

In both places political parties emerged to agitate for devolution. There was a strong feeling in Scotland and Wales that they were neglected by the major parties. In the second election of 1974, the Scottish Nationalist Party won eleven seats and 30 percent of the Scottish vote. Shaken by losses in one of Labour's strongholds, Wilson came out in favor of devolution, although the left wing of his party saw devolution as a threat to a socialist economy and a reversion to the loyalties of the preindustrial age.

The Conservative Party was the party of the Union, and Thatcher was a strong unionist. A major problem was that devolved areas would be represented in both the Parliament of the United Kingdom and their own assemblies, which, to the English, seemed palpably unfair. Opinion in the Conservative Party began to solidify against devolution, and Thatcher decided to oppose Labour's devolution plan.

As Callaghan's problems mounted, he sought to strengthen his position in Parliament by making an alliance with the Liberals. At their insistence, he agreed to referenda in Scotland and Wales on devolution, a proposal that also assured him the support of the Scottish and Welsh Nationalist Parties.

Labour backbenchers opposed to devolution countered by amending the bill to require that devolution be supported by 40 percent of those eligible to vote.

In Scotland, the referendum was met with apathy; Scottish nationalism was limited to a small but articulate minority. The referendum passed by a slim majority, but a low turnout meant that those in favor were well below the required 40 percent of the total electorate. The majority of the voters in Wales were opposed. The Scottish Nationalist Party was furious and abandoned its support of the Callaghan ministry.

The Triumph of Margaret Thatcher

In the disastrous winter of 1978–1979, the developing crisis reached a climax. British workers were hard hit by unemployment and Callaghan's misguided incomes policy. Many workers felt they had no choice but to fight the guidelines of their own Labour government. A new factor was the increasing size and militancy of the public-sector unions, with many members who were among the lowest-paid employees in the country.

The remnants of the social contract gave way in November 1978 when the Ford Motor Company ended a nine-week strike by giving its workers pay raises of 17 percent. Truck drivers called a national strike demanding similar raises, and British Rail was afflicted with numerous one-day strikes. The winter was unusually cold, and for the first time since 1963, the entire United Kingdom was covered with snow, disrupting transportation and communications. As strikes spread, violent mass picketing took place in many parts of the country. The front page of the popular tabloid, *The Sun*, showed Callaghan, tanned and beaming, as he returned from a vacation trip to the West Indies. The headline screamed: "CRISIS? WHAT CRISIS?"

The ultimate disaster of the 1978–1979 "winter of discontent" came when more than a million public employees went on strike. Now equipped with television sets, the British public were appalled by scenes of garbage piled up in the streets, sick people (including children) turned away from hospitals, schools closed, and the dead unburied. The tabloid newspapers printed screaming headlines: "Pickets Rule," "No Mercy." It was a political and moral defeat from which the Labour Party could not recover. At that point, the national consensus that had been crumbling for a decade collapsed.

As leader of the Conservative Party, Thatcher challenged the unions head on. She called for limitations on picketing, secret ballots before strikes were called, and no-strike agreements with workers in vital services. "There will be no solution to our difficulties," she declared, "which does not include some restriction on the powers of the unions."

Callaghan knew that the tide had turned against him and the policies of Labour. He realized that anything his government attempted to do would be resisted by his own party and would not be credible, either to the international financiers, who held Britain's fate in their hands, or to the British people.

In March 1979, the Scottish Nationalists vented their frustration by moving a vote of No Confidence, and Thatcher leaped into the fray. On the night of the vote, even the catering staff in the Houses of Parliament was on strike, so that the members had to provide their own meals. Thatcher feared that some of her Conservatives might wander off to nearby restaurants and miss the crucial division. The smaller parties would determine the outcome.

It was a tense moment as the members filed through the lobbies to register their votes. The Liberals, the Scottish Nationalist Party, and most of the Ulster Unionists voted against the government. When the tally was announced, the opposition motion had won, 311–310. The five-year maximum between elections was coming to an end, and Callaghan was forced to go to the country at the worst possible time. Parliament was dissolved in April and an election was called for May.

Polls showed that Thatcher was well behind the likable Jim Callaghan in personal popularity. She won because the Labour government and the Labour Party had been discredited, and she offered new leadership and a fresh start. In her campaign speeches, Thatcher advocated a strong foreign policy, reduction of the income tax, drastic cuts in public spending, and sound money. She was committed to free enterprise, a competitive market economy, and restriction of trade unions' power. She presented Labour as the party of inflation, wage controls, and strikes. She promised that Labour's legislation requiring local authorities to establish comprehensive schools would be repealed. She called for greater personal opportunity and responsibility. And she made clear her commitment to Victorian middle-class values: strong families, home ownership, personal savings, educational opportunities, law and order.

As the campaigns unfolded, it became clear that the key issue was trade union power, which most of the British public felt had become too great. Thatcher made clear her determination to confront the problem by establishing "a fair balance between the rights and duties of the trade union movement." She promised legislation to limit trade union privileges, including restrictions on picketing and strikes in essential services. Within the Conservative Party there was great anxiety at provoking a confrontation with the unions that might result in the kind of disastrous defeat inflicted on Heath in 1974. Immune to such fears, Thatcher charged ahead.

Another issue was immigration. The National Front decided to make a major effort, fielding over 300 candidates and claiming access to the free political broadcasts on radio and television. Opponents of the National Front mobilized large demonstrations against it. In a working-class area of south London, a violent clash took place with three hundred people arrested and one person killed. Firm police control of parades prevented most of the violent confrontations from which the National Front derived much of its publicity.

The election was held on May 3, 1979. With 44 percent of the popular vote, the Conservatives won a slim majority of 43 seats in the 635-member House of Commons. Labour received 37 percent of the vote, the lowest since 1931—an emphatic rejection. The Liberals garnered a respectable 14 percent. The Scottish and Welsh nationalist parties lost heavily, suggesting that some of their former support had been a protest vote. With less than 1 percent, the National Front collapsed. It was apparent that many of its supporters had voted Conservative, largely on the basis of Thatcher's strong stand on immigration.

The major change in voting patterns was a massive swing of lower-middle-class skilled workers to the Conservatives. As they prospered, they had developed middle-class lifestyles and aspirations, and they no longer identified with the cloth-capped Labour Party of yore. They inclined to the views of the Conservative Party, although they had deserted Heath in 1974. They had had enough of high taxes, high inflation, wage controls, and strikes. They were turned off by the unrealistic proposals of Labour's left wing. They looked for leadership that would restore a sense of national unity and bring order to the workplace and the streets. They had been frightened by the industrial disruptions of "the winter of discontent."

One beneficiary of the Conservative victory was John Major, a personable Londoner of modest background, who was a surprise victor in the prestigious constituency of Huntingdonshire.

The next day Thatcher went to Buckingham Palace, where the queen authorized her to form a government. Thatcher was now prime minister, with a mandate for change.

CHAPTER TWO

~

The Beginnings of Thatcherism, 1979–1983

The Prime Minister

Margaret Thatcher came to power at a time of national breakdown that had resulted in widespread distress. She shared the public sense of crisis, and her election in 1979 was a result of her evident determination to do something about it. Thatcher stated bluntly that her goal was to restore pride and vigor to a nation in decline. She saw herself as an agent of change—a "conviction politician" with no interest in trying to revive the failed consensus of the past. She set out to turn the Labour revolution of 1945–1951 on its head: instead of a planned economy, a market economy; instead of nationalized industry, free enterprise; instead of strong trade unions, limited union power; instead of an expanded welfare state, a body of public services that were efficient and economical.

She proclaimed her commitment to a diminished role for government, fiscal responsibility, tough control of crime and public disorders, and sturdy British patriotism. The piecemeal, hit-and-miss steps by which her reforms were implemented were pragmatic adjustments to the realities of leadership in a democracy but did not change the underlying consistency of her purpose.

Several weeks were required before the Thatchers could move into No. 10 Downing Street. When Margaret and Denis occupied the small prime minister's flat at the top of the building, she was back where she came from—living over the shop!

Their daily life was simple. As much as possible she continued a practice of their earlier years, having breakfast together. Beyond that, her hours were irregular, and she made a meal or a snack whenever time permitted. Like many busy people, there were times when she resorted to the freezer and the microwave. She slept about four hours per night. Her time and energy were devoted to her work. She relied on Denis to handle everyday matters: "Anything I wanted he could provide," she said, "and he was always *there*."

Thatcher usually met with the queen once a week to discuss government business. Queen Elizabeth is intelligent, conscientious, and experienced, having consulted with seven prime ministers before Thatcher. Although these meetings were strictly private, it was said that Thatcher and the queen did not get along well. A cartoon of the time showed Thatcher saying to the queen: "You look after the weddings, and I'll look after the government."

When Thatcher began her ministry, she had to establish herself in the eyes of her Cabinet, the Conservative Party, and the British public. She had to find Conservatives who shared her view that Britain needed a radical change of direction—not only from the policies of Labour, which were discredited by "the winter of discontent," but also from the paternalistic "One Nation" Toryism of the past.

Initially, political realities dictated that she choose ministers who carried weight in the Conservative Party, most of whom had served in the Heath ministry. Among these were Sir Geoffrey Howe, chancellor of the Exchequer, and Lord Carrington, foreign and commonwealth secretary. William Whitelaw, deputy prime minister and home secretary, was noted as a conciliator, and as such he became a valued member of her team. Michael Heseltine, a property tycoon and publisher with strong connections to business, was the heir to the interventionist and pro-European views of Edward Heath. He was appointed secretary of state for the environment, which dealt with local government, housing, and urban problems.

During the years of opposition, Sir Keith Joseph had been the principal influence in defining Thatcher's economic views. He became minister for industry. Heath was passed over for foreign secretary, the post that he really wanted. He rejected Thatcher's offer of ambassador to the United States.

Power in British government is exercised through the major departments. The Cabinet office supervises the work of the departments as directed by the prime minister. Within No. 10, the policy unit worked closely with the prime minister to shape the day-to-day decisions needed to develop and implement policy.

In her early years, Thatcher met frequently with the full Cabinet, as she sought to impose her views on a body that was divided and often skeptical. She was opinionated and outspoken, and at times she revealed a shrewish nature as she shouted down those who disagreed with her. Unwilling to reply in kind to a woman, some of the men gave up and con-centrated on their own departments. Thatcher preferred to use small com-mittees of Cabinet members, which moved matters along more efficiently and were more easily dominated.

The Thatcher ministry floundered in its first two years: economic condi-tions were desperate, the prime minister was inexperienced, and the Cabinet was disrupted by personality and policy clashes. By 1981, Thatcher had a clearer idea of where she was going, and she reshuffled her Cabinet to bring it more in line with her ideas. At that point the Thatcher ministry finally hit its stride.

Thatcher also worked to establish her leadership of the Conservative members of the House of Commons. As a maverick in her own party, her par-liamentary support was shaky. She gave considerable attention to the Con-servative backbenchers, who had made her the party leader. She knew the importance of their goodwill. In her earlier years, she was a frequent visitor to the Commons' tearoom.

Getting Going

The Thatcher ministry took office at a time of worldwide inflation and re-cession, aggravated by sky-high oil prices resulting from the overthrow of the Shah and the Islamic revolution in Iran. Inflation peaked in 1980 at 21 per-cent, and the Gross National Product fell. Unemployment was at 1.3 million in 1979 and over 2 million by 1981.

Thatcher's immediate goal was to reduce inflation, which in her opinion dis-couraged business investment, led to short-term speculation and profiteering, and penalized saving. In that objective she was supported by public opinion; most people were not unemployed and were shocked by runaway inflation.

She accepted the monetarist argument that government contributed to inflation by excessive spending and borrowing. Stringent efforts were made to keep money growth within narrow limits, although Thatcher soon dis-covered how difficult it was to measure the money supply. High interest rates were imposed to reduce business and consumer borrowing. Interest rates were already at 14 percent when Thatcher took office. In November 1979, they were raised to 17 percent and remained at or near that level for the next year.

Thatcher rejected the idea that inflation could be checked by controls on prices or wages. She made no effort to restore full employment by subsidizing failing industries. These she repudiated as the discredited policies of Labour. If the state managed its own finances properly, she believed, the market would make the necessary adjustments in prices, wages, and employment.

She was fortunate that one recurrent problem of the past—the balance of payments—was greatly diminished. By 1979, North Sea oil had become productive, and high oil prices brought in foreign currency that stabilized the pound at a comparatively high level. The strong pound helped to reduce inflation, because it made imports cheaper. It was damaging to industry, because it made exports more expensive, but declining inflation was seen as the precondition of industrial revival.

In the first three years, the economic crisis overwhelmed all other concerns. Howe's 1979 budget was the first installment of Thatcherism. He announced that the primary objectives were to cut public spending and increase personal incentives by reducing direct taxation, which, he believed, "would leave room for commerce and industry to prosper." Income tax was sharply reduced: the base rate fell from 33 percent to 30 percent, and the top rate was cut from 83 percent to 60 percent. Although cuts in income tax poured more money into an already inflated economy, in Thatcherite ideology this policy, so advantageous to the wealthy, would benefit the economy by encouraging entrepreneurship and investment.

To soak up purchasing power, the burden on consumers was increased. The VAT (value added tax), a kind of sales tax, and the motor fuel tax were raised, as were National Insurance contributions. These increases fell mainly on middle- and low-income people. The nationalized utilities were permitted to increase their artificially low prices, which was a further addition to the cost of living. The main objection to Howe's budget was the unfairness of his approach, for income tax cuts benefited well-to-do people, while consumption taxes fell heaviest on low-income families and the poor.

Heavy cuts in public spending were announced in all branches of government except the police, defense, and the National Health Service (NHS). Tight cash limits were imposed on all departments, which had to cope with inflation out of existing budgets. Expenditures for housing and local government were hit hard, and education suffered lesser cuts. Reductions were also made in subsidies to the nationalized industries, which led to more unemployment. Increased costs for pensions, unemployment benefits, and other social security payments ate up the savings that were made. Total expenditures actually rose by about 6 percent, but that was less than might have been expected, given the rate of inflation.

At first the fiscal and monetary policies of the Thatcher ministry seemed to have aggravated the twin problems of inflation and recession. In the next year consumer prices, to most people the most important economic indicator, rose by 18 percent. High interest rates choked off domestic investment and sucked in "hot money" from abroad, creating a strong pound that damaged exports. North Sea oil, in most respects a fortunate asset, had a similar effect.

Economic output in the next two years fell by 5 percent. Manufacturing output fell by 15 percent, and investment by 30 percent. Large private companies and the nationalized industries showed heavy losses. By 1983, unemployment had risen to 3 million, with few prospects for new jobs to replace those irretrievably lost. Industrial relations were torn by acrimony and strikes. Riots, both economic and racial, broke out in London, Liverpool, and other hard-hit industrial cities.

Despite double-digit inflation, Thatcher clung firmly to her belief that only the market could resolve Britain's problems in a manner that would last. From 1979 to 1981, the retail price index rose an average of 14 percent annually. Wage inflation kept pace: the unions got wage increases averaging 16 percent in 1979 and 20 percent in 1980. People with jobs were holding their own; the blow fell heaviest on people living on fixed incomes and the unemployed.

After this disastrous beginning, Thatcher realized the contradiction between cutting income taxes and fighting inflation. The decision was made that the fight against inflation must take precedence over tax cuts intended to stimulate economic growth. Only reduced public borrowing could check inflation, and the way to do that was to raise taxes and cut spending. Much as she regretted giving up her premature tax cuts, Thatcher had the courage to raise income taxes in a recession, an unorthodox policy that eventually succeeded.

The moment of truth for the Thatcher government came in 1981. Howe's budget included increases in the income tax (actually not adjusting for inflation, then running at about 18 percent), another increase in National Insurance contributions, and a wide variety of new consumption taxes and other charges. NHS charges were increased. Higher education took severe cuts, and university expansion was stopped in its tracks.

Steps were taken to reform social security in ways that would reduce costs. Since 1965 benefits for sickness and unemployment had been indexed on the basis of wages, which the government thought made it too tempting to live on benefits rather than return to work. In 1982, benefits were changed to an index based on price inflation, which usually was lower. Pensions were also indexed to prices, which produced great savings in the National Insurance Fund. Sick pay for the first eight weeks was charged to employers (with some reimbursement) rather than being paid out of National Insurance because employers would be strict in granting sick leave if they had to pay for it.

Eventually fiscal restraint, tight money, and unemployment brought inflation down. In 1982, the inflation rate began dropping and reached 4.5 percent in 1983. For the next five years inflation remained around 5 percent, a level that undergirded a period of strong economic growth.

Oil revenues and the strong pound made possible a free-market step of the greatest consequence: abolition of the exchange controls that had been in place since World War II. Sterling was freed to become a world currency again, and British investors could seek the best possible returns anywhere in the world. London's role as a financial center was enhanced, and the growth of overseas investments made Britain an integral part of the emerging world economy.

Local Government

Local government in Britain was largely an extension of the central government, which funded 60 percent of local government expenditures. Local government employees had proliferated to carry out government programs. These employees were unionized, and the unions used them to influence local authorities and turn out votes for the Labour Party. Thatcher believed that local governments, especially those in large cities that were dominated by Labour and the unions, were swollen, inefficient, inordinately costly, and often corrupt. Local government spending was an impediment to her efforts to control inflation.

During the years in opposition, Thatcher had spelled out three principal reforms: control of local government spending; sale of council houses, which would reduce political influence and enable tenants to own their own homes; and reform of the rates, the property tax on homes and businesses. She was determined to make local governments efficient and economical, an objective shared by Heseltine, secretary of state for the department of the environment, who brought to his office the perspective of a successful businessman.

The Local Government Act of 1980, introduced by Heseltine, strengthened central control of spending by fixing the spending of each unit of local government at the level deemed necessary to maintain uniform national services. The Greater London Council, led by "Red Ken" Livingstone, defied the government and adopted a "municipal socialist budget," an example followed by the councils of the other metropolitan counties. They increased the rates, a step that fell heavily on owners of business and homes, most of whom were Conservatives, and used the money to increase the number of public employees, keep public transport inexpensive, and fund social programs.

In 1983, the government responded with the Rates Act, which put a cap on rates. Heseltine proposed an independent Audit Commission to audit the books of local government units and evaluate expenditures. This institution proved to be highly successful in bringing local expenditures under control.

A major activity of local governments was public housing. In 1980, local governments were restricted in the funds they could use to construct council houses. For the next decade, housing was the spending area receiving the largest cuts. Councils were required to raise rents to fair-market levels. Low-income tenants received financial assistance (Housing Benefit), but those who could afford to pay were no longer living in subsidized housing.

The most important step was the sale of council housing. As much as possible, Thatcher wanted ordinary working people to own their own homes, which she saw as an inducement to personal responsibility. In 1980, the Housing Act gave tenants of council houses the right to purchase their houses at low prices and on easy terms. The longer they had been tenants, the greater the discount, up to a 50 percent discount from market value. The increases in rents dictated by the government made it advisable for tenants to buy, if they could afford it. More than a million council houses were sold during the 1980s. Heseltine stated that the legislation "lays the foundation for one of the most important social revolutions of our time." It also helped convert some working-class voters into Conservatives.

By 1990, most of the desirable houses had been sold, with the remaining public housing consisting of high-rise flats occupied by the poor in estates riddled with crime, drugs, and disorder. Three-quarters of the people in public housing were in the lowest 40 percent of income, and 60 percent of them were unemployed.

Housing sales were an important source of income for the Treasury, rising from £472 million in 1979–1980 to more than £2 billion in 1986–1987. Owner-occupiers of houses increased from 56 percent to 71 percent. Much of the increase was due to sales of council houses to working-class people who had expected to rent all their lives.

Social Issues

During this period of inflation and unemployment, the safety net held. Although Thatcher gained a reputation for hostility to social programs, she continued the main commitments to social security, the National Health Service, and schools. Training programs for young people were introduced to assist them in preparing for the changing world of work. In some cases the training was a valuable investment in the future; in others, the programs may have done little more than keep restless youths off the streets, in itself an accomplishment of some social utility.

One factor in Thatcher's electoral victory had been her commitment to a reduction of immigration. In a population of 53 million whites, Britain had 1 million people of West Indian origin and an equal number of Asians. Conservatives claimed that British civilization was threatened; workers feared competition from immigrants; and some immigrant communities had a high incidence of crime, family breakdown, illegitimacy, and disorder. An English nationalist to the core, Thatcher shared the uneasiness of many of her countrymen about pockets of poorly assimilated immigrants. The challenge was to prepare legislation that was undeniably racist without appearing to be racist.

The solution adopted was a new definition of British citizenship that sloughed off the long-standing claims of Commonwealth residents. The Nationality Act of 1981 defined British citizenship as something other than being a subject of the queen. Full British citizenship went to people who resided in Britain or were closely related to citizens. The eligibility of Commonwealth immigrants for citizenship was restricted to people who had one parent or grandparent born in the United Kingdom.

The Nationality Bill had considerable support in both parties: the Conservatives were strong nationalists, and Labour wanted to protect jobs and keep wages up. The bill was strongly opposed by immigrant groups and the churches. It faced opposition in the House of Lords, where the Archbishop of Canterbury was a prominent opponent. Passage of the Nationality Act terminated the right of millions of former imperial subjects to settle in Britain. Essentially, the question of Commonwealth immigration was settled. Thatcher had fulfilled her campaign promise.

Political Parties

The Thatcher ministry got off to a turbulent start, and the Cabinet and House of Commons were filled with contention and acrimony. Led by Heath, some of the former leaders of the Conservative Party criticized Thatcher's financial and economic policies, which they declared were doctrinaire and damaging. They were concerned about the collapse of British industry and the devastation brought to the old industrial areas. They wanted to maintain social harmony, despite differences of income, education, and occupation. They were call "wets," a term applied to a timid schoolboy who cries easily. The Thatcherites remained resolutely "dry-eyed," as the bad news kept coming in.

By 1981, the strain of the Thatcherite economic policy was beginning to show. Within the Conservative Party, Thatcher's policies underwent a drumfire of criticism from Heath and other "one Nation" Conservatives. One prominent Conservative urged the party to remember "its well established tradition of the protective role of the state." Harold Macmillan, now Lord Stockton, recalled the human tragedies of unemployment in the 1930s, which he had seen firsthand as a young MP for Stockton. The Archbishop of Canterbury called on the Church to be the conscience of the nation. He declared "the costs of the present policies, with the continuing growth of unemployment are unacceptable."

In 1980, the backbench 1922 Committee had supported the government's policy, but by 1981, even the backbenchers were calling for a change. They were supported by 364 economists who signed a letter to the *Times* calling for an end to the economic squeeze. Thatcher insisted that the worst was over. Britain, she said, is like a patient "who for a time is suffering from both the illness and the medicine." When the suggestion was made that it was time for a "U-Turn" like Heath's in 1972, she replied: "You turn if you like. The lady's not for turning."

By 1982, the economy was in a position to revive, but a heavy price had been paid in unemployment and bankruptcies. Most of the burden had been borne by industrial workers, retired people, and the poor. Inflation and spending restraints had damaged public services, both national and local. Thatcher's popularity had reached a low point. A poll showed that only 25 percent of the British people were satisfied with her performance as prime minister, and only 18 percent were satisfied with the Conservative government.

In the meantime, John Major had taken the first steps in the political career that would lead to No. 10 Downing Street. His career exemplified the democratic Britain that had emerged from World War II. His father was an elderly, down-and-out former entertainer; his mother had been a dancer in his father's traveling show. Major grew up in Brixton, a poor and racially mixed part of London. He attended a grammar school, but he did not attend a university, leaving school to seek his fortune at age sixteen. He held a variety of low-paid jobs and was briefly on welfare before taking a job in a bank, which included a period of time in Nigeria. In his autobiography, Major tells the story of his irregular family background and upbringing, in a straightforward and entertaining way.

Major decided early in life that he wanted a political career. He joined the Conservative Party in his Labour-dominated constituency of Lambeth, where his intelligence, charm, and rapport with working-class people enabled him to be elected to the borough council. He lost a try for a seat on the Greater London Council, but in the campaign, he met his wife, Norma, a dressmaker and designer who was an avid fan of opera. He next turned his attention to winning a seat in Parliament. His candidacies in predominantly Labour constituencies in London in the two elections of 1974 failed, but he gained experience in campaigning.

As a Londoner from a working-class neighborhood, Major expected to be elected from a London constituency. It was a surprise in 1979 when he was selected as the candidate for Huntingdonshire, a pleasant rural county near London that was a safe Conservative seat. He won handily in the election of May 1979 and took his seat in the House of Commons led by the new prime minister, Margaret Thatcher. He became one of the Tory whips, where he learned the art of dealing with other MPs in the process of moving the government's agenda through the Commons. Given the differences among the Tory members, it was a challenging assignment.

Defeat in the election of 1979 brought a dramatic change in the Labour Party. In 1980, James Callaghan retired from the party leadership. Michael Foot, a scholarly intellectual lacking leadership ability or experience in the higher offices of government, succeeded him. Bitter differences broke out between the Labour MPs who had supported Callaghan's moderate policies and the left-wingers, who felt that Callaghan had sacrificed the principles of the Labour Party to the forces of international capitalism. Usually identified with the left, it was Foot's task to hold his contentious party together.

Within the Labour Party, the left wing intensified its demands for radical solutions to Britain's problems: withdrawal from NATO and the European Economic Community (EEC), unilateral nuclear disarmament, price controls, increased public expenditure to restore full employment, renationalization of certain industries, abolition of the House of Lords, and an end to private education and medicine. These policies had little support among the British people and contributed to the precipitous decline of the Labour Party.

Activists centered in London and major industrial cities aggravated differences within the party. They sought to reduce the powers of the party's parliamentary leaders by making them more responsible to the National Executive Committee (NEC) and local constituency organizations. In the past, Labour MPs had chosen the party leader, but that was changed to an electoral college representing MPs, constituency organizations, and the unions. Activists known as "the loony left" promoted efforts to improve the status of women, ethnic minorities, and gays and lesbians. In some cities, including London, they gained control of local government, which they used to promote their agenda.

In 1981, the Labour Party broke wide open. Four moderate leaders left the party to establish the Social Democratic Party (SDP). Led by Roy Jenkins, one of Labour's most distinguished and experienced members. They argued that Britain needed a party of moderate reform that would strike a balance between Thatcherism and socialism and was not dominated by the unions and the radical left.

The Social Democrats advocated a mixed economy with extensive public investment, decentralization of government, an improved welfare state, a firm commitment to the EEC, support of NATO, and efforts for multilateral disarmament. With four leaders who were experienced and well regarded, the SDP had instant credibility. More than twenty Labour MPs joined the rebels. The media, with their incessant search for novelty, gave extensive attention to the new party, which hired a public relations firm to help the process along.

In June, the Social Democrats joined with the Liberal Party to form a centrist force that would be attractive to moderate voters who rejected both Thatcherism and socialism. Jenkins became the leader of the SDP–Liberal Alliance in the House of Commons and the country, with David Steel, leader of the Liberals, in a subordinate role. The stated purpose of the Alliance was to "break the mould of dogma and class conflict" that characterized the two major parties. The SDP–Liberal Alliance was a precursor of New Labour and Tony Blair's "Middle Way."

At first the Alliance achieved remarkable success, reaching 44 percent in the opinion polls in the fall of 1981, as the Conservatives and Labour sank to 27 percent each. Despite the blaze of publicity, support for the SDP–Liberal Alliance was shallow and was based mainly on dissatisfaction with the two major parties. As the Thatcher government took hold, the Alliance began to slip; by April 1982, the three parties were virtually even at 33 percent in the polls.

During those grim days of inflation, recession, and unemployment, the monarchy provided a bright spot. In July 1981, His Royal Highness, Charles, Prince of Wales and heir to the throne, was married to Lady Diana Spencer. The wedding took place in St. Paul's cathedral with great pomp and ceremony and was televised throughout the world. On that grand occasion, the magic of the British monarchy was seen at its most bewitching. The next year the birth of a son seemed to secure the future of the dynasty. Five years later, the royal family added Miss Sarah Ferguson, who was married to Prince Andrew, Duke of York, the queen's second son. Few anticipated the unhappy outcomes of those royal marriages.

Privatization

Thatcher was devoted to the principles of free enterprise, competition, and the market economy. In her view, public ownership of major industries meant that they became politicized; without the test of the free market, they became inefficient and uncompetitive. For political reasons, they were not permitted to fail and required subsidies to preserve jobs.

Selling off the nationalized industries was a logical outcome of Thatcherism, but it began tentatively, almost as an afterthought. The first privatizations were of industries that did not have strong political constituencies and were not widely known to the public. These included the National Freight Corporation (1980), part of British Aerospace (1981), Cable and Wireless (1981), British Oil (1982), British Rail Hotels (1981), and Associated British Ports (1983). The entire National Freight Corporation was sold to its employees. The price of the shares rose so rapidly that employees who did not take up their quota of shares soon regretted it.

The privatizations had the additional advantage that they brought much-needed funds into the Treasury, a consideration that became increasingly important as privatization moved on to larger industries. In 1979–1980, the income from privatizations was £377 million; by 1988–1989, it was more than £6 billion. Apart from any economic merit that privatization might have, it became an important factor in the finances of government.

The Trade Unions

The first three years of the Thatcher ministry were tormented by strikes. In 1979, Britain had its worst year ever, with 4.5 million workers on strike at one time or another and almost 30 million workdays lost due to strikes. Thatcher's policy was to keep the government out of private-sector strikes, allowing the workers to face the loss of their jobs if they priced their employer out of the market. She believed that workers were more concerned with preserving their jobs than in engaging in political and industrial confrontations. "Millions of British workers," she said in 1979, "go in fear of union power." Polls showed that she was right: up to 80 percent of workers favored the government's proposals to reform and limit the unions.

The major problem was strikes in the nationalized industries, which had been sheltered by Labour from market competition. Almost immediately the leadership of the National Union of Mineworkers (NUM) challenged the Thatcher government and the National Coal Board. Substantial sums had been invested in improving the best mines, which could produce all the coal that Britain needed, and many less-efficient pits faced closure. Thatcher was not prepared for the kind of confrontation that had destroyed the Heath ministry. The "hit list" of mines to be closed was withdrawn, and the National Coal Board was given an additional subsidy.

Thatcher realized that a confrontation with the miners was likely to take place eventually, and she did not want to be caught unprepared, as Heath had been. She found that neither the Coal Board nor the main users of coal had stockpiled coal at the plants where it would be needed. She insisted that preparations be made to make it possible to withstand a coal strike in the future.

In 1982, the moderate president of the NUM retired and was succeeded by Arthur Scargill, a militant firebrand who was a bitter enemy of the National Coal Board. Scargill immediately demanded a 31 percent pay raise. The rules of the NUM required a ballot before calling a strike. Scargill campaigned hard for a "Yes" vote, but the miners, fearful of losing their jobs, voted 61 percent against. Foiled, Scargill bided his time and waited for a better opportunity.

The most damaging strike was at British Steel. In addition to picketing British Steel plants, pickets were also posted at private steel companies that were trying to remain open. Attempts were made to block imports of steel, although some steel was getting through. Unlike users of coal, users of steel had accumulated large stocks in anticipation of the strike.

One way or another, the major steel users, such as the auto industry, were able to get the steel they needed. After three months, the strike was settled with a compromise. The government agreed to an 11 percent raise, and the steel workers gave in and accepted a productivity agreement that closed some old, inefficient plants. Thatcher had given in to strikers, but she had avoided an all-out confrontation before she was ready for it.

With British Steel back in production, it was necessary to take the steps needed to make it profitable in the future. Thatcher brought in Ian MacGregor, a tough-minded American manager (born in Scotland), to lead the corporation. MacGregor began cutting jobs and closing inefficient plants. At that point, Thatcher was willing to provide additional investment capital for British Steel, which changed from being the least efficient producer in Europe to one of the best.

Thatcher faced another test at the nationalized auto manufacturer, British Leyland (BL). From a market share of 33 percent in 1974, BL cars had fallen to 20 percent in 1979. The unions at BL were notoriously disruptive, and under Labour governments they had usually gotten their way. The company had steadily lost market share to private competitors like Ford, whose models were more attractive and costs were lower. It was a sad day for car lovers in 1980 when BL ended production of the MG sports car.

In 1980, a strike for higher wages was threatened at BL. In this instance, management simply announced that it would begin paying the wages it had

proposed and urged the workers to show up. At a time of high unemployment, almost all employees reported for work, and the strike did not take
place. When a similar crisis arose in 1981, the workers voted to accept BL's
offer rather than face closure of the plants.

BL was rewarded with an infusion of cash from the government, despite
Thatcher's general principle that nationalized industries must stand or fall on
their own merits. The political and social consequences of shutting down BL
were too much to accept. People have strong feelings about cars, and the
British public wanted to preserve the last large British carmaker.

Galloping inflation had penalized workers in the public sector. In 1981,
the civil service unions responded with a series of strikes that interrupted the
Inland Revenue (the British equivalent of the IRS), issuance of passports and
driver's licenses, air traffic controllers, and other essential public services.
Eventually they settled for the government's offer of 7.5 percent. The general
public had shown little sympathy for the civil servants, with their secure jobs
and comfortable pensions.

More serious was a nationwide strike in 1982 in the NHS, whose many
low-paid workers had suffered severely from inflation. Unwilling to leave the
British people totally without health care, the union called for "rolling disruptions" from one hospital to another. After eight months, the Health Service workers, making little headway with the government and seeing the
backlog of patients mounting, gave in. The nurses, whose pay had fallen far
behind the private sector, received a decent increase, but low-paid ancillary
workers got very little. The Thatcher ministry had won a victory, but it was
not a victory to be proud of.

Unlike Heath, Thatcher moved cautiously to limit the powers of the
unions. She was fortunate that the unions had discredited themselves with
the public and many of their members by irresponsible strikes at a time of
great economic stress. Thatcher's step-by-step approach seemed reasonable
to the unions, compared to what they had been led to expect, nor did they
think that her government would last long enough to accomplish its purpose.
They did not realize what was happening to them until it was too late.

The Employment Act of 1980 required 80 percent approval to establish
a closed shop, restricted sympathy strikes, and limited picketing to the
worker's place of employment. The Employment Act of 1982 provided
that unions engaging in illegal labor practices, including mass picketing,
could be sued for civil damages and fined or held in contempt of court.
The problem of wildcat strikes and other shop-floor disruptions was dealt
with by making the national unions responsible for local violations of the
law or the labor contract.

The legislation of 1980 and 1982 brought the judges into labor relations, a group typically unsympathetic to the unions. By offering a remedy in the civil courts, strikes would be depoliticized, since government intervention would be replaced by judicial decisions arising from complaints brought by employers. Government would enter the picture only if violence erupted, in which case the police and the criminal justice system would become involved.

The newspaper business had some of the most powerful and combative unions, for the printers were determined to preserve the obsolete methods and work rules that were threatened by new technology. For more than a year, the *Times* and the *Sunday Times*, the most prestigious British newspapers, had been shut down due to a conflict between the owners and the employees concerning this matter.

Although a compromise settlement was reached in 1981, the owners decided to sell out to Rupert Murdoch, an Australian tycoon, who was the owner of two tabloid newspapers, *The Sun* and the *News of the World*. Much as they disliked Murdoch and his insistence on efficient labor practices, the unions decided to come to terms with him to save their jobs. Murdoch, however, had more tricks up his sleeve, which were revealed in due time.

The Conservative victory in 1979 marked the beginning of the end for the political influence of organized labor, tied as it was to the Labour Party. At first the Trades Union Congress (TUC) was unconvinced that the Thatcher government meant what it said about taming the unions. As unemployment grew, the TUC assumed that a crisis of such dimensions would require the government to change its policies. When Thatcher held to her course, it became clear that the government had abandoned the historic goal of full employment. A hostile government, an unsympathetic public, and mass unemployment brought to an end the political and economic power of organized labor.

By 1982, inflation was falling, and the economy was beginning to recover. Thatcher had gained respect with the public for her leadership and toughness, although she was not personally popular. She had assembled a Cabinet that would work with her, often grudgingly, and she had faced down Heath and other heavyweights in the Conservative Party. It had been a rough beginning, but the Thatcher Revolution was on its way.

The Cold War

Thatcher was a child of the World War II era, and in her early years, she had been imbued with the World War II spirit of democracy versus dictatorship.

When the war ended and the Cold War began, she saw the tensions between the Western democracies and the Soviet Union in the same light.

She recognized the importance of American political leadership, economic strength, and military power as embodied in the North Atlantic Treaty Organization (NATO). She saw the United States as the guarantor of free-flowing global trade, so vital to the island kingdom. She held firmly to the idea of a "special relationship" between the United States and Great Britain, with Britain serving as a link between the United States and its allies on the European continent.

Thatcher brought a new assertiveness into British foreign policy. She was determined to reverse the image of Britain as a once-great power in terminal decline. Although Britain could not rival the superpowers, she was convinced that Britain could play a significant role in world affairs and should be able to defend itself and its remaining dependencies. Despite the fiscal squeeze, she supported the NATO decision for a five-year program of increased military spending. And she blew the trumpet of British nationalism loud and clear!

Her reforming zeal did not extend to the Foreign and Commonwealth Office or the Ministry of Defence. A review of defense needs was undertaken in 1981, but it had little effect other than a recommendation to reduce the navy, which proved embarrassing when Argentina invaded the Falkland Islands. The five-year NATO buildup was sustained until it ran out in 1985, when military expenditures began to decline.

Thatcher was determined that Britain would maintain its own nuclear deterrent. She decided to adopt the powerful, submarine-based American Trident missiles to replace the obsolete Polaris missiles. When the Soviet Union began installing medium-range nuclear missiles that could reach targets in Western Europe, NATO decided that it had to be prepared to retaliate in kind. The decision was made to place powerful, accurate American cruise missiles (a medium-range missile) in Germany and Britain.

The new missiles were politically controversial, for a strong antinuclear movement had come into existence. In addition to those who opposed nuclear weapons on military and moral grounds, others questioned whether Britain could afford the high cost of being a nuclear power, especially since NATO already had access to powerful American nuclear forces.

Britain's nuclear deterrent was opposed by the Campaign for Nuclear Disarmament (CND). The objective of the organization was to eliminate nuclear weapons throughout the world and to make Britain the leader of the antinuclear movement by abandoning nuclear weapons unilaterally. The Labour Party had shown sympathy with the organization, and many prominent Labour figures were members.

The antinuclear cause was dramatized by large numbers of women who established a "peace camp" at Greenham Common, north of London, where the cruise missiles were to be installed. In April 1983, the CND organized a vast demonstration with participants linking arms from Greenham Common to an ordnance factory fourteen miles away. Although there were gaps in the chain, the demonstration was proclaimed a success.

In 1983, the first cruise missiles arrived at Greenham, despite violent demonstrations at the base. The general public thought otherwise. Polls showed that two-thirds of the British public favored retention of nuclear weapons along with strong conventional forces.

President Ronald Reagan

The inauguration of Ronald Reagan as president of the United States in January 1981 brought a kindred spirit to the White House. Thatcher was eager to restore "the special relationship" that had faded during the 1960s and 1970s. President Reagan responded favorably, for they had much in common. They shared similar ideas about reducing the role of government, cutting taxes and spending, and firm opposition to Soviet militarism and expansion. He respected her intelligence and knowledge, and she responded to his charm.

Despite their personal friendship, the Reagan foreign policy was at times embarrassing to Thatcher. In 1982 Israel, stung by Palestinian attacks from Lebanese territory, invaded south Lebanon to destroy the settlements of the Palestinians. This invasion provoked an invasion by Syria into northern and eastern Lebanon, and the Lebanese government fell apart.

The Reagan administration, with much fanfare, sent American troops to Lebanon to preserve the unity of that small country. The president called on America's allies for support in forming a multinational force for this purpose. Thatcher assessed the chances for success in this venture as almost nil, but she wished to preserve her relationship with the president. She sent a small contingent of troops, as did France. The multinational force accomplished nothing, and the American and other troops remained stationary in their positions.

In October 1983, a terrorist drove a truckload of explosives into Beirut airport and killed 241 American marines housed there. Shaken by this disaster, Reagan pulled American troops out of Beirut, leaving his allies to deal with the situation. British and French troops were withdrawn the next year, and the Lebanon fiasco came to an end.

When the Americans left Lebanon, some American forces were rerouted to attack the small West Indian island of Grenada, which had come under the control of a communist leader. The ostensible reason was to destroy an airfield that the Grenadans were building with Cuban assistance. The Reagan administration claimed that Grenada was becoming a threat to hemispheric security. Some American students on the island were portrayed as potential hostages.

Thatcher urged Reagan to exercise restraint. Britain had an important interest, for Grenada was part of the Commonwealth, and the queen was the formal head of state. The British high commissioner in the islands was not aware of any dangers. Thatcher urged the Reagan administration to hold back until a serious threat (if any) emerged.

Needing a public relations "victory" to offset his fiasco in Beirut, Reagan invaded the tiny island without warning. The United States vetoed a Security Council declaration that the invasion was a violation of international law. A heavily armed American force landed and easily overpowered 600 Cuban construction workers armed with rifles. Although the Grenadans had no airpower, the U.S. Air Force was brought into the fray, and American "precision bombing" struck a hospital, killing fifty patients.

The British public viewed this made-for-TV war as an irresponsible exercise of superpower might, and the British press expressed its resentment that a part of the Commonwealth had been attacked without obtaining British consent. Thatcher was embarrassed that her efforts to maintain a "special relationship" with Reagan had been ignored.

The European Community

While showing her determination to maintain good relations with the United States, Margaret Thatcher displayed readiness for confrontation with the European Community (EC). She was determined to challenge the domination of the Council of Ministers by France and Germany and to resist the bureaucratic regulations of the European Commission in Brussels. Her blunt manner and outspoken ways made her an unwelcome colleague at meetings of the Council of Ministers. She was accused of "hand bagging" at ministerial meetings: making her point by whacking those vexatious foreigners with her handbag.

"The Iron Lady" insisted that the terms negotiated by Heath for admission into the EC were inordinately expensive. The EC was funded by contributions from the member countries based on domestic VAT and tariffs imposed by the EC on imported manufactured goods and foodstuffs. Britain had an active trade and imported much of its food. The result was a contribution that was disproportionate compared to countries that were more self-sufficient.

Since agriculture was a relatively small part of the British economy, Britain received less in agricultural subsidies, which comprised the bulk of the EC budget.

In her first meeting with the Council of Ministers, Thatcher insisted in no uncertain terms that the situation could not continue. The EC leaders agreed to study the budget and Britain's contribution to it. In 1984, after the interminable haggling typical of the EC, agreement was reached that Britain would receive an annual rebate of two-thirds of its excess contributions. Thatcher declared that she was satisfied, and remarked: "We are trying to be good Europeans."

At the root of Britain's continuing problems with the European Community was a difference of opinion concerning its purpose and character. Breaking down national borders within the EC had led to strong economic growth, but in the process, the Community had developed a complex regulatory system managed by a large bureaucracy in Brussels. Within the EC, the system worked to regulate competition among members and protect established interests. In relation to other countries, the EC was protectionist.

With her belief in free enterprise and market competition, Thatcher's economic philosophy ran counter to that of the EC. Britain was a country with important Atlantic and global interests. The EC had adopted tariffs and other obstacles to imports from nonmembers, which threatened Britain's economic ties with other parts of the world. When Thatcher complained to President François Mitterand of France that the EC was protectionist, he replied: "That was the point of it."

Economic integration required predictable exchange rates among the member states. To achieve this objective, the EC had established the Exchange Rate Mechanism (ERM), which required each member of the EC to follow policies that would keep its currency in a stable relationship with the others. Thatcher flatly refused to join the ERM. She believed in free markets, including free exchange rates among national currencies. The strongest currency in the ERM was the West German mark, and Thatcher, nationalist that she was, did not want the British currency tied to West Germany.

The EC had also developed a strong movement toward political unity, which Thatcher staunchly resisted. She was determined to protect British sovereignty, especially in respect of foreign policy, defense, and the national currency. Although Britain was unquestionably part of Europe, for four centuries the British people had also looked outward and found a destiny overseas. Her efforts to push the EC in a direction more congenial to Britain were unsuccessful. Under Thatcher, Britain was always the misfit in the EC.

Britain cooperated with the EC in one respect—the establishment of a European Parliament, directly elected by the voters in each member country. The United Kingdom has seventy-eight members. Concerned as she was with preserving national sovereignty, Thatcher was determined that the European Parliament would be nothing more than a "talk shop," and such it has remained, albeit an expensive one.

The Falklands War

Just as Thatcher's popularity had reached its lowest point, she was given a new lease on her political life by General Leopoldo Galtieri, the president of Argentina, whose regime was noted for its disdain for human rights and the "disappearances" of thousands of its people. In April 1982, the Argentines invaded the Falkland Islands (known as the Malvinas to the Argentines), a barren, windswept archipelago located off the southeastern coast of Argentina. The claims of Britain and Argentina to the islands were lost in obscurity and the islands had little economic value. There could be no question that the eighteen hundred people who lived there were British and had no desire to be ruled by General Galtieri.

Negotiations concerning the fate of the islands had been taking place since 1965 and continued right up to the day of the invasion, but Britain felt no sense of urgency about the matter. A review of defense spending had produced plans to eliminate most of the surface fleet, including the two aircraft carriers. Despite reports of unusual Argentine military activity, the Foreign Office and the British public were totally surprised when reports arrived that Argentine naval and ground forces had arrived at Port Stanley, the only city on the Falklands, and were landing troops.

Thatcher reacted like a lioness whose cubs were threatened. A hastily improvised armada of more than one hundred ships and 27,000 men, including aircraft carriers and destroyers, was sent on a fifty-day voyage to the rescue. There were forty-four warships and 10,000 ground troops. The *Queen Elizabeth II* and other cruise ships were requisitioned as troop ships. The queen's second son, Prince Andrew, was a helicopter pilot on one of the aircraft carriers and went off to the South Atlantic with his mates.

In Parliament, there was general agreement that a firm response was necessary, but the government was heatedly attacked for its failure to anticipate the Argentine action. There was strong criticism of a defense policy that emphasized NATO and missiles at the expense of the Navy. Lord Carrington, foreign secretary, took the blame for the debacle and resigned.

Led by Thatcher, a Cabinet committee was established to serve as a War Cabinet. All parties supported the war, although the Labour Party hoped that a display of British willingness to use force would lead to a resolution of the dispute without actual fighting. Public opinion rallied to support the war. Britain was no longer a major power, but the British people still had their national pride and a glorious naval history going back to Sir Francis Drake and the defeat of the Spanish Armada. They were not going to be pushed around by a second-rate country like Argentina, especially one ruled by an unsavory dictator.

Through it all Thatcher held to her course with Churchillian determination. Now it was the turn of the Argentines to be surprised, for they had not expected such a prompt and vigorous response. The members of the European Community and the Commonwealth immediately promised their support and imposed economic sanctions on Argentina. After intense debates, the United Nations Security Council passed a resolution condemning Argentina's invasion and demanded immediate withdrawal as a preliminary to negotiations.

Despite Thatcher's efforts to establish a "special relationship" with Reagan, the first response of the United States was to attempt to mediate the dispute. The Reagan administration looked to Latin American dictators as bulwarks against communism. They did not want a humiliating defeat for the Argentines, which would probably bring the downfall of the Galtieri regime. While the British force was heading southward at full speed, Secretary of State Alexander Haig shuttled between Washington, London, and Buenos Aires with a proposal for a neutral administration of the islands until a permanent settlement could be reached.

When Secretary Haig's efforts got nowhere, the United States belatedly imposed economic sanctions on Argentina. From the outset, the U.S. Department of Defense supported the British task force by providing fuel, ammunition, weather forecasting, and satellite communications that contributed significantly to the success of the operation. Throughout the Cold War an Anglo-American "intelligence community" had knitted the two countries together, providing information about possible foreign threats. Ties between the U. S. and British navies were close.

As the armada proceeded southward, there were many who had second thoughts. The Labour Party urged further efforts at a settlement through the United Nations. Even some members of the Cabinet were getting cold feet. An amphibious landing on a defended shore in the stormy South Atlantic 8,000 miles from home was by no means a sure thing.

There were two main islands, East and West Falklands, and about one hundred smaller islands. Linked with the Falklands were the island of

South Georgia and the Sandwich Islands. By the end of April, South Georgia, 800 miles eastward, had been captured, and the British naval task force was approaching the Falklands. A 200-mile exclusion zone around the Falklands was declared, within which any Argentine ship or plane would be attacked.

When the Argentine cruiser *General Belgrano* approached the zone in a threatening manner, she was torpedoed by a British submarine and sank, with the loss of almost 400 lives. Although they were not under attack, the escorting Argentine destroyers fled the scene at full speed, not remaining to pick up survivors. Thereafter the Argentine navy remained in port. *The Sun*, the most popular of the tabloid newspapers, filled its front page with a picture of the *Belgrano* sinking and a screaming headline: GOTCHA!

The Argentines fought back with land-based fighter-bombers firing air-launched Exocet missiles that sank several British warships. Later, Argentine pilots, flying at the extreme limit of their range, attacked British ships engaged in landing troops.

In mid-May, with winter approaching in the Southern Hemisphere, British commandos established beachheads despite fierce Argentine air attacks. After more troops were landed, British forces advanced on Port Stanley. The Argentine soldiers proved to be cold, frightened, ill-trained recruits. They put up a token resistance, well aware that they were no match for British regulars and had been abandoned to their fate.

On June 14, the Argentine forces surrendered and the Falklands War ended in a triumph that thrilled the nation. Britain lost 255 men killed with almost 800 wounded. Six British ships were sunk and ten damaged, and nine carrier planes were lost. The Argentines had 652 men killed. The Argentine junta fell from power, and Thatcher had won a classic military victory.

The Election of 1983

In her first three years, Margaret Thatcher had been one of Britain's most unpopular prime ministers. Polls had shown her approval rating as low as 20 percent, and at times the Conservative Party was rated lower than Labour or the SDP–Liberal Alliance. With the victory in the Falklands War, that changed. Public approval of Thatcher's handling of the war soared from 60 percent in the first few weeks to 84 percent when victory was achieved. At the beginning of the war, the three major parties were virtually even in the polls. When the war ended, the Conservatives were at 52 percent.

By 1983, the polls showed the Conservatives at 44 percent, Labour at 35 percent, and the SDP–Liberal Alliance at 20 percent. The economy was improving and with it public confidence. In January, 22 percent of the public said they expected the economy to improve; by April, just before the election, that figure had risen to 36 percent. Steps had been taken to bring the public finances under control and to curb the power of the unions. Inflation had fallen to 4 percent and wages were increasing at double that figure, although unemployment was still at 3 million. The long-standing Rhodesia problem, a disruptive factor in the Conservative Party, had been resolved in 1981, when the colony became the independent state of Zimbabwe, with a democratic constitution that gave power to the black majority.

Taking advantage of these favorable omens, Thatcher announced that a general election would take place in June 1983, although Parliament still had a year to go. The Conservative election manifesto indicated that the reforming spirit of Thatcherism would continue. Income taxes would be further reduced. The manifesto promised continuing privatizations and trade union reform. The most important new thrust was reform of local government, limitation of increases in the rates, and abolition of the Greater London Council and the other metropolitan counties.

With the left wing in command, Labour's election manifesto was a declaration of war on Thatcherism: increased spending to reduce unemployment, exchange controls to reduce the influence of international capital movements, repurchase of nationalized industries that had been privatized, expansion of public ownership to new industries such as electronics and pharmaceuticals, repeal of legislation restricting the powers of the unions, improved social benefits, increased spending on the National Health Service and the building of council houses, and withdrawal from the European Community. Defense was an important issue, as Labour committed itself to unilateral nuclear disarmament and withdrawal from NATO.

The bookish Michael Foot was respected within the Labour Party, but his bumbling inability to control his own party diminished any claim he might have to lead a government. Labour was embarrassed by the Militant Tendency, a small extremist group that advocated abolition of the monarchy and other institutions of central government, and predicted civil war if its demands were not met. Expulsion from the Labour Party did not remove the public's identification of the militants with Labour's left wing.

Saddled with candidates and policies rejected by most of the public, Labour Party moderates faced defeat with a sense of resignation, hoping that it would serve to demonstrate the electoral fatuity of the left. One Labour MP called the party's manifesto "the longest suicide note in history." Labour's support in the polls dropped from 36 percent to 28 percent over the four-week election period. The tabloid papers were unsparing in their mockery of Foot and Labour. The *Daily Mail* ran a cartoon showing Foot as an elderly tramp, dragged along the street by his dog while tripping over his walking stick. "DO YOU SERIOUSLY WANT THIS OLD FOOL TO RUN BRITAIN," the headline screamed.

The SDP–Liberal Alliance had become an important factor in electoral politics as a nonsocialist alternative to Thatcherism. The Liberal leader, David Steel, was an attractive campaigner, and Roy Jenkins, leader of the Social Democrats, provided intellectual power and a sense of strong leadership. Its main promise was to launch an all-out attack on unemployment through public works and special programs for the long-term unemployed.

Labour's losses were the Alliance's gains. From 15 percent in the polls at the beginning of the campaign, the SDP–Liberal Alliance rose to 26 percent. Polls showed that if both opposition parties were combined, Thatcher would probably lose.

The election gave the Conservatives 42 percent of the vote, Labour 28 percent, and the SDP–Liberal Alliance 25 percent. The Thatcher ministry was still a minority government in terms of the popular vote, although it had 397 seats in the House of Commons, as compared to 209 for Labour and 23 for the Alliance. The Conservatives swamped Labour in London, the Southeast of England, the Midlands, and the West. Labour carried the industrial North and Scotland. The Liberals carried Wales, their stronghold.

The realignment of British politics that had begun with Thatcher's victory in 1979 was taking shape. The Conservative Party had the support of the middle-class, homeowners, and white-collar workers in the growing financial and service-industry sectors. Thatcher's ability to win and hold a large body of working-class voters (especially skilled workers) was an important factor in her electoral victory; it was estimated that fewer than half the trade union members voted Labour. The SDP–Liberal Alliance had done well in the popular vote and could look forward to becoming the main opposition party. The Conservatives and the SDP–Liberal Alliance were both middle-class parties, and the future seemed to lie with them.

Labour was the big loser. With 28 percent of the vote, Labour narrowly escaped coming in third. Over the previous twenty years, the industrial working class, the bedrock of the Labour Party, had declined to less than half the labor force. Union membership had fallen, and the excesses of the 1970s had discredited union leadership.

Labour still had strength in the declining industrial areas of the north of England and Scotland, where factories were closing and unemployment was high. With the exception of the impoverished high-rise housing estates of major industrial cities, Labour was virtually wiped out in the prospering south of England. In the previous twenty years the white-collar suburban middle class had grown, and such people were not attracted to a political party advocating socialism and dominated by the trade unions and urban radicals.

Some commentators declared that the Labour Party was finished. Within the Labour Party, however, a group of moderates refused to accept defeat. Labour still had a base of approximately 200 seats to build on. The disaster of 1983 provided the impetus for the development of New Labour.

~

CHAPTER THREE

The Heyday of Thatcherism, 1983–1987

Established Leader

Margaret Thatcher worked hard to maintain a strong public image. She re-made herself into "Maggie," the well-turned-out woman who appealed to middle England. She consulted a former television producer, who changed her hairstyle and clothes, and helped her modulate her somewhat shrill voice. She presented her ideas and policies through carefully prepared speeches, assisted by a playwright who brightened her style and added bits of humor. She was quick-witted and well informed and made effective use of television interviews. The Tuesday and Thursday periods for "Prime Minis-ter's Questions" provided an opportunity for her to present the brief state-ments preferred by the press and television.

Thatcher was more than a party politician. She dominated her Cabinet, although she could not ignore their advice and risked serious embarrassment if she pushed them too far. Nor could she take for granted the support of the Conservative MPs, who normally maintain a kind of tribal unity behind their leader. Her style and policies appealed to the Conservative backbenchers, and she was especially effective among the party activists who attended the annual Conservative Party conferences.

She was, in some ways, a populist, who appealed beyond her Cabinet and party to middle- and working-class people. "I want to see one nation," she said in 1983, "but I want everyone to have their own personal property stake. I want them to have their own savings that retain their value, so they can pass things on to their own children, everyone strong and independent of government" (Riddell 1991).

While Thatcher made herself widely visible in the United Kingdom and in world affairs, she rarely spoke in the House of Commons, apart from the obligatory "Prime Minister's Questions." On the average, she gave a speech in Parliament about every forty-five days.

She steadfastly opposed televising the Commons' debates until 1989, when public pressure made it necessary to give way. Then the public discovered that she was very good at Question Time and usually came out the winner.

Having established herself politically, Thatcher reshuffled her Cabinet to bring new energy and fresh ideas to her second ministry. Sir Geoffrey Howe moved to the Foreign and Commonwealth Office and was replaced as chancellor of the Exchequer by Nigel Lawson, a rising star. Michael Heseltine, a handsome, strong-willed publisher and property tycoon, moved from Environment to Defence. In 1981, Sir Keith Joseph became secretary of state for education and science, where he began developing the Thatcher ministry's plans for reform of the schools. Another Cabinet shuffle in 1985 brought Douglas Hurd, a distinguished figure in the Conservative Party, into the Cabinet as home secretary.

John Major continued to serve as a whip, where he gained an intimate knowledge of the members of Parliament and their special concerns. Since the whips exist to forward the government's agenda—at times they could be intimidating to individual members—John Major would hear them out and do what he could to be helpful.

In 1984, Major became a senior whip with responsibility for Treasury business in the House of Commons. In this role he became familiar with the business of the Treasury—the heart of British government—and began a career in the Treasury that eventually led him to the top.

The Economy

Thatcher's economic goal was to make Britain competitive in the emerging world economy, and to a considerable extent she succeeded. She wanted to establish an "enterprise culture" by encouraging business and reducing disincentives imposed by government. She advocated tax cuts for individuals and corporations, deregulation of industry, breaking down restrictive trade practices, support for scientific and technological research, and introduction of training programs to prepare workers for new kinds of employment. Some evidence of success was seen in a rapid increase in the number of new businesses and the self-employed. Business leaders expressed a new sense of freedom and opportunity.

Whatever the reason, in 1983 the British economy began a period of growth, admittedly from a depressed level. In the four-year period, 1983 through 1986, the Gross Domestic Product increased by 8 percent, industrial production by 7 percent, productivity per worker by 13 percent, and exports by 21 percent.

With inflation at 5 percent, consumer confidence and spending rose and a demand-side upswing began, strengthened by similar growth in the United States and other countries. Employed persons benefited. During the four-year period, the retail price index rose by an annual 4.7 percent while earnings grew at an average of 7.7 percent. Imports increased by 30 percent as British consumers went on a binge, buying foreign cars, television sets, and cameras, and enjoying holidays abroad. North Sea oil helped keep the balance of payments healthy and sterling remained strong.

At the Exchequer, Nigel Lawson continued the Thatcherite fiscal policy: shift taxation from incomes to consumption, control spending, reduce public borrowing, and keep inflation down. Revenues were growing, bolstered by income from North Sea oil and sales of nationalized industries. Expenditure was tightly controlled and the rate of increase was well below the growth of the revenue, gradually whittling down the need to borrow. In 1984, Lawson cut the tax rates on corporations, balancing the losses incurred with new revenue gained from removing a cluster of unwarranted corporate tax exemptions.

In 1985, the basic exemption for the personal income tax was substantially raised, giving tax relief to many low-income people. Homeowners were given a boost by increasing the tax deduction for mortgage interest. As revenues grew, Lawson promised to cut the income tax base rate from 30 percent to 25 percent, beginning by knocking off 1 percent in 1986 and another 2 percent in 1987. The top rate remained at 60 percent until 1988.

Deregulation proceeded, as banks were permitted to lend on mortgages, and building societies (savings and loan associations [S&Ls] in the United States) were permitted to act more like banks. Deregulation of hire purchase (installment buying) encouraged consumer spending and debt. Lawson's tax cuts brought an unsettling reminder of the Heath ministry as house prices rose rapidly, especially in London. Lending institutions were flush with cash; mortgage loans were easily available at 100 percent of value and at moderate interest rates. Buyers were willing to take on large mortgages in the expectation of further price increases.

Under Thatcher, London expanded its role as one of the world's great financial centers. The commitment of the Thatcher ministry to the global market was dramatically demonstrated in October 1986, when the stock market was opened up to foreign and domestic traders ("the Big Bang"). The Stock Exchange was required to remove trading restrictions that it had imposed on its members, including fixed commissions. The stock trading, merger, and takeover boom in the United States spread to Britain, with much of the activity financed with borrowed money.

Of course, the boom could not last, and a sudden drop on the New York Stock Exchange in October 1987 brought the party to an end. Heavy losses were incurred, and the volume of shares traded declined dramatically, leading to mergers and layoffs in brokerage firms. To cushion the shock, Lawson poured money into the markets, further increasing inflationary pressures.

Despite excesses, the boom unleashed by the Big Bang was valuable to British financial institutions. The stodgy, tradition-bound ways of the past were replaced by a new, aggressive mentality that made the City a center of money and investment in the emerging world economy. It has been estimated that 50 percent of the increase in the national wealth during the 1980s came from financial services.

The enterprise culture was less evident in manufacturing, where employment fell from 7 million in 1979 to 5 million by 1990. British firms failed to put enough money and effort into research and development. British banks preferred short-term loans to established firms rather than the long-term commitments needed to build new industries. The response of industrialists to growing demand was sluggish, and imports rose to satisfy growing consumer demand.

The result was continuing high unemployment, which averaged 3.1 million from 1983 through 1986. The high point was 1986, when it peaked at 3.3 million, most of the unemployed coming from manufacturing industry. This loss was partially offset by an increase in low-paid service jobs, many of them held by women and part-time workers. The number of employed adult male breadwinners declined.

Privatization

During Thatcher's second ministry, privatization became a major feature of Thatcherism. Privatization continued with the disposal of the remainder of British Aerospace (1985), the National Bus Company (1985), Associated British Ports (1985), Jaguar (1984), some naval shipyards (1985–1986), and the factories of the Royal Ordnance. Selling off the nationalized industries was politically advantageous in many ways: it brought money into the Treasury, it helped fund tax cuts, it relieved the taxpayers of costly subsidies, it eroded the political base of the Labour Party, and it forced the unions to deal with private employers (who might downsize or go out of business if costs became too high) rather than engage in political strikes.

The Thatcher ministry pushed energetically to make these industries marketable. With aggressive new leadership and unhampered by trade union recalcitrance, productivity (admittedly from a low base) rose more rapidly in the nationalized industries than in the private sector. One commentator remarked that Thatcher was the best manager the nationalized industries ever had. Harold Macmillan (Lord Stockton) compared privatization to a family selling off the Georgian silver.

Privatization was acceptable in manufacturing industry, where a competitive market existed, but public utilities such as telephones, gas, electricity, and water were another matter. People were reluctant to remove these basic services from public ownership. The Thatcher government argued that privatizing public utilities would bring in new management and private capital to extend and modernize them. It was recognized that privatizing the public utilities would require nonpolitical regulatory bodies to control rates and monitor service.

The telephone system had begun as part of the Post Office. The two were separated in the 1960s, but British Telecom continued the bureaucratic, unionized culture out of which it had arisen. The British telephone system was obsolete at a time when communications in other advanced countries were being revolutionized.

In 1984, the Thatcher ministry proposed the sale of British Telecom, the largest share offer ever made to that time. Lawson proposed mass-marketing the shares to the general public, rather than relying on bids from major investors. The shares were offered in lots of varying sizes with a modest down payment. More than a million people applied for the smaller batches—so many, in fact, that larger lots were broken up into smaller lots, and institutional investors that had applied for the larger lots got nothing. The unions urged employees of British Telecom to boycott the sale, but 95 percent of them bought shares anyway.

By the end of the month, the price of the part-paid shares was almost double the down payment, and many holders of the small lots sold out, taking a quick profit. Eventually, institutional investors (including union pension funds) ended up holding the lion's share anyway. Although the Labour Party criticized the government for selling the shares too cheaply, the Conservatives gloated that now 5 percent of the adult population were shareholding capitalists.

The effects of privatization came slowly, and in 1987 a rash of public complaints shocked Telecom into action. Investment was doubled; new up-to-date equipment was introduced; delays in installation declined; and prices fell. Telecom suddenly showed interest in its customers. Responding to complaints that there were not enough pay phones and that too many of them were not working, the company quickly added 45 percent more pay phones, and the number functioning rose from 77 percent to 95 percent. A regulatory body called Oftel was established that kept prices below inflation, and yet British Telecom flourished. It was a striking example of the benefits of privatization.

One of the shortcomings of private enterprise was revealed when Telecom began removing the beloved red pay boxes, designed by the distinguished architect Sir Giles Gilbert Scott, that had been a familiar fixture on British streets since 1906. Many of them were ripped out, shipped to the junkyard, and replaced by sleek, modernistic designs. The discerning public was appalled at the loss of a minor but ubiquitous part of the nation's public architecture.

The successful privatization of British Telecom in 1984 led to the privatization of British Gas in 1986. British Gas had been nationalized shortly after World War II. It was a giant of British industry. It distributed gas to British factories and households, explored for gas in the North Sea oil fields, and sold and serviced gas appliances at retail.

The first North Sea gas fields were opened up in the 1960s. In the next twenty years, British Gas built an elaborate network of gas mains and pipes that provided cheap, clean energy to British homes and industries and ended the gloomy fogs and killing smogs that had been a feature of life in British towns. When privatization took place, natural gas provided 50 percent of British energy, and coal was declining rapidly.

Seeing the success of Telecom, British Gas was more than willing to be privatized. The privatization plan gave British Gas a twenty-five-year monopoly on the distribution of gas, with the exception of large industrial users, where competition was permitted. The monopoly was justified on the grounds that no competitor could compete with its unparalleled distribution system. A regulator of prices and services (Ofgas) was established.

The sale of British Gas was a deal even larger than British Telecom. An elaborate publicity campaign was undertaken to secure a maximum return, and 40 percent of the shares were reserved to be sold in small lots to gas customers on an easy payment plan. Almost 4,500,000 people applied for shares, including most of the employees of the company. The shares sold out immediately, and by the end of the year, holders of part-paid shares had a profit of

30 percent over their initial payment. Tony Blair, speaking for Labour, complained that the shares had been sold too cheaply.

Many who bought shares in Telecom and British Gas did so only to turn a quick profit. Most of the shares of the privatized industries ended up in the hands of institutional investors. Nevertheless, from 1979 to 1989, the number of individual shareholders in Britain increased from 3 million to 9 million. Thatcher had added millions of new shareholders to her "people's capitalism" and perhaps to the Conservative Party.

Privatization of the National Bus Co. led to a dispute between those who wished to keep it as one company and those who wished to break it into separate companies to encourage competition. The executives wished to keep it as one company, like Telecom and British Gas. The decision was made to break up the company and deregulate the buses, which would permit new companies to enter the bus business.

Stiff resistance was encountered in Parliament from some Conservative backbenchers, who feared that service on lightly traveled routes would be discontinued. Labour, of course, was opposed. Eventually the necessary legislation was passed, and a plethora of bus companies competed for passengers. With better and more frequent service, ridership increased after years of decline.

In 1985, a surprising storm blew up that nearly brought the downfall of the Thatcher ministry. It concerned a company called Westland, which was Britain's only manufacturer of helicopters. Although Westland had good products, it faced bankruptcy unless it was taken over by a larger company that could provide additional capital and technology. For some time, Westland had been cooperating with the American company, United Technologies, which manufactured Sikorsky helicopters. Some of Westland's products had been Sikorsky designs manufactured under license. United Technologies made an acceptable bid to purchase a share of Westland, and the company and the workers favored this offer.

Michael Heseltine, defence secretary, was independent and strong willed. He resented Thatcher's dominating manner in the Cabinet and her opinionated unwillingness to listen to other points of view. Since Westland produced helicopters for the British armed forces, he declared that a company of strategic importance should not be permitted to come under American influence. He attempted to put together a European consortium including Westland that would build military helicopters. He saw his proposal as a step toward further cooperation with Europe in military procurement.

The pro-Europeans in the Conservative Party supported Heseltine. Thatcher felt that such a decision should be left to the company, which supported the United Technologies bid. Thatcher refused to proceed further on Heseltine's proposal, especially since the European consortium had not appeared.

Heseltine was furious. At the next Cabinet meeting, he went head to head with Thatcher in a shouting match and angrily resigned. The result was a row in the Conservative Party and the press about Thatcher's alleged autocratic and devious methods. Heseltine was a tall, handsome man with long blond hair and great rhetorical skills. He was a popular figure, who traveled throughout the country, speaking at Conservative meetings. His willingness to stand up to Thatcher made him seem like a potential rival. Thatcher herself was shaken by the sudden furor that Heseltine had aroused. He had dramatized the division within the Conservative Party concerning relations with Europe, and had brought out widespread uneasiness at the pace and direction of Thatcherite reform.

Another nationalized industry that Thatcher wanted to privatize was British Leyland (BL), Britain's only large manufacturer of automobiles and trucks. The jewel in BL's crown, Jaguar, was successfully privatized in 1984, when it was sold to Ford. Leyland's other products (Rover, Land Rover, Range Rover, and BL trucks) were losing market share to imported cars or cars manufactured by the British subsidiaries of Ford and General Motors. Thatcher knew that nationalized industries needed to be reformed before they could be privatized, and with aggressive leadership, some parts of BL were becoming profitable.

In 1985, General Motors made a favorable offer for Land Rover, Range Rover, and BL trucks. Ford made an offer for Rover. These would be the first large nationalizations that went to foreign corporations, and the prospect of foreign ownership was a shock to British national pride.

Thatcher discovered that powerful emotions could be aroused by the auto industry. An outcry arose in Parliament and the press that Americans were taking over Britain's last auto manufacturer, although Ford and General Motors had long produced cars in Britain that were manufactured by British autoworkers. Workers at Rover welcomed privatization, which would help protect their jobs. Shocked at the reaction, the American companies abandoned the deal.

With the Westland affair fresh in mind, Thatcher could not afford another political dustup. To end the public clamor, Rover was sold instead to British Aerospace, a privatized company, which had no interest or experience in manufacturing cars. British Aerospace, in turn, entered into an arrangement with Honda, giving Honda entry to the British car market. Leyland Bus was sold to Volvo, a Swedish firm. Leyland's van business was sold to a Dutch firm. So the foreigners won after all, but not the Americans.

The Trade Unions

The election of 1983 put Thatcher in a position to reduce further the power of the trade unions, which she held responsible for much of Britain's economic decline. The Employment Acts of her first ministry were strengthened in 1984 by legislation that ended the self-perpetuating power of union leaders by requiring that they be reelected every five years. A strike could not be called without a secret ballot of all members who would be involved, and unions would be legally liable for damages resulting from a strike held without a favorable vote.

The legislation of 1984 included an attack on another Thatcherite grievance: the use of union funds for political purposes, almost always for support of the Labour Party. The law required prior approval by secret ballot. In this instance, Thatcher had mistaken the attitude of the members, who supported the political use of union funds. They had lost confidence in the efficacy of the strike, but they were still willing to take political action to advance their interests.

The crucial test of Thatcher's determination was the coal strike of 1984. At issue was the decision of the National Coal Board to close money-losing pits. The coal industry had long been in decline. In 1914 there had been a million miners, in 1946 seven hundred thousand, and by 1983 the number had shrunk to two hundred thousand. New sources of energy, especially oil and natural gas, had cut the use of coal in half over the previous ten years. The deeper and more modern coal pits in the Midlands were still profitable, but in other parts of the country, old and inefficient mines with thin seams of coal required subsidies from the taxpayer.

By 1983, Thatcher was ready to deal with the problems of the coal industry, knowing that the necessary cutbacks would provoke a strike of the kind that had brought down Sir Edward Heath in 1974. She prepared for a strike by moving Ian MacGregor, who had performed well in transforming British Steel, to the chairmanship of the Coal Board. MacGregor was a tough, resolute manager, and he began making plans to close unprofitable pits. The Coal Board quietly accumulated large stocks of coal and located them at the generating plants and steel mills that were the principal users of coal. Other major users were advised to accumulate inventories.

Fleets of tank trucks to carry oil to generators were leased, painted in innocuous colors, and hidden away for use when needed. Anticipating major confrontations, Thatcher established an agency that would mobilize police from all over the country to stop illegal practices such as secondary strikes, mass picketing, and violence.

It was important that the Coal Board divide the miners to prevent a complete shutdown. The mines of Nottinghamshire in the Midlands were efficient and profitable; those miners were unwilling to challenge the Coal Board and possibly lose their jobs. Workers in the inefficient mines were offered generous terms to give up their jobs, and many of them decided it was better to take the payments than strike. The miners left to challenge the Coal Board were those who were most militant and who worked in the least desirable pits.

None of this deterred Arthur Scargill, feisty leader of the National Union of Mineworkers, who was determined to block all closures and force a confrontation with the Coal Board over this issue. Apart from an understandable desire to keep up the membership of his union, Scargill was a fiery demagogue who carried deep resentments toward the government. His motives were as much personal and political as economic. He hoped to repeat the victory that the miners had gained in 1974, when shortages of coal had shut down the nation and ended the Heath ministry.

Scargill, however, was holding a weak hand, for the circumstances of 1984 differed greatly from those ten years earlier, when coal was still the essential fuel. After the excesses of the 1970s, many unions had become resigned to the changes taking place in British industry. Most of the miners did not want to strike and had rejected several previous strike ballots. The Thatcher ministry and the Conservative majority in Parliament, victorious in two elections, were hostile. The Labour Party was severely weakened, and the public had lost sympathy with strikers.

Scargill called for a strike in March 1984. In so doing, he was limited by the requirement of his union that the decision be made by the miners voting in a secret ballot. He did not ballot his members because he knew that he would lose. Where regional ballots were taken, the strike was rejected. To avoid a strike vote, Scargill persuaded militant miners in some regions to strike, and they were used as pickets to prevent other miners from working. Gangs of strikers called flying pickets went to power plants to stop the coal from getting to the generators. Other pickets went to mines that were still operating, and violence broke out between striking and nonstriking miners.

The flying pickets violated the law against secondary picketing, which brought the police into the conflict. The British public was astonished to see on their television screens hundreds of police equipped with riot gear streaming into strike areas from other parts of the country, guarding power plants and protecting long lines of trucks bringing coal. Wives and children of the strikers appeared and engaged in angry confrontations with the police. Clashes between the miners and the police won public sympathy for the police and the rule of law. The Archbishop of Canterbury, however, spoke up in support of the strikers.

The Central Electricity Generating Board was the government's command post, for it was essential to keep the generators operating and the lights on. The workers at the generating plants were persuaded that it was their job to keep the power flowing. One of them pointed out that his ninety-year-old mother depended on electricity to keep her warm; if "the electric's off," he said, "she's finished." High earnings due to extensive overtime strengthened his resolve.

Convoys of independent truckers brought coal to the power stations from those mines that were still working, making big money but facing threats, abuse, and sometimes danger from the pickets. The most important factor was the increased use of oil. Generating plants were hastily converted from coal to oil, and tank trucks brought the oil to the plants. Every driver who owned his own truck made a fortune during the strike, hauling oil day and night until he or his truck collapsed. Nuclear plants operated constantly at hotter levels than ever before.

With high unemployment, Scargill's call for support from the rest of the labor movement was not answered. The steel workers declared that they would keep making steel with whatever coal they could get. Leaders of the transport workers and railway men expressed support, but their members continued working and moving coal. When the Trades Union Congress (TUC) executive voted to support the strike, one of the members stated: "Our men will not obey, and the union leaders who voted for it know it will not stick."

Scargill had hoped for support from the dockworkers, who had their own grievances. In July, the dockworkers went out on strike in support of the miners. They were prepared to block imports of coal, but the Coal Board did not intend to import coal, to avoid alienating those miners who remained at work. The dockworkers' strike affected the importation of ore for British Steel and imports of food, but enough ports continued working to meet all needs.

The dock strike lasted only ten days, and then it collapsed. There was much featherbedding on the docks, and the dockers feared that after the strike their hiring system would be changed with extensive loss of jobs. A second dock strike in August was effective in only a few ports and soon ended. The failure of the dock strikes made it even clearer that Scargill was doomed.

Thatcher, as was her policy, stayed aloof from the strike, which she stated firmly was between the mineworkers and the Coal Board. She made it clear that there would be no government bailouts and that profitable and unprofitable pits would go down together if a satisfactory settlement were not reached. She was prepared to call in troops to preserve order, but the Generating Board, who managed the power plants, persuaded her that such action would only lead to sympathy strikes.

Efforts to reach a negotiated settlement were frustrated by Scargill's refusal to consider closure of any mines whatsoever. As more strikers returned to their jobs, coal production began to return to nearly normal levels. By March 1985, almost a year after it had begun, the strike had ended in total defeat for Scargill and the miners whom he had led into a disaster. The number of coal miners was reduced by 40 percent, but the reduced number produced 85 percent of the coal that had been produced before the strike.

The effects of the coal strike on Britain were great. The Falklands War and the coal strike were the decisive events in establishing Thatcher as a national leader. She had won the battle that Heath had lost ten years earlier. Beyond the coal industry, it was evident to workers that strike action would not bring government intervention nor would it win public sympathy. It might not even bring support from other unions. At a time of high unemployment, workers were concerned about protecting their jobs, which might disappear if their factory or industry were needlessly disrupted. Public opinion had turned against strikes that were intended to secure gains for some by making everyone else suffer. The efficacy of the strike—Labour's ultimate weapon—had been blunted, if not destroyed.

The decline of the trade unions was seen in another failed strike. The print unions were among the most militant elements in the British labor movement, and they were still smarting from the concessions they had made in 1981. They insisted on excessive numbers of printers, their work rules were highly restrictive, their paid hours grossly inflated, and the quality of their printing was low.

Rupert Murdoch, owner of the *Times*, the *Sunday Times*, *The Sun*, and the *News of the World*, was determined to introduce computerized technology into the newspaper business, making large numbers of printers redundant. He built a new, picket-proof building on cheap land in the former docklands, away from Fleet Street where newspapers had been located for more than two centuries. He installed the latest computerized printing equipment and recruited technicians to operate it. Many of them were members of the electricians union.

Murdoch knew that the printers would strike, as they had so often in the past. Since they were among the most literate and best-paid workers in Britain, they would be able to sustain a long and unified walkout. He also realized that the Employment Acts of 1980, 1982, and 1984, with their restrictions on sympathy strikes and picketing, gave him the leverage he needed to overcome the resistance of the unions, which would be desperate.

After a long period of negotiations, the unions declared a strike in January 1986. Murdoch dismissed all the strikers, and his new plant went into full operation. It was evident that the new technology would revolutionize the newspaper business. The printers, living in the past, refused to accept the brutal fact that their skills had been rendered useless by technology, and their jobs had ceased to exist.

Murdoch had prepared for the strike as carefully as Thatcher had for the coal strike. The printers union assumed they could count on the sympathy of the transport workers and railroad unions, who would refuse to deliver newspapers that had been printed while the workers were on strike. To counter this tactic, Murdoch had organized his own delivery system using independent truckers. He had built a second high-tech, computerized plant in Glasgow to serve Scotland and the north of England. He could deliver his morning papers overnight to every newsstand in the British Isles.

The legal prohibitions against secondary strikes left the printers without support from other unions. Some unions attempted to support the printers with sympathy strikes, but Murdoch obtained injunctions prohibiting them from picketing and other forms of strike action. When the printers attempted to shut down Murdoch's new printing plant, "the battle of Wapping" took place, as police struggled with mass pickets. In one confrontation at Murdoch's dockland printing plant, 175 police officers and demonstrators were injured.

Thatcher adhered to her policy that strikes were a matter for management and labor. She refused to intervene, except to enforce the law against mass picketing. The strike failed and organized labor had taken another heavy blow. Murdoch's technology provided such profitable economies that the other papers soon followed suit. They moved out of Fleet Street to the docklands and built new, computerized plants that no longer needed the skills of the printers.

The trade unions continued to play an important role in British industrial relations, but the Thatcher years deprived them of their most potent weapon—the strike. A combination of Thatcherite legislation, long-term unemployment, and the failures of the miners' and printers' strikes convinced organized labor that strikes, apart from brief stoppages to underline a point, would not succeed and might recoil on the workers involved.

The recession of 1979–1982 hit hardest the industries in which the unions were strongest: manufacturing, mining, construction, docks, and railways.

Privatization of key industries weakened their leverage. In 1979, British trade unions enrolled 13.5 million workers, or 57 percent of the potential membership. In 1986, the figure was 43 percent of the potential membership, and in 1992, it was 35 percent.

The largest decline was in the manufacturing sector, where membership declined from 65 percent in 1980 to 44 percent in 1990. Job growth has taken place largely in sectors that typically have been difficult for unions to organize: the self-employed, clerical jobs, service industries, small business, and new factories in small towns and rural areas where unions were weak. Unions have remained strongest in the public sector.

Local Government

Thatcher was a centralizer. She believed that irresponsible local governments jeopardized her efforts to control inflation, lower public spending (including local spending), and reduce taxes. Local governments were required to "contract out" many responsibilities to private firms: garbage collection, building and vehicle maintenance, catering, and the like. Some employees formed their own firms and bid for the contracts.

The great grievance of the Thatcherites was a long-standing one: the rates, which were taxes on homes and businesses based on the presumed rental value of the property. The government subsidized local authorities with block grants based on population and other factors. In the past, these grants had provided 60 percent of the money for local government, but with the financial squeeze, grants had fallen to about 48 percent by 1988. Local authorities responded by raising the rates.

Approximately 60 percent of the local rates were paid by businesses, and homeowners paid the remainder. Of 35 million voters in England, 18 million paid rates and 6 million of those had their rates paid by Housing Benefit or otherwise reduced. The majority did not pay rates at all. Since most Labour voters were renters, Labour councillors in industrial towns did not hesitate to impose heavy rates on homeowners, who tended to be Conservatives. High rates were also imposed on business property, despite the negative effects on jobs.

The Greater London Council (GLC) and the councils of some other industrial cities, among them Liverpool and Sheffield, had come under the control of left-wing extremists ("the new urban left") referred to by the tabloids as "the loony left." They raised the rates and increased spending on their pet projects. They filled local government jobs with their partisans, expanded welfare services for the poor and unemployed, and made grants of public money to special-interest groups such as public-housing tenants, feminists, gays, lesbians, minorities, and peace groups. Some of their activities were fully justified, given the problems created by long-term unemployment and other social ills.

The GLC, led by "Red Ken" Livingstone, was Thatcher's thorn in the flesh. From 1981 to 1986 Livingstone increased GLC expenditures by 170 percent. He greatly expanded the number of employees and other dependents and made generous grants to activist groups. He claimed to be creating "urban socialism" as the people's alternative to Thatcherism. He hung red flags on the GLC building across the Thames from the houses of Parliament, invited foreign revolutionaries to the council chambers, and posted a banner listing the figures for unemployment. In 1981, the GLC cut fares on the London Underground by 32 percent, a popular step, and raised the rates to make up the difference. The government intervened and London Transport was nationalized.

In 1984, legislation was passed capping the rates of the GLC and seventeen other local government units, most of them controlled by Labour. The GLC flatly rejected the cap. In Liverpool, the Labour councillors refused to submit a budget based on the legal limits. To demonstrate their resistance, they issued dismissal notices to all city employees, which were later recalled. Then the council overspent its budget and pledged its reserves to borrow from international bankers.

Thatcher's answer to urban noncompliance was a demonstration of raw power, fueled not a little by anger. In 1985, the Thatcher ministry proposed abolition of eighteen urban councils whose fiscal management was regarded as irresponsible. Labour controlled all but two. The list included the six metropolitan counties established by the Heath ministry plus the GLC.

This step had considerable public support locally, but met resistance from members of both parties in Parliament. In addition to predictable opposition from the Labour Party, many Conservatives criticized these proposals, for they reversed changes made by Heath. Opposition also came from representatives of the arts, environmental protection, public health, and other special interests that received financial support from the threatened local governments. The proposal came close to defeat in the House of Lords, where many Conservative peers objected strenuously.

Despite resistance, the bill became law and responsibility for managing these urban areas fell to the thirty-three London boroughs and the districts of the other metropolitan counties. One of the last acts of the GLC was to distribute its massive assets among favorite groups and causes, an action later reversed by the High Court. Fifteen years later, the GLC building was offered to the new municipal government of London established during the ministry of Tony Blair.

The European Community

Thatcher's abrasive personality and nationalistic outlook involved her in frequent controversies within the European Community (EC), where her willingness to accept confrontation had earned her the nickname "Attila the Hen." In the 1980s, the EC was expanded to include Greece (1981), Spain (1986), and Portugal (1986), economically weak and politically unstable countries that were admitted as a way to support their struggling democracies.

At first the British thought that the new members would dilute the grip of France and Germany on EC affairs. Instead, those countries, sometimes lumped with Italy as "Club Med," needed the regional subsidies doled out by the EC, and they clung closely to their paymasters.

Thatcher was pleased as the EC moved toward an internal free market, which she saw as the major reason for British membership. The crucial step was taken in 1986 with the Single European Act, which would eliminate all barriers to trade among the member states by 1992. In the euphoria of the moment, Thatcher chose to ignore the preamble to the act, which envisioned a political and monetary union, an oversight that came back to haunt her.

By that time about half of Britain's trade was with the other members of the EC, as opposed to 20 percent with those same countries twenty-five years earlier. Nevertheless, British trade still had a global dimension, as Britain traded more outside the EC than any other member. Britain's major grievance was that the single market did not include financial services and air transport, industries in which Britain was strong.

In 1986, Britain and France agreed to build a tunnel under the English Channel connecting England and France. The decision brought out ancient rivalries between the two countries, with reminders of the importance of the Channel as a defensive barrier in wars with Philip II of Spain, Louis XIV, Napoleon, and Hitler's Germany. In reality, NATO and European unity had rendered these objections meaningless. The major problems were financing, much of which was expected to be provided by private capital, and the environmental effects of increased traffic in the congested southeast of England.

Neil Kinnock and the Foundations of New Labour

After its failure in the election of 1983, the Labour Party chose a new leader, Neil Kinnock, a charismatic Welshman from Labour's left wing. Kinnock had been an MP since 1970, but he had never held Cabinet office. He was an eloquent and witty speaker, who could arouse the Labour Party's rank and file. He knew that Labour could not win without dropping some of its more extreme policies.

At this point, the political career of Tony Blair began. Blair was born in Edinburgh and lived for a time in Australia before his family settled in Durham, in the northeast of England. Like John Major, he had theatrical ancestors: his father, who was adopted by a shipyard worker in Glasgow, was the offspring of two comic-hall actors.

After a distinguished military career in World War II, the elder Blair, a man of great ability and ambition, became a lecturer in law at Durham University and a successful barrister in Newcastle upon Tyne, a short commute by train from Durham. The family was not wealthy, but enjoyed a solid middle-class standard of living. Tony's father was a staunch Conservative, whose ambition to pursue a political career was cut short by a stroke when Tony was eleven.

Tony Blair was educated at Fettes, a highly respected public (i.e., private) school in Edinburgh. He was a good student and athlete, a charmer who always wanted to be the center of attention, and a hard worker who was determined to succeed in everything he did. After completing school, he spent a gap year in London, where he managed aspiring rock bands and became the lead singer of one of them. He wore the long hair and eccentric clothes typical of rock musicians. His friends agree that, unlike his colleagues, he never used drugs. In 1972, he went to Oxford, where he studied law, became a devout Christian, and developed a philosophy of Christian socialism that emphasized the importance of good communities in nurturing good people.

From Oxford, Blair went to London, where he studied law and served his apprenticeship with Derry Irvine, a Scottish barrister. There he met his future wife, Cherie Booth, who was also a student of Irvine. Like her husband, Cherie had a theatrical ancestry. Her father was a professional actor descended from a theatrical family: its most famous (notorious) member was John Wilkes Booth, who assassinated Abraham Lincoln. Cherie and Tony were married in 1979.

Both the Blairs were devoted to the Labour Party. Tony identified himself with the moderates, but Cherie was more left wing. In 1983, Tony was elected MP for Sedgefield, a Labour-dominated constituency near Durham, his hometown. Cherie was the Labour candidate in another constituency. She was defeated and resumed her career as a lawyer.

Another new member of the class of 1983 was Gordon Brown, a graduate of Edinburgh University, who had been active in Labour politics in Scotland. Brown was obviously a "comer." Blair and Brown shared an office in the Parliament building. John Smith, a Scottish lawyer and a member of the leadership team in the House of Commons, was well acquainted with Brown from their associations in Scotland. He knew Blair through Derry Irvine, Blair's legal mentor. Smith helped Blair and Brown move quickly into roles as spokesmen for the shadow ministry.

Kinnock put Peter Mandelson, whose grandfather had been a major figure in the Attlee government, in charge of public relations. Mandelson was charged with changing Labour's image with the public. One step was to replace the red flag with a red rose (sans thorns) as Labour's symbol. Mandelson brought a degree of sophistication and professionalism to the advertisements and other media relations of the Labour Party that helped give it a more modern public image. His massaging of Labour's message brought the American term, "spin doctor," into the vocabulary of British politics.

Kinnock's approach was resisted at the grassroots by left-wingers, many of whom were young, well-educated, articulate public sector employees. In the depressed industrial towns, they were strong in local government and the constituency organizations. They believed that Labour had lost in 1979 and 1983 because it had failed to radicalize and energize its base, the urban working class. A considerable number were members of the National Union of Public Employees (NUPE) or the National Union of Teachers (NUT), both threatened by Thatcherite reforms. They looked to the annual party conference as an outlet for their views. They also were active at the constituency level in selecting (nominating) or deselecting candidates for Parliament.

Despite strong opposition within his own party, Kinnock began chipping away at Labour's more controversial policies. One difficulty was to develop a response to privatization, especially sales of council houses, which ran counter to the party's socialist roots but had been accepted enthusiastically by the public. Another was Thatcher's legislation limiting trade union power, which was popular, even among many union members. The excesses of Scargill in the miner's strike damaged the image of organized labor, and Labour was further discredited by the actions of "the loony left" in London and elsewhere.

The most difficult issue to resolve was unilateral nuclear disarmament, which had gained new urgency with the development by the Americans and the Soviet Union of medium-range nuclear missiles of great power and accuracy. Most of the public accepted the need for some kind of nuclear deterrent, although there were serious questions concerning the kind of nuclear weapons needed, where they should be installed, and how they would be controlled. Kinnock attempted, but failed, to modify Labour's commitment to unilateral nuclear disarmament. He went into the next election vulnerable to the charge that Labour could not be trusted to defend the country.

The Election of 1987

In 1987, Thatcher decided that the time was opportune for an election, a year earlier than required. The polls showed that the Conservative Party was rising after a slump in 1985. At the end of 1986, the Gallup poll found the Conservatives at 41 percent, Labour at 32 percent, and the SDP–Liberal Alliance at 23 percent. Thatcher's personal ratings had risen to 38 percent favorable.

As she undertook to lead her party in a third election campaign, Thatcher could state that her early goals had been achieved: the economy was humming, inflation was under control, the pound was strong, banks were lending freely to businesses and individuals, the housing market was buoyant, consumers were spending, and exports were increasing. Unemployment was high but was concentrated in the north of England, Scotland, Wales, and Northern Ireland, while the south was thriving with new white-collar and white-coat industries.

There was widespread concern with crime in the inner cities and the large housing estates, and Thatcher's commitment to vigorous law enforcement was unquestioned. Her most popular policies had been the sale of council houses and limiting the powers of the unions. She indicated that she was now ready to give more attention to social problems: schools, health, and crime.

The Conservatives appealed to the middle class and people with middle-class aspirations. Professional and white-collar workers, the most likely Conservative voters, were now 40 percent of the workforce. Many skilled workers owned their own homes and were making good money in steady jobs. With the decline of manufacturing, Labour's working-class, unionized constituency was melting away.

Neil Kinnock's efforts to give Labour a moderate tone had little influence on the electorate, and his ongoing struggles with the left wing further weakened Labour's appeal. Labour had important issues on which to run: the decline of manufacturing industry, persistent high unemployment, and the shortcomings of the public services. Kinnock proved to be an effective television campaigner, and he hit hard at the moral shortcomings of Thatcher's "uncaring" leadership.

Labour's weak spot was its views on foreign policy and defense, where Thatcher was strong. Kinnock affirmed the commitment of Labour to NATO, but he continued to advocate unilateral nuclear disarmament and the closing of American nuclear bases in Britain. The Conservatives depicted Labour's defense policy as British soldiers with their hands in the air.

In the election of 1983, the Social Democrat–Liberal Alliance had shown signs of becoming a major party, and it had continued to achieve successes in by-elections. But the new party lacked an established power base. Its appeal to voters in the opinion polls was an expression of dissatisfaction with the two major parties that was unlikely to translate into votes in national elections. Its few members in Parliament were unable to influence policy or gain much attention in the media.

The Alliance also had internal problems. Roy Jenkins, one of the founders of the Social Democrats, retired from the leadership and was succeeded by David Owen. David Steel continued as leader of the Liberals, although incapacitated for a while by ill health.

For the SDP–Liberal Alliance, the election of 1987 was vital: if the Alliance could pass Labour and become the second largest party, it could begin to accumulate the votes of those who opposed Thatcherism. The Alliance parties supported economy in government, a market economy, the European Economic Community, and NATO. They promised a more vigorous attack on unemployment, racial tensions, and regional disparities. They were divided on the nuclear deterrent.

When the election results were tallied, the Conservatives had won a commanding majority of seats with only 42 percent of the votes. Thatcher's victory in 1987 was less a result of her own popularity, which was beginning to wane, than popular mistrust of the alternatives. The Conservatives lost seats in the north of England, Wales, and Scotland, where unemployment remained high, but they dominated the south, where Labour won only three seats outside of London.

The Conservative Party gained 54 percent of the middle-class voters and held the support of the skilled workers. Conservative support among men continued to rise, although Labour gained among women, who saw Labour as the more "caring" party. The Conservatives were strong among the over fifty-fives, whose voting percentage is always high.

Labour improved slightly to 31 percent of the vote, but much of that came from the declining industrial areas of Scotland, unskilled workers, people who were dependent on pensions and public aid, and inhabitants of large council housing estates. The main strength of the Labour Party was in the public-sector employees, the unions, and local government—segments of the electorate hard hit by Thatcherism.

The Alliance parties garnered a disappointing 23 percent. Eventually, the two parties merged to form the Liberal Democratic Party, conceived as "the natural alternative to Thatcherism." Paddy Ashdown, an effective speaker who performed well on television, became the leader.

The Liberal Democrats continued to be strong in "the Celtic fringe"—the west of England, Wales, and Scotland. They were also competitive in local government elections in many parts of England. Their overriding objective was some form of proportional representation, for without that they would never gain seats in the House of Commons commensurate with their strength with the voters.

Thatcher's three electoral victories indicated that a major political realignment had taken place. The electoral success of Thatcherite conservatism was based on something more than a strong leader or unattractive opponents. It was because of policies suited to the demographic and economic developments that were changing the social structure and regional orientation of the United Kingdom. Thatcher's third victory guaranteed that the changes brought by Thatcherism—for better or for worse—were irreversible. The personal leadership of Margaret Thatcher had been the crucial catalyst that had made these things happen.

~

CHAPTER FOUR

The Fall of Margaret Thatcher, 1987–1990

Margaret Thatcher Riding High

After her victory in the election of 1987, Margaret Thatcher seemed to be at the peak of her power. Resistance within the Cabinet and the Conservative Party had been quelled, and her political opposition had once again tasted defeat. Despite appearances, signs of political weakness were present. Some of the major figures in the Conservative Party disliked her confrontational leadership and disagreed with her attitude toward the European Community. Cabinet reshuffles were frequent, as were dismissals and resignations.

Only three members of her 1983 Cabinet were still in office in January 1990. Something is to be said for bringing in young talent, such as John Major, Douglas Hurd, and Kenneth Baker, but extensive turnover is disruptive to any government and disturbing to party MPs. Thatcher's incessant activity was unsettling to many. She had never been a popular leader, and in three elections her party had never won more than 44 percent of the vote. A poll in 1989 showed that 67 percent of the respondents disliked her, but 63 percent respected her.

Her style can be described as "presidential," in that she was more a national leader than a party leader. A portent of future difficulties was seen in her domineering ways toward her Cabinet. Increasingly, she relied on her own judgment and a "kitchen cabinet" of personal advisers in No. 10. Instead of working together to achieve agreed policies on major issues, Cabinet members found it best to devote their attention to the administration of their own departments.

Sir Geoffrey Howe continued at the Foreign Office, Douglas Hurd as home secretary, and Nigel Lawson at the Exchequer. John Major entered the Cabinet as chief secretary to the Treasury, where his main responsibility was to keep track of spending and set departmental budgets in the annual spending review. In this role he met with ministers to discuss, and usually whittle down, their spending requests. His grasp of detail and emollient manner made his objections easier to take. This experience gave him an intimate knowledge of where the money went—the key to any government.

As a political leader, Thatcher took for granted the support of Conservative voters, and she was still able to bring down the house at Conservative conferences. She charged ahead on her agenda, although many of her objectives were not popular. In a poll taken in 1988, it was found that 39 percent of the population said they were "Thatcherist" in that they favored a capitalist, market-oriented society, while 54 percent said they were "socialist." Although 70 percent of the people polled saw Britain as Thatcherist, only 40 percent wanted it to be that way. The strong British sense of community prevailed over her individualism.

The Economy

In Thatcher's third ministry, the results of Thatcherism began to be seen. From 1985 to 1989, the Gross Domestic Product expanded by 14.5 percent. Corporate profits were buoyant, inward investment was strong, and exports continued to rise. Manufacturing industry had struggled back to 1979 levels, although its share of the total economy had shrunk. Inflation, as measured by consumer prices, held steady at about 5 percent, while earnings grew about 8 percent.

People who were employed were doing well and willing to spend. Unemployment fell from a peak of 3 million in 1986 to below 2 million. One disturbing sign was a trade deficit, resulting from declining revenues from North Sea oil, the consumer boom, and failure to improve British competitiveness in such items as automobiles, household appliances, and electronics.

The public revenue grew by 37 percent in that same period, while spending growth was held to 21 percent. The main spending increases were for health and community care (12 percent), education (8 percent), and law and order (14 percent). The main reductions were in defense (9 percent) and housing (40 percent). Savings in subsidies to council housing were to some extent offset by Housing Benefit paid to low-income people.

Nigel Lawson believed that cutting the income tax would free up money for new investments, increase productivity, and thus meet growing consumer demand. With the economy growing and the revenue in surplus, tax cuts became feasible. In 1988, Lawson reduced the top rate of the income tax from 60 percent to 40 percent and the basic rate to the promised 25 percent. Intermediate bands (brackets) were eliminated. Personal allowances were raised, and corporation and inheritance taxes were reduced.

As wages rose and unemployment fell, the demands on the National Insurance Fund declined, and by 1988 the fund was in balance: pensions and other benefits were being paid entirely out of the money coming in. In October 1987, Lawson boasted to the Conservative Party conference: "We have turned a budget deficit into a budget surplus. For the first time in living memory we are repaying the national debt." The media, always looking for striking personalities, hailed Lawson as "the miracle man."

The British economy had long been led by financial services, and the boom was especially noticeable in banking, foreign exchange, and insurance. Manufacturing investment in plant and equipment belatedly began to increase, and industrial production rose. The principal growth was in the service industries, which in 1988 employed 68 percent of the workforce.

More than 3 million new jobs were created from 1983 to 1990. Women, many of them in low-paid, part-time clerical or service occupations, filled a large proportion of the new jobs. Employment of women increased by 15 percent from 1985 to 1990, while male employment held steady. In 1990, 48 percent of employees were women. Approximately 20 million young people entered the workforce in the 1980s, and they were available to take the new jobs.

The main beneficiaries of Thatcherism were the wealthy and the middle class. From 1979 to 1989, the incomes (after taxes) of the wealthiest 10 percent increased by 65 percent per married couple. The incomes of the poorest 10 percent fell by 14 percent. The wealthiest also benefited most from the decrease in income taxes: from 1979 to 1989, their taxes fell from 52 percent to 36 percent of income, while the taxes of those with average incomes remained virtually the same.

Geographical divisions became pronounced. London and its great urban sprawl were generally well off, although London also had some of the worst poverty and social disorder in Britain. The East and the Southeast were doing well. The West of England was holding its own. The industrial areas of the Northeast and Northwest were badly depressed. Some cities, such as Birmingham and Manchester, were thriving as regional centers of banking, retailing, and services. Many others, however, had lost the industries that had provided jobs, and there was little likelihood that new, high-tech industries would locate there.

The dark side of Thatcher's Britain was unemployment. During "the winter of discontent" that had brought her to power, unemployment had been approximately 1.3 million, or 4.9 percent of the labor force. In 1981, unemployment was 2.5 million (9.4 percent). In 1986, it was 11.8 percent; and in 1990, when she left office, it had fallen back 5.8 percent. Many of the unemployed had held jobs that would never return, or lived in areas that would not generate new jobs. One result was the emergence of a large underclass. From 1979 to 1987, the number of people below the poverty line doubled, and almost 20 percent of the children qualified for school meals.

Privatization

The Thatcher commitment to privatization had been strengthened by the successful sales of her second ministry, and the process continued with unabated vigor. Each privatization helped to fund tax cuts, won political support from business, and further weakened the Labour Party. As to creating a "share-holding democracy," most of the small purchasers regarded the undervalued shares as a chance to turn a quick profit, and large investors and institutions soon owned the bulk of the shares.

British Airways had been high on the privatization list, but for years the airline had been losing money, and it could not be sold until that situation was changed. In 1983, a new chairman was appointed with the assignment of making the airline salable. By 1987, he had succeeded by cutting its bloated staff while improving service, at which time the airline was successfully privatized.

Other privatizations that took place in 1987 were Rolls Royce (aircraft engines) and the British Airports Authority, which included Heathrow and Gatwick airports. Rolls Royce stock doubled the first day, giving a quick preelection profit to the 2 million people who had applied for shares. Tony Blair, Labour's spokesman on economic matters, complained that it was a breach of trust "to undervalue shares for the purpose of attracting investors." It was notable, however, that Neil Kinnock said nothing, realizing the popularity of the shares among the voters.

The largest privatization of the year was the government's remaining 31.5 percent of the shares of British Petroleum. It was the largest stock offering ever made, anywhere. All the stock could have been sold to institutions without difficulty, but a significant portion was reserved for small investors and a massive advertising campaign was undertaken. However, the sale coincided with the stock market crash of October 1987, and it was less successful than expected.

Privatization of British Steel was another long-term goal, but the steel industry had to be made profitable before it could be sold. A vigorous program began to introduce modern technology, shed jobs, and close unprofitable plants. The costs in unemployment and disruption of communities were high, but by 1988 British Steel had become one of the largest and most profitable steel companies in the world. In that year British Steel was successfully sold to a consortium of British and overseas investors, with 23 percent reserved for an estimated 500,000 small investors. Once again the Labour Party complained "British Steel is being offered at this bargain basement price for sordid political reasons."

The Thatcher government broke new ground with the privatization of the water and electricity companies, natural monopolies essential to public well-being. These companies needed massive amounts of new capital to keep pace with technology. Furthermore, their long-established managers and employees, with their set ways of doing things, were slow to respond to new needs and management practices.

Britain's nationalized water system was comprised of ten companies serving major river basins, such as Thames Water and Severn-Trent Water. In addition to providing water and sewer services, these companies had a variety of environmental responsibilities, including maintaining the purity of rivers, flood control, management of wetlands, and protection of wildlife. When the water companies were privatized, the National Rivers Authority was established to deal with environmental matters, and the privatized water companies were limited to water and sewerage. Under the National Rivers Authority, British waterways became among the purest in Europe.

Sale of the water companies to investors took place in 1989. To make the companies salable, the government wrote off their debts, provided generous tax breaks, injected a considerable amount of cash for capital improvements, and offered the shares on easy terms. The shares were highly attractive, and the offer was five times oversubscribed. A regulatory office (Ofwat) was set up to regulate prices and monitor the quality of service.

The electricity industry was complex, and not all parts were attractive to investors. In 1988, a complicated privatization plan was proposed. Twelve regional electric companies delivered electricity to consumers. Shares in these companies were sold to the public in 1990 and were a popular investment. An office to regulate the industry (Offer) was established.

To rationalize the industry, the power stations were organized into two separate generating companies that were successfully privatized. The National Grid carried electricity from the generating companies to the regional electric companies. The National Grid was turned over to the twelve electric companies, but it was required to purchase electricity from the cheapest source, thus introducing competition between the two generating companies. Private companies were encouraged to enter the power generation business, selling electricity either to the twelve regional companies or to the National Grid.

Investors rejected privatization if it included Britain's outmoded nuclear power plants. There was considerable environmental opposition to nuclear power, especially concerning the disposal of nuclear waste. Accordingly, the nuclear plants were withdrawn from the sale.

In 1990, the Ports Bill was passed to sell off the Port of London Authority and other ports still owned by the government. The two major privatizations that still remained in the planning stage were British Coal and British Rail.

The Channel tunnel project proceeded, despite engineering difficulties and overspending. In 1990, the French and British segments of the tunnel met under the Channel after three years of work, but vast overruns had been incurred.

Problems also arose with the new roads and the high-speed rail system needed to connect the tunnel with London. The rail network and existing roads were clearly inadequate, but Britain insisted that it could not afford extensive new construction. Residents along the proposed route did not want increased road and rail traffic in their communities. Differences also emerged in deciding on the best route to bring the trains into London.

Thatcher was closely involved in efforts to promote the British armaments industry through exports. Her largest arms deal (£20 billion) was the sale of Tornado aircraft and support equipment to Saudi Arabia in 1985. In 1988 and 1989, she made trips to Nigeria, and British foreign aid to Nigeria was greatly increased. Two years later, a British manufacturer won a large contract to supply battle tanks that the Nigerian military used in 1992 for a political coup.

When British Aerospace had an opportunity to make large weapons sales in Malaysia, the Thatcher ministry sweetened the deal by promising economic aid to build a dam in the interior, although consultants had reported that the project was not viable. In 1988, the arms deal was signed, and in 1990, the agreed aid for the Pergau Dam was paid. Although this arrangement was not unusual in the highly competitive world of international arms sales, when revealed in 1994, it proved embarrassing to those involved.

In the 1980s Iraq, under Saddam Hussein, was seen as a bulwark of Western interests against Iran, which had come under the rule of the ayatollahs. Western countries, including Britain, were eager to sell weapons to Saddam, and Britain used its long-established connections in the Middle East to advance the interests of British arms manufacturers.

In 1985, the brutality of the Iraq–Iran War led the United Nations to prohibit the export of weaponry to either of the belligerents, and Britain agreed to support the sanctions. In 1989, a British company, Matrix Churchill, had an opportunity to sell machine tools to Iraq that could be used to make weapons. The company claimed that they were for civilian use, and several junior ministers joined to "interpret" the guidelines in a manner that would allow the sale, informing Thatcher and the foreign secretary (John Major) in a perfunctory manner. Letters written by one of the ministers to Members of Parliament stated that the policy had not changed, when to some extent it had.

Although Thatcher was not directly implicated in the Matrix Churchill affair, it seems likely that her determination to support the British armaments industry by making sales abroad influenced the decisions made by the junior ministers. They had reason to think that they were carrying out her policy, although it was better that she not know too much about it. In this instance, as with the Pergau Dam, Thatcher had contributed to a political scandal in waiting.

The Superpowers

In her third ministry, Margaret Thatcher gave more attention than before to foreign policy. By 1987, Thatcher was an established world figure who drew attention wherever she went. Few political leaders have been able to resist the siren song of foreign affairs, and in this respect, she did not differ from others. In the television age, the temptation to strut on the world scene is strong.

The personal friendship of Thatcher and President Ronald Reagan was real, but its influence on the relations of the two countries should not be exaggerated. The "special relationship" was severely tested in 1986 when Reagan decided to unleash a midnight bombing raid on Tripoli to punish Colonel Muammar Gaddafi, ruler of Libya, for his support of terrorism. Other European countries refused Reagan permission to dispatch bombers through their airspace. They regarded the raid as a violation of international law, an action that could only injure innocent people, and a display of military force for domestic political consumption.

Despite these considerations, Thatcher repaid Reagan for his support in the Falklands War by allowing him to use British bases for the raid. She insisted on a careful definition of targets, limiting them to places used to support terrorists. Despite American claims of precision bombing, when the raid was carried out bombs were scattered all over Tripoli, hitting friend and foe alike, including the French embassy.

When the news came to Britain of civilian casualties, the British press and public were shocked at scenes of physical destruction, weeping mothers, and angry mobs promising retaliation. The raid encouraged the view that the United States was a reckless superpower ready to use airpower against any weak country that aroused its ire. BBC coverage of the attack was so critical that the Conservative Party Central Office found it necessary to publish a rebuttal.

Reagan proclaimed victory, but Gaddafi continued to support international terrorism, although more discreetly. Two years later Gaddafi got his revenge when a terrorist bomb brought down a Pan American Boeing 747 over Lockerbie, Scotland, killing 258 passengers and 11 inhabitants of the town.

Thatcher's most important contribution to the superpower relationship was her reaction to the rise of Mikhail Gorbachev to power in the Soviet Union. She recognized that a new kind of Soviet leader had emerged who held out the prospect of an end to the Cold War. In response to friendly British overtures, Gorbachev visited London in December 1984 and Thatcher declared: "I like Mr. Gorbachev; we can do business together."

Gorbachev became general secretary of the Communist Party and de facto leader of the Soviet Union in March 1985. Thatcher realized that Gorbachev did not represent fundamental change: his objective was to make the system work better through *perestroika* (restructuring) and *glasnost* (openness to criticism). It was evident that Gorbachev intended to continue the Soviet Union's role as a great power and rival of the United States.

The major issue between the two superpowers was nuclear weapons, where American technological advances were causing anxiety in the Soviet Union. The Soviet Union was most concerned by the American development of the Strategic Defense Initiative ("Star Wars"), a complex system in space intended to defend the United States against intercontinental ballistic missiles.

If successful, the Strategic Defense Initiative (SDI) would leave the Soviet Union exposed to American missiles without the ability to retaliate. Many in the West questioned whether SDI would ever work, but the Soviets took it seriously. It seemed to them that the United States was gaining a technological edge that the crumbling Soviet economy could never match.

Thatcher was a supporter of nuclear weapons, which she felt had maintained the peace in Europe by negating the vast Soviet superiority in conventional forces. But she was convinced that the key to nuclear deterrence was nuclear balance. SDI held out the possibility that the nuclear balance would be upset, possibly provoking the Soviet Union to undertake a nuclear war before the American missile defense was in place.

Thatcher had the ear of President Reagan, and she had won the respect of Chairman Gorbachev. Her most important influence was probably her ability to explain Reagan and Gorbachev to each other. She made it clear to Gorbachev that the West would not let down its guard in respect to nuclear weapons and would continue to resist Soviet expansion in Third World countries. She visited Washington in December 1984 and again in February 1985, where she encouraged Reagan to continue with "Star Wars" research, but she urged that testing and implementation be done in a measured manner that would not push the Soviet Union to desperate actions.

The climax arrived in October 1986, when Reagan and Gorbachev met at Reykjavik, Iceland, to discuss nuclear disarmament. Both were ready to make substantial cuts in their nuclear arsenals, but the Soviets insisted that the United States abandon "Star Wars," which Reagan refused to do.

Carried away by enthusiasm for disarmament, Reagan proposed doing away with all nuclear weapons within ten years, a prospect that appalled Thatcher. She hurried off to Washington to remind the president that nuclear weapons had preserved the peace for forty years and should not be abandoned. By that time the moment for extensive nuclear disarmament had passed, and the nuclear standoff continued until the collapse of the Soviet Union brought the Cold War to an end.

In March 1987, Thatcher made a triumphant visit to Moscow as the guest of Chairman Gorbachev. In addition to public appearances, where she was well received, she talked frankly with Gorbachev about the Cold War, nuclear weapons, disarmament, human rights, and Gorbachev's plans for economic development. The relationship was cemented by the Soviet president's visit to London in 1987. Gorbachev made a second stop in Britain in 1989, which Thatcher reciprocated later in the year. As Gorbachev sought to work his way through the daunting problems of the Soviet Union, its Eastern European empire, and the superpower rivalry with the United States, perhaps Thatcher served as a useful and unthreatening interpreter of Western views.

In 1989–1990, the world scene was dramatically changed by events in the Soviet Union and Eastern Europe. The Soviet economy continued its precipitous decline, aggravated by President Gorbachev's reform policies. Within the Soviet Union, subject nationalities in the Baltic area, Ukraine, Georgia, and the Muslim regions claimed the right to manage their own affairs. The Soviet empire in Eastern Europe crumbled as one country after another threw off Soviet control and ejected its Communist rulers. In November 1989, the Iron Curtain was breached, and thousands of refugees fled to the West.

The major issue was the impending reunification of Germany. With her memories of World War II, Thatcher was appalled at the prospect of a powerful, united Germany dominating Europe. As usual, she was outspoken in her views, but events made her objections irrelevant. In October 1990, the East German state collapsed and was absorbed by the Federal Republic of West Germany to create the German Federal Republic. In November, the Conference on Security and Cooperation in Europe declared that the Cold War had ended.

The inauguration of President George Bush in 1989 weakened the relationship with the United States that had been so important to Thatcher. The Bush administration decided that American foreign policy should draw closer to Germany, which was seen as the new center of power in Europe. Bush and Secretary of State James Baker seemed to view Thatcher as a tiresome woman offering advice that was neither wanted nor heeded. They would soon find that they were mistaken.

The European Community

Despite her resolution to be "a good European," Thatcher, with her free-market views and global perspective, continued to be a troublesome factor in the European Community (EC). In that respect, she was in tune with the British public, which was slow to accept Britain's relationship with Europe. The EC was more unpopular in Britain than in any other member state, with the exception of Denmark.

In 1990, only 50 percent of the public thought that membership in the EC was "a good thing." Nevertheless, Britain derived substantial benefits from the single market: 53 percent of British exports went to member states in 1990, compared to half that amount twenty years earlier.

Jacques Delors, president of the European Commission, continued to press for closer political and economic unity. He proposed to replace national currencies with a single European currency, managed by a European central bank. Thatcher stated her objections in a speech at Bruges (September 1988) in which she declared: "We have not successfully rolled back the frontiers of the state in Britain only to see them reimposed at the European level, with a European super-state exercising a new dominance from Brussels." The European Community should be a union of sovereign states, she declared: "France as France, Spain as Spain, Britain as Britain, each with its own customs, traditions, and identities."

In the same speech, she reiterated British internationalism. While asserting that Britain's destiny was in Europe, she added: "That is not to say that our future lies *only* in Europe." She was determined to keep Britain open to the wider world and to move the EC in the same direction.

With the breakdown of the Iron Curtain, Thatcher saw Eastern Europe as a great new responsibility for the West. She urged expansion of the EC to Poland, Czechoslovakia, Hungary, and other newly freed states. This proposal would necessarily loosen the bonds of the EC by making the Common Agricultural Policy, uniform employment and social policies, and regional subsidies unworkable.

Expansion to the East threatened the centralizing policies of Jacques Delors. For that reason it was, for the foreseeable future, unacceptable to many of the member countries.

The Emergence of a Crisis

In her third ministry, Thatcher turned her attention to the social role of the government, especially in regard to social security, the National Health Service (NHS) and schools (see chapter 5). She found that the way of the reformer is hard. These institutions were intimately involved in the lives of ordinary people, and any attempt to meddle with them was bound to create anxiety.

Civil servants, doctors, nurses, teachers, and social workers resisted changes that were untested and ran counter to accepted ways of doing things. Teachers and nurses engaged in long and bitter strikes, which were eventually resolved by increases in pay. Pensioners, the unemployed, and others dependent on the welfare state were inclined to think that the reforms would not make life any better for them. Although they wanted better services, the general public was uneasy at the pace of change. Thatcher had pushed the country further and faster than it was willing to go.

The crucial problem was a financial crisis, as inflation revived. Nigel Lawson had adopted a "flexible" monetary policy based on interest rates, exchange rates, and other economic indicators. To cushion the shock of the stock market fall in 1987, he had lowered interest rates and poured money into the economy, which further stoked the fires of inflation.

Like Sir Edward Heath in 1972, Lawson found that the boom that his tax cuts and loose monetary policy had unleashed had gotten out of hand. Money from his tax cuts had not gone into investment but into speculation, houses, and consumption. Wage settlements averaging 9.25 percent and a great expansion of consumer credit through hire purchase and credit cards fueled inflation, which reached 8 percent in 1989.

A major culprit was mortgage lending, as banks and building societies competed with each other and made mortgages at 100 percent of inflated values. House prices rose steeply; people bought houses at prices unimaginable just a few years before. The boom sucked in foreign goods, and the balance of payments turned sharply against the pound. In 1988, Lawson raised interest rates to 10.5 percent and then to 13 percent to fight inflation and raise the level of the pound in international markets. It seemed that monetary policy alone could not stem the tide.

As inflation took off, the financial community urged participation in the Exchange Rate Mechanism (ERM). The ERM used the strong West German mark as its standard, and member countries were expected to stabilize their exchange rates with the mark. It was thought in the City that membership in the ERM would bring salutary discipline to the British economy and thus reduce inflation and improve the balance of payments.

Lawson was close to the financiers and sympathetic to this view. Sir Geoffrey Howe, the foreign secretary, was a strong advocate of full British participation in the EC. He supported Lawson in urging membership in the ERM, which would be a clear signal of Britain's commitment to Europe. While this decision was pending, Lawson pushed interest rates as high as 15 percent to fight inflation and keep the pound in step with the strong German mark.

Thatcher disagreed with Lawson on fixed exchange rates. She believed in the rationality and inescapability of markets, in money as well as other items. "There is no way to buck the market," she said.

Thatcher had come to office in 1979 determined to reduce inflation and the stifling effects of high interest rates. Ten years of painful effort and sacrifice seemed to be going down the drain. The British economy had flourished since she and Howe had removed exchange controls and allowed the pound to float to its market level. Now Lawson had put in place a surreptitious variant of the fixed exchange rates that had been so damaging in the past. Observers noted increasing tension between the prime minister and "the miracle man." When Thatcher turned to Sir Alan Walters, her former economics adviser, to give her independent advice, a showdown appeared imminent.

In July 1988, as she was preparing to leave for a European summit in Madrid, Howe and Lawson came to No. 10 and issued an ultimatum: agree to join the ERM by a fixed date or they would resign. Thatcher could not face the political fallout that would result from the resignation of the two most distinguished members of her Cabinet. Reluctantly, she issued a statement in Madrid that Britain would join the ERM when British inflation had fallen to European levels.

Tangling with Lawson and Howe put Thatcher up against two strong-willed individuals with their own constituencies in the City and in the Conservative Party. As tensions mounted she backed off, and in June 1989, she announced her support for Lawson's policies. Lawson conceded that a decision concerning membership in the ERM could wait another year.

The Poll Tax

As leader of the Conservative Party in opposition, Thatcher had promised to reform the system of rates, the local government tax on homes and businesses. The rating system had been reviewed in 1981 and again in 1982, but no decision had been reached. By 1987, property values had risen dramatically. In 1985, a revaluation (reassessment) of property in Scotland produced large increases in valuations, resulting in steep increases in the rates that businesses and homeowners had to pay. Property owners in Scotland were in an uproar. No revaluation of business and residential property had been made in England since 1973, and it was recognized that sharply higher valuations would bring a similar reaction there.

The Conservatives were the party of small business and homeowners, who bore the burden of the rates. Approximately two-thirds of the population paid no rates or had their rates paid for them by the welfare system. The Thatcherites charged that Labour-controlled councils in large cities imposed high rates on the people who were well off to fund low-cost rents, bus fares, and other popular services.

In the previous decade, Howe and Lawson had cut the support grants to local governments from 60 percent of spending to 40 percent. Local governments had made up the difference by pushing the rates even higher. People and businesses moved to places with lower rates, leaving the central city worse off than before.

With her victory in the election of 1987, Thatcher felt strong enough to undertake a drastic reform of local government finance and get rid of the hated system of rates. Seeking a replacement, the decision was made that the only way to curb local government spending was to require everyone to pay something, which would make local authorities responsible to the general public for their stewardship of local government funds. The poll tax was first introduced in Scotland, where ratepayers were up in arms against the rates, but the full effect of the new system was not yet clear.

Early in 1988, a bill was introduced for England and Wales to replace the rates on homes with a uniform community charge (poll tax) on every person over eighteen years of age. The maximum poll tax per household was expected to be about £200, roughly half the average under the rates. Rebates based on the ability to pay would lower the tax progressively from 100 percent to 20 percent. There were lower charges for students and people with low incomes. If local governments spent excessively, they would have to increase the poll tax to cover the cost. It was expected that the general public (not just homeowners) would become a pressure group to restrain local government spending in order to keep the poll tax low. If local pressures were not effective, the central government would have the power to limit poll tax charges (capping).

Business property remained under the rating system, but a national level was set for business rates to keep businesses from moving from high-rated communities to those with lower rates. The income from business rates was assigned to communities on a per capita basis, so that local governments with large businesses would not have an advantage over those with none, and councils would not be tempted to squeeze businesses for all they could get.

Thatcher made the decision for the poll tax, despite strong opposition in the Cabinet, Parliament, and the country. Likely political fallout was minimized. Problems of administration and collection were ignored, although people are considerably more mobile and easily concealed than houses. Tumultuous debates took place in the House of Commons, where Thatcher faced a backbench revolt reminiscent of the overthrow of Heath in 1975. When the final vote was held in January 1990, 31 Tories voted against it, including Heath and Heseltine.

The poll tax was introduced in England and Wales in March 1990. Although the system seemed logical in the abstract, it aroused a storm of protest when applied. Homeowners were glad to be relieved of the rates, but they were astonished at the size of their poll tax charges. Inflation and unemployment had increased the costs of local government, while the government had cut its support grants. Some authorities imposed a stiff poll tax to undertake projects that would not have been affordable under the old system of rates.

Poll taxes averaged £400 per household, and the rebates to low-income people still left them with a poll tax they could not afford. It was found that 73 percent of households and 82 percent of individuals would pay more in poll tax than they had paid before in rates. People soon forgot their complaints about the rates and focused their outrage on the new system.

People without children who owned expensive houses and paid high rates were better off paying the poll tax. Families with a modest house and several adult children living at home paid more in poll tax than they had in rates, as did elderly women living in little old houses with a low valuation. Renters, especially those with large families, who had paid no rates at all, were hit hardest. Thatcher had intended that people who objected to the poll tax would rise up against the spending of their local councils. Instead they blamed her!

It was not enough to say, as Thatcher did, that the wealthy paid their share of taxes in other ways while renters received local government services and paid no rates at all. She tried to point out that local authorities set the level of the poll tax, and their ambitious spending plans were the cause of the problem. She declared that every citizen should be proud to make a financial contribution to the community, a view of taxes not commonly found among ordinary mortals.

Complaints rained down on Conservative MPs, and Thatcher faced a full-blown crisis in her own party. Business interests, to whom Thatcher was usually sensitive, opposed the new business rates. People flatly refused to reveal how many adults lived in their house, especially since young adults came and went. Landlords in tough neighborhoods were threatened to keep them from revealing the number of adults living in their properties. In March 1990, a demonstration in Trafalgar Square against the poll tax resulted in a riot where cars were burned and more than three hundred police officers were injured. In a desperate effort to calm the situation, the government set limits to "excessive" increases in spending and funneled large subsidies to local governments to keep the poll tax down—the very antithesis of Thatcherism.

Stormy Weather

From the beginning of her ministry, Thatcher had been unpopular among many Conservatives, and that continued although she had won three elections. Within her Cabinet, she met resistance from Howe and Lawson. Prominent Conservatives out of office, including Heath and Heseltine, criticized her domineering manner and her evident willingness to run the whole show. Her support of the poll tax cost her the support of many backbenchers.

Disputes concerning Britain's relationship with Europe led to the breakdown of her long relationship with the foreign secretary, Sir Geoffrey Howe. In July 1989, Thatcher decided that it was time to get Howe out of the Foreign Office. She handled the matter badly. After various efforts to avoid an open breach, Howe was removed from his prestigious post, which included use of an attractive country house that he enjoyed. Understandably, Howe resented this obvious demotion, papered over with the nominal roles of deputy prime minister and leader of the Conservative Party in the House of Commons.

As the successor to Howe at the Foreign Office, Thatcher chose John Major. The appointment astonished everyone. Thatcher indicated that she wanted a foreign secretary who shared her views, although Major's views on foreign policy, if he had any, were quite unknown. More likely, she wanted someone whom she could dominate and who had not been indoctrinated with the pro-European views of the Foreign Office.

Clearly, she recognized Major as a talented politician, although press speculation that he was her chosen successor was wide of the mark. Despite his lack of experience in foreign affairs, Major was a quick study, and he soon was able to hold his own in international conferences.

With Howe out of the Foreign Office, Lawson realized that his own position was slipping. He was a man of great ability and self-confidence, who insisted that the chancellor of the Exchequer should have the paramount role in shaping economic policy.

Lawson was an articulate and colorful figure, who enjoyed public attention. He forgot that Thatcher had brought him into the limelight, a fatal mistake in an underling. His disagreement with Thatcher about the ERM was irreconcilable. In October 1989, Lawson resigned. Perhaps he realized, although he would not admit it, that the inflationary crisis facing Britain was partially of his own making.

Major, who had scarcely had time to settle into the Foreign Office, replaced Lawson as chancellor of the Exchequer, the post he had always wanted. It was left to this young, inexperienced politician to deal with the economic crisis. Douglas Hurd, a pro-European and former follower of Heath, replaced Major at the Foreign Office.

These surprising changes shook the Conservative Party and startled political observers. A warning shot was fired later in the year when a little-known backbencher, Sir Anthony Meyer, decided to give Conservative MPs an opportunity to show their dissatisfaction by standing as a candidate in the annual leadership election. When Meyer received thirty-three votes, with twenty-seven abstentions, it was clear that Thatcher was in trouble within her own party.

At the Exchequer, Major continued Lawson's policies. The fight against inflation dictated that taxes and interest rates could not be cut. At the Foreign Office, Hurd was convinced that good relations with the other members of the EC required joining the ERM. Opinion among political, financial, and business leaders was almost unanimous that the only way to contain inflation was to link sterling with the German mark by joining the ERM. Lacking views of his own, Major was swept along by the tide.

Major's main challenge was to persuade Thatcher. An election was due in 1992, and Major felt the need to unite the party. With a political storm brewing, Thatcher found that she could not have everything her own way. Eventually, she was worn down by the insistence of her Cabinet. In October 1990, Thatcher impulsively agreed to join the ERM without conditions, a political decision taken without adequate preparation or consultation with the EC. It was a fateful decision that Thatcher and Major would regret.

The year 1990 was decisive for Thatcher. When the year opened, her government faced serious difficulties: inflation was rising; the economy was floundering; the Conservative Party was riven by disputes over Europe; the poll tax was widely hated; and the Labour Party, with vigorous leadership and renewed confidence, was leading in the polls. Thatcher had become the most unpopular prime minister since polls had begun. In March 1990, polls showed that only 20 percent of the public was satisfied with her performance. Her belief in rugged individualism and a competitive market was not widely shared.

To keep peace with the ERM, Britain was compelled to keep interest rates high to maintain the required relationship with the other currencies, and by mid-1990, the full effects were being felt. Most British houses were bought with variable rate mortgages. Mortgage rates rose to 15 percent, and mortgage payments almost doubled. House prices began to fall as people unloaded houses that they could no longer afford. Millions of people who had bought during the boom were stuck with negative equity—the mortgage was higher than the sale value of the house. It was a political disaster equal to the poll tax.

The shiny new office towers had high vacancy levels. The new shopping malls that were just coming into service had difficulty paying their way. Banks and insurance companies that had prospered during the boom found that their portfolios were burdened with nonperforming mortgages and unsecured loans that were unlikely to be repaid. Construction slowed and workers drawn into the building trades by the boom were laid off.

The politicians and the public began to think that Thatcherism and prosperity were not synonymous. The Conservative Party fell to 30 percent in the polls and suffered heavy losses in the local elections in May. Later in the year, a by-election in Eastbourne, a Tory stronghold, was lost to the Liberal Democrats in a spectacular upset. The Conservative Party was stunned.

Crisis in the Persian Gulf

At this crucial moment, a foreign policy crisis distracted Thatcher from her growing problems at home. In August 1990, Saddam, the brutal dictator of Iraq, suddenly invaded the adjacent ministate of Kuwait, which he claimed should be Iraqi territory. When news of Saddam's invasion arrived, Thatcher was in the United States attending a conference. Suddenly, President George Bush realized that Britain was an important power after all, and he rushed to Colorado to meet with her.

The invasion brought back memories of the Falklands War, and Thatcher again rose to the challenge. She was influential in encouraging Bush to organize an international alliance that would resist Saddam, defend the other states of the Arabian Peninsula, and expel the Iraqis from Kuwait. She promised full British support, and immediately British forces were on their way to the Gulf. "This was no time to go wobbly," Thatcher told the president.

A legal basis for action was established when the United Nations Security Council condemned Iraq's aggression and demanded the restoration of the government of Kuwait. An embargo was imposed on Iraq and the Western powers were authorized to enforce it, but it seemed evident that overwhelming force would be needed to expel Saddam from his conquest. Kinnock declared Labour's support for armed resistance to outright aggression.

With Saudi Arabia as a base, an allied force of half a million military personnel, with massive amounts of equipment and supplies, was assembled to defend the Gulf states and restore the independence of Kuwait. The United States supplied most of the troops, support forces, and communications, but Britain sent forty-five thousand well-trained troops. France and other countries also contributed. Thatcher's contention that a well-prepared, well-led power of medium rank could still play an important role in world affairs had been confirmed.

The Fall of Margaret Thatcher

While the Gulf crisis was in progress, the turmoil in the Conservative Party came to a head. Many Conservatives were anxious about the unpopularity of their leader, which rubbed off on the party. Prominent figures in the party, among them Heath, Howe, Lawson, and Heseltine, opposed her confrontational relations with the EC. The poll tax was a continuing aggravation. Kinnock was beginning to look prime ministerial, and the changes he had made in Labour's policies made the party look ready for government. Newspapers that had previously supported the prime minister declared that she had become an electoral liability.

The poll tax gave her enemies within the party their opportunity, for Thatcher would not abandon the poll tax, and with the poll tax in place, Conservative chances in the next election were dim indeed. The Conservative conference in October 1990 was gloomy, for it was evident that the poll tax spelled doom with the voters.

Howe precipitated Margaret Thatcher's downfall. At the European Union summit in Rome she declared that, if necessary, she would veto Jacques Delors's plan to establish a single European currency. She followed that with a hard-hitting anti-European speech in the House of Commons. Her reply to the plans of Jacques Delors for political union was "No. No. No." The next day Howe resigned, and in November he replied with a stinging attack on her leadership, especially on relations with Europe.

Howe was widely respected in the House of Commons, and the speech had a great effect on the Conservative MPs and the public. Major and Hurd attempted to rally the troops, but Howe had unleashed a powerful feeling that could not be stopped. Finally a prominent Conservative had openly challenged Thatcher. Differences over relations with Europe, which would eventually shatter the Conservative Party, had broken wide open.

The next day, with the Conservatives' annual leadership election approaching, Heseltine, a colorful figure who had kept himself in the public eye by making speeches at Conservative meetings throughout the country, declared himself a candidate for the leadership. He cited the prime minister's unpopularity and promised to replace the poll tax. Heseltine and his supporters were using the same method that Thatcher had used to displace Heath.

But Thatcher's situation was different. When she had gained the leadership, Heath had been defeated in two elections, and the Conservative Party was out of office. In November 1990, she had won three consecutive elections, the Conservatives had been in power for eleven years, and the next election was two years off. The victor in the Falklands was preparing Britain for war in the Gulf. Rejection seemed unthinkable.

Thatcher was mistaken. Despite her electoral successes, she had not changed the core of the Conservative Party. Many of the leaders and rank-and-file members were not Thatcherites and felt uncomfortable with Thatcherism. Unlike the Falklands War, which concerned British citizens, the war in the Gulf did not bring an upsurge of popular support. Thatcher had held her leadership position by her ability to appeal beyond her party to the voters and win elections. When it became evident that she could not win the next election, the Conservative Party was ready to dump her.

Confidently, Thatcher went off to Paris to a summit meeting and was out of the country when the leadership election took place. No effort was made to rally her followers or mount a campaign in the media, although Heseltine was busy doing interviews. Major, who had declared his support, was at home recovering from long-scheduled dental surgery. Her absence meant that those who voted against her did not have to look her in the eye while doing it. On the first ballot, she defeated Heseltine by 204 to 152 with 16 abstentions, but she had fallen 2 votes short of the required majority plus 15 percent, and a second ballot would be required. A simple majority would decide the second ballot.

Thatcher hurried back from Paris in a desperate effort to stem the tide, but it had become clear that she could not unite a divided and shaken party. She had great news: the treaty marked the end of the Cold War—the prize that she had sought throughout her entire political career.

But it did not matter. When she met individually with members of her Cabinet, one by one they made lukewarm pledges of support but added that she could not win. They saw Heseltine as a disruptive figure. They argued that the only way to stop him was for her to step down and allow other candidates to come forward. She knew that she was finished. In the meantime, Norman Lamont and other friends of Major were promoting him as her successor, while others favored Hurd.

On November 22, 1990, Thatcher tearfully informed her Cabinet that she intended to resign her office and the leadership of the Conservative Party. "It's a funny old world," she remarked. Six days later she went to Buckingham Palace and tendered her resignation to the queen.

That afternoon Thatcher returned to the House of Commons, full of fight and fire. The House of Commons was jammed, as members packed the benches and crowded into every available space. In one of the greatest speeches of her remarkable career, she reviewed the plight of Britain when she took office, enunciated the principles that had guided her, and reviewed the accomplishments of her three ministries. She reiterated her view of the European Union and Britain's place within it.

The House of Commons rocked, as the Tories cheered and the Labour benches jeered. Suddenly she stopped and exclaimed: "I'm rather enjoying this!" One Tory member rose to his feet, pointed toward her likely successors—Heseltine, Hurd, Major—and cried out: "You'd wipe the floor with this lot!" When she finished, the Tories gave her a standing ovation. Everyone knew that a giant was passing from the scene.

Thatcher's resignation shocked the politicians, the media, and the public, who had become accustomed to her presence—like her or not. Howe declared that it was time for a "team approach" to Cabinet decisions. Heseltine announced that he would regard it as a "huge honor" to lead the Conservative Party.

Howe and Lawson launched a final dart at Thatcher by endorsing Heseltine. Thatcher's resignation made it possible for other candidates to come forward. Hurd was a moderate with pro-European views. Major was seen as a noncontroversial figure who would provide time for the divisions in the party to heal. He stated that he wanted to achieve "a country that is at ease with itself."

Major agreed to stand for party leader, and his supporters, led by his Treasury colleague, Lamont, organized an energetic five-day campaign that included canvassing of members and media interviews. Major promised to do something about the poll tax, take a commonsense position regarding the EC, and do all he could to restore unity to Conservative Party. He expressed his concern for the millions of ordinary people who had not benefited from the changes of the past decade.

Thatcher supported Major, mainly because it seemed that he could defeat Heseltine. The Thatcherites favored Major as one who would continue the Thatcher agenda; others saw him as a competent administrator, who would consolidate the changes that had taken place but go no further. The pro-Europeans noted his acceptance of the ERM, and assumed that he would be responsive to their desire for closer relations with Europe. The backbenchers, who had dealt with him over the years as a whip and in his subsequent offices, knew and liked him.

Major frequently visited the Commons tearoom to chat with the members, while Heseltine was arrogant and aloof. During the leadership campaign, Major gave several television interviews, in which he showed that he was informed, articulate, and personable. For the first time, the British public took a hard look at John Major. They liked what they saw.

When the ballot was taken on November 27, John Major was two votes short of a majority. Some voted for him because he was not Thatcher; some because he was not Heseltine. Few thought that he was ready to be prime minister. Most of his votes came from the center and right of the party; most of those who had voted for Thatcher voted for Major. The distinguishing factor seemed to be that those who voted for Heseltine were more positive toward Europe.

Hurd and Heseltine withdrew, and Major became the new leader of the Conservative Party and prime minister. Heseltine realized that his opportunity to reach the top office had vanished. However, by challenging Thatcher, he had given the Conservative Party an opportunity to make a fresh start. "He who wields the knife never wears the crown," he said.

The fall of Thatcher was as astonishing as her rise to the highest office in 1979. During those eleven years, she had dominated the British political scene and made herself a world figure. What had happened to bring her to such a sudden and bitter end?

Perhaps she had stayed in office too long. The leadership and confidence that were welcome when she first became prime minister had become an imperious manner that led her to ignore or defy political advice, of which the poll tax was the most damaging example. Frequent Cabinet dismissals and reshuffles had created many influential enemies in the Conservative Party.

Her many trips abroad weakened her grasp of public opinion at home. Hers was an executive mentality: apart from the mandatory "Prime Minister's Questions," she seldom participated in parliamentary debates. Her visits to the House of Commons tearoom, which had been frequent early in her ministry, became a rare event in her later years. She had outlasted and, to some extent, resolved the issues that had brought her to office. For one reason or another, she had worn out her welcome.

CHAPTER FIVE

~

Thatcherite Reform

The Civil Service

Margaret Thatcher believed that Britain's decline was partially due to a government that was costly, inefficient, and hidebound. She was determined to reform British government, as a necessary step in reforming other institutions that were also functioning badly.

The core of British government was the civil service, and she began there. The British civil service was world famous for its impartiality, competence, and devotion to good government. At the top of the civil service were approximately one hundred permanent secretaries ("mandarins"), almost all of them urbane gentlemen educated at Oxford or Cambridge in liberal studies. Their responsibility was to assist the minister in running his department by providing information and advice while helping him to avoid mistakes that would be politically or personally embarrassing. They were the top of a civil service pyramid of 720,000 employees.

Critics commented that the top echelon of the civil service lacked professional expertise in economics, science, and other technical fields, and were separated by their education and social class from commerce, industry, and the lives of ordinary people. Thatcher had many populist views: one of them was that the top levels of the civil service were a privileged elite who looked on themselves as an estate of the realm, rather than as a body of administrators with work to do. She was convinced that the civil service was riddled with poorly defined responsibilities and without cost-benefit accountability. In the upper levels she suspected a genteel "old-boy" network that encouraged logrolling and buck-passing. She believed that the structures and routines of the civil service were inefficient and unresponsive to the needs of a dynamic nation. She was determined to ride herd on them, and during her ministries she reduced the total number by about 20 percent.

Thatcher was a great admirer of successful businessmen, and she sought to introduce into the civil service the practices of large businesses. She asked Sir Derek Rayner of Marks & Spencer, a highly regarded retail chain, to serve as her adviser on efficiency in government.

Rayner established an "Efficiency Unit" at No. 10 to conduct investigations of departments, looking for ways to achieve better performance and save money. He discovered that the Ministry of Agriculture was breeding its own rats for research at a cost of £30 per rat when they could be bought commercially for £2. Rayner pushed for a reduction of paperwork. The claim was made that twenty-seven thousand forms were eliminated and another forty thousand were redesigned. Some savings were made, although the civil service complained that many of the supposed savings were illusory.

Rayner's most important step was to begin decentralizing administration. He began by establishing semiautonomous "cost centers" managed by administrators with minimal supervision by the responsible department. A new system of financial management was introduced to define objectives, measure results, and assess costs.

Sir Robin Ibbs, who succeeded Rayner as head of the Efficiency Unit, proposed to dismantle the hierarchical, bureaucratic, departmental structure of the civil service, replacing it with semiautonomous agencies. At the top would be a core group of 50,000 civil servants with policy-making responsibilities. The remaining 550,000, who performed administrative or routine functions, would be organized into agencies largely independent of ministerial control. They would be managed by responsible executives as "businesses." People who dealt with these agencies would be "customers."

In 1988, his proposals were formalized in a program entitled Next Steps. Change began slowly with rather distinct agencies, such as the Stationery Office, which issued official publications and ran a chain of bookstores scattered throughout the country. When Thatcher left office, there were thirty-four agencies employing 80,000 people.

Social Security

Margaret Thatcher came to office in 1979 as a critic of the welfare state on two principal grounds: it was too expensive, and it sapped individual initiative and responsibility. She discovered that public pressure demanded greater expenditure, not less. A poll in 1987 showed that 61 percent of the public wanted better public services and would accept some increases in taxes for that purpose. Actually, the flourishing public revenue of the late 1980s meant that Britain could afford higher expenditures for social services, even while Nigel Lawson was cutting taxes.

Although Thatcher was continually accused of making "cuts," the total spending of the welfare state (adjusted for inflation) on housing, education, health, and social security increased from £72 billion in 1979 to £85 billion in 1989. Health and community care increased by 37 percent. Paradoxically, Thatcher's blunt criticisms overshadowed her efforts to improve the system, and the public never trusted her as a custodian of the welfare state.

Norman Fowler, secretary of state for social services (1981–1987), undertook four elaborate reviews in an effort to reform and rationalize the hodgepodge of benefits that had accumulated over the years. He began with pensions. The basic state pension, which was the same for everyone, was modest, and millions of people who depended on it received a welfare supplement. The majority of people who had been employed in steady jobs had acquired a second pension: either a company pension or the state-sponsored pension called SERPS. The most important reform was to make company pensions transferable from one employer to another, thus ending the penalty for changing jobs.

Money paid into SERPS was spent as it came in, thus piling up huge obligations that later governments would have to pay. Fowler wanted to abolish SERPS, although existing obligations would be met. The pensions industry could provide a second pension for people who did not have a company pension. Then Lawson weighed in. He needed SERPS contributions to fund tax cuts. The eventual decision was to keep SERPS but reduce the benefits that would be paid, thus easing the burden on future generations.

The Fowler reviews found that the social security system was riddled with benefits that encouraged dishonesty and cheating and were a disincentive to work at low-paid jobs. Limiting benefits to low-income people ("means tests") led to cheating and other devices to beat the system. If the head of a household became employed at low wages, his income after taxes might be no more than living on benefits ("the poverty trap").

When she tackled these problems, Thatcher found that social security benefits were built into people's lives and were not easily untangled. She faced a powerful poverty lobby that played upon the sympathy typical of the British public for people in distress. Furthermore, many of the benefits were politically sensitive because they benefited the middle class too. People who were better off insisted they had a right to the benefits whether they needed them or not.

The most conspicuous example was Child Benefit, which went to mothers with ample income as well as to mothers with low incomes. Thatcher's attempt to base Child Benefit on need encountered stiff opposition within her own party; middle-class mothers, who used the money for childcare, school fees, and the like did not want to lose Child Benefit. Eventually Thatcher decided to "let it wither on the vine," by fixing the cash amount without adjustment for inflation. Income Support, a means-tested program for families, was increased to compensate low-income mothers.

Since she was unable to make major changes, Thatcher had to settle for a codification and clarification of the social security system. Some of the older benefits were replaced with new ones. The act established uniform criteria for means testing, Family Credit provided a supplement to households where one member was employed, and Income Support assisted the elderly or families caring for children or a disabled person. Eligibility for Housing Benefit was rigorously defined so that it did not discriminate against people employed in low-paid jobs.

John Major, then minister of state at social security, was intimately involved in drafting this legislation and seeing it through the House of Commons. The effects of these changes were moderate: the elderly, incapacitated, and workers' families with children got something more; the unemployed got something less. Increased expenditures for unemployment benefits meant that there was no overall saving in the cost of social security. In this respect, as in so many others, the state could not be rolled back.

The National Health Service

Britain was the only major industrial state to maintain a national, publicly funded health service, including medical care, prescriptions, and hospital care for all its people. The mission of the National Health Service (NHS) was greater than it could possibly fulfill. People could go to the doctor as often as they wished at no cost to themselves, and some abused that privilege. The NHS also owned and operated the hospitals, which employed a huge workforce carrying out a wide variety of duties in thousands of buildings of varying size, age, and suitability.

Despite constant complaints about its shortcomings, the NHS was the most cherished institution of the welfare state. A major problem was the growing demand for health care due to advances in medicine and the aging of the population. Although the demand for health care is virtually limitless, by any standard the NHS was underfunded. At a time when other major industrialized nations were spending up to 10 percent of the Gross National Product on health care, the NHS struggled with 6 percent.

Every year the funding of the NHS increased, but never fast enough to keep up with medical costs and the increase of health needs. Thatcher's view was that the NHS was badly administered. The NHS was essentially an assemblage of physicians and hospitals, who did their thing and sent the bills to the government. Thatcher set out to nationalize and rationalize the NHS. When she was criticized for failing to support it adequately, she replied: "The NHS is safe only with us, because we will see that it is prudently managed and financed."

As with the civil service, Thatcher turned to a businessman to recommend efficiencies. In 1983, she appointed Sir Roy Griffiths, managing director of the Sainsbury supermarket chain, to review the administrative structure of the NHS and make recommendations for improvement.

Griffiths was aghast at what he found. The Department of Health and Social Security had general responsibility for the NHS, which supervised the services of family doctors, specialists, and hospitals in a clumsy, costly three-layered structure of regional, area, and district health authorities. Local social services ("community care") for the elderly, handicapped, and mentally ill were administered separately but linked loosely to the NHS. The NHS was the biggest employer of labor in Europe but had no clear lines of authority and scarcely knew how many people were on its payroll. "If Florence Nightingale were carrying her lamp through the corridors of the NHS today," Griffiths said, "she would almost certainly be searching for the people in charge."

Griffiths recommended establishing a central management board and professional management staffs for the regional and district health authorities. Although additional staff would add to the administrative costs of the NHS, he believed that they would more than pay for themselves by improved efficiency. In 1982, the NHS was decentralized into approximately two hundred compact districts. Two years later the government established general managers in the health authorities, a step that infuriated physicians and employee unions, who had been pretty much running the NHS on the local level to suit themselves.

Fowler carried through a number of reforms to make the NHS more efficient. Hospitals were required to ask for bids from private firms for ancillary services such as catering, cleaning, and laundry. The fiercest battle was with the doctors and pharmaceutical companies, when doctors were required to prescribe generic drugs if they were available. These changes aroused cries from Labour, the doctors, the pharmaceutical companies, and the unions that the NHS was "in danger."

In an institution as large as the NHS, things inevitably went wrong. Waiting lists lengthened and districts ran out of money before the end of the fiscal year. In 1986–1987, the media were filled with medical horror stories, inevitably attributed to lack of adequate funding. In the House of Commons, the semiweekly "Prime Minister's Questions" became a nightmare of accusations and pathetic anecdotes. The media barrage was intensified just before the 1987 election, when two stories appeared on the same day: one told of a boy whose heart surgery had been long delayed; the other reported Thatcher's admission that she used private medicine because she got prompt attention.

The British Medical Association complained that the Health Service was "under-funded, under-mined, and under threat." The nurses made well-justified claims for pay increases that were backed up by one-day stoppages and other disruptions. It was pointed out that large numbers of doctors and nurses were leaving the NHS for the private sector or other countries, especially the United States.

In 1987, the Thatcher ministry proposed to impose charges for periodic dental and eye checkups. The proposal was seen as a violation of the principle of preventive medicine that might be further extended in the future. A revolt of Conservative backbenchers took place, in which the Labour Party joined enthusiastically. The British Medical Association declared its opposition. The nurses again resorted to a strike to protest their low pay.

In January 1988, Thatcher established a committee of ministers, chaired by herself, to make a comprehensive review of the NHS. The report of the committee was entitled *Working for Patients*. One result of the report was the separation of the Department of Health and Social Security into two separate departments. Kenneth Clarke, an ambitious junior minister, became secretary of state for health, with a brief to reform the NHS. He promised to overhaul its "ramshackle bureaucracy" and run it in a businesslike manner. John Major, now chief secretary to the Treasury, provided additional funds to give a substantial pay raise to the nurses and catch up with unmet needs.

The Thatcher ministry's reform proposals were introduced in 1989 and passed in 1990 as the ministry was coming to a close. The legislation fundamentally changed the role of the district health authorities. Instead of operating a health service, they would contract with providers of medical care—the "purchaser-provider split." The district health authorities received government funding based on a formula that included population, age of the population, and other factors affecting health needs. With those funds they would contract with the doctors and hospitals to provide services.

The hospitals would compete with each other to get the contracts on which their continued existence depended. If the district authorities were dissatisfied, they could take their business elsewhere (if an alternative provider existed), and the hospital would suffer the consequences.

A similar principle was introduced concerning the doctors. Groups of doctors with more than seven thousand patients could separate from the district management. They would receive funds directly from the NHS that they would use to purchase the services of specialists and hospitals in meeting the needs of their patients. Under this system, specialists and hospitals would compete to obtain referrals from the fund-holding doctors, who held the moneybags. Patients were allowed to change doctors freely and to seek attention at hospitals where the waiting list was shorter.

Proposals for change within an institution as popular as the NHS provoked a furious debate. The Labour Party objected to introducing market considerations into an institution that had been established as a public service. The British Medical Association complained strenuously at introducing "the competition culture" into the practice of medicine. The bishop of Birmingham described the reforms as "unchristian" because they treated patients as consumers, in contrast to the example of Jesus.

Another part of the act provided funds for "community care" of the elderly, infirm, or disabled. Under the existing system, local authorities maintained homes for people who needed residential care. With the new system, local authorities closed down their custodial homes, since the government would pay for care in private facilities. With an open checkbook, entrepreneurs built new, up-to-date facilities, and the cost of community care rose from £10 million in 1979 to £2 billion in 1991.

Legislation in 1990 ended the abuse by making local authorities directly responsible for community care. As with the fund-holding doctors, the local authorities would receive funds from the central government and would provide care in the home of the individual or a relative or in a nursing home. Much as Thatcher mistrusted local authorities, she had to accept the reality that they were on the spot and could make better judgments about need.

Schools

In her third ministry, Thatcher acted aggressively in dealing with schools. Although it was generally recognized that education in Britain's best schools was excellent, in many less prestigious schools the level of student accomplishment fell short of what was needed in an advanced society. Parents were fed up with schools that were places of incompetence and disorder, head teachers who failed to exercise discipline over staff, teachers who failed to teach, students who did not learn, and the lack of accountability.

Conservative critics declared that the existing school curriculum did not give enough attention to fundamental subjects such as reading, writing, mathematics, science, geography, and history. Teachers were criticized for emphasizing the personal development of the student rather than verifiable gains in knowledge and skills. To this was added the complaint that schooling did not adequately prepare young people for employment in business and industry.

Thatcher responded to these complaints with school legislation that was the most important since the Education Act of 1944. As was usual with Thatcher, the legislation established strong central authority over the schools in respect of standards and budgets. The legislation prescribed a national curriculum of three core subjects: English, mathematics, and science, and six other subjects: geography, history, arts, music, a foreign language, and physical education. Assurances were given that the new curriculum would include sufficient time for religious education.

The national curriculum made it possible to introduce national achievement tests at ages seven, eleven, fourteen, and sixteen. The results of the tests would be published, which would permit a national evaluation and ranking of schools. Teachers were opposed to "league tables" (like American baseball standings) that might reflect unfavorably on them. This dispute remained unsettled under Thatcher.

The ministry's plans for school reform were embodied in legislation in 1988, but not until after long and heated debates. Management of the schools was transferred from the local education authorities to the governing boards of the schools. Parents were authorized to decide by a vote whether the school would "opt out" of local control and receive its funding directly from the Treasury. The governors of these "grant-maintained" schools would choose their own headmaster and teachers, select the students that they would admit, shape their own curriculum (in accord with the national curriculum), and manage their budget as they thought best. The Inner London Education Authority, hotbed of teacher militancy, was abolished.

Universities

Although an Oxford graduate herself (or perhaps because of it), Thatcher had little sympathy for the universities. She was inclined to think that the universities were bastions of privilege and dilettantism, generally radical in politics, and producing graduates unprepared to enter into the real world of work. She felt that universities needed drastic reform to bring them to modern standards of productivity and efficiency.

Her views were partially a matter of cost. She insisted that university expansion could no longer continue. In 1981, a 15 percent cut over three years was imposed. The total number of students that could be admitted to British universities was reduced, and many programs and research activities were curtailed or eliminated. Building projects were cut back, and early retirement programs were introduced to reduce the number of faculty. Oxford University retaliated by refusing to confer an honorary degree on the university's most famous alumna, but Oxford had been around for eight hundred years and could afford to annoy the prime minister.

The universities lost their cherished independence when a fundamental change was made in the operations of the University Grants Committee (UGC), which allocated government funds to the universities. Instead of lump-sum grants to be used by each university at its own discretion, grants were earmarked for specific purposes. Funding for teaching was separated from funding for research. Reviews of departmental strengths and weaknesses were undertaken in a variety of subjects. In short, the UGC was given greater control in pursuit of the Thatcherite principle of accountability.

In her third ministry, Thatcher kept up the pressure on the universities to limit growth and costs. The University Grants Committee was replaced by the Universities Funding Council, which provided funds to the universities with specific performance guidelines. At least half the members of the council were to be drawn from outside the field of education, presumably to keep the universities relevant to societal needs. The Council also had a full-time staff to exercise close supervision and keep the paperwork flowing.

Financial support of the universities was curtailed, and universities were warned that increased enrollments would not bring additional funding. The principle was announced that programs should be determined, not by student demand, but by the needs of the competitive economy that the Thatcher ministry was building. To promote the Thatcherite economy, grants were skewed toward science and engineering, for which there was small student demand, while popular subjects, like the humanities and the social sciences, were starved.

Inspectors given the Orwellian title "Academic Quality Assessors" were sent to evaluate university-sponsored research. Tenure was abolished for future university appointments. Proposals to abolish free tuition ran afoul of middle-class resistance. Overseas students, however, were required to pay the full cost of their education, a step that made miniscule savings but carried a heavy cost in British influence and prestige in the Commonwealth countries.

The polytechnics and colleges of art or technology, with their career-oriented programs, were favored as more in accord with the needs of the national economy. Their lower costs per student and their ability to absorb increasing numbers made them attractive to the cost-conscious Thatcher ministry. They continued to grow rapidly, until by 1987 their enrollments surpassed the universities' enrollments. In 1988, the polytechnics were removed from local management and funding and put under the Polytechnics Funding Council.

The Environment

With her emphasis on economic growth, Thatcher gave low priority to protection and improvement of the environment. She wanted to encourage industrial development, not introduce environmental controls that might be an added burden on industry. Privatization was another consideration: the sale of the electric power industry would be jeopardized by introducing strict controls on coal-burning generators; the sale of nuclear plants would be made difficult by tight environmental restrictions on their operations and wastes. Strict controls on water quality would affect the salability and price of the water companies.

One factor that increased the involvement of the Thatcher government in the environment was the need to implement policies required by the European Community. Another was the growth of the environmental ("green") movement, which drew most of its strength from middle-class, suburban, small-town, and rural people. Elections for the European Parliament provided a way for people to make a statement, and in the European election of 1989, the Green Party received up to 20 percent of the vote in some areas.

As a trained chemist, Thatcher liked to keep in touch with scientists. They convinced her that greenhouse gases and loss of the ozone layer were threats to the livability of the planet. In 1987, the Inspectorate of Pollution was established within the Department of the Environment. However, this office was given modest resources, and its mandate was limited to industrial pollution. The Control of Pollution Act (1990) extended its authority to disposal of household and industrial wastes. The next year the government signed an international agreement to reduce the emission of substances that injured the ozone layer, but environmentalists were not pleased when more use of nuclear power was recommended as one way to do it.

In the 1980s, a small dark cloud appeared on the horizon in the form of "mad cow disease" (bovine spongiform encephalopathy), a fatal disease that destroyed the brains of cattle. It was found that the disease was spread by adding the offal of infected sheep to cattle feed as a protein supplement. This practice was prohibited in 1988, and the only solution appeared to be to destroy all cattle born before that date.

Such a drastic action could not be undertaken hastily, and a Tory government was inclined to take the time needed to obtain scientific verification before inflicting such a blow on one of its important constituencies. In 1990, a frightened public insisted that British beef be banned from schools and hospitals. A year earlier, the United States had banned the importation of British beef.

Law and Order

Thatcher was a forceful advocate of the "law and order" strand in British conservatism, with its emphasis on maintaining personal safety, private property, and the authority of government. In 1979 and 1980 racial tensions in major cities led to riots that Thatcher and her Conservative constituencies were determined to control.

In 1981, riots broke out in Brixton, a run-down, racially mixed part of south London. They began with a major police operation to arrest burglars and muggers who infested the area. More than a hundred police officers were involved and hundreds of youths (mainly black males) were arrested or stopped and searched. The riot that followed lasted for three days and hundreds of people were injured, including many police officers. Although most of the rioters were black, they were joined by white youths, and all races participated in the looting that followed.

The next day there were clashes in another part of London between white skinheads and Asian immigrants. When the police attempted to restore order, the mob turned against them. During the summer similar riots broke out in Liverpool (Toxteth), Manchester (Moss Side), and other cities. In every case the police were the initial target of the rioters, and looting followed.

Lord Scarman, a respected judge, was named to conduct an inquiry into the Brixton riot. The *Scarman Report*, which was presented later that year, pointed out the problems created by unemployment, poor housing, ethnic conflict, and low educational achievement. Scarman noted that there was a high level of street crime in these neighborhoods. When the police cracked down, black youths felt they were victims of racial prejudice. Scarman concluded that the immediate cause of the Brixton riot was the anger of young black males toward the police.

The police defended themselves by saying that blacks committed the most crimes, and no racial prejudice was involved. While faulting the police for not maintaining better relations with the community, Scarman in general commended the conduct of the police in dealing with the riot.

In his report, Scarman advocated strengthening police forces to deal quickly with riots while urging special training to make the police sensitive to racial resentments. He urged "positive discrimination" to overcome the sense of negative discrimination felt by the black population. The report also called for an independent body to investigate complaints of racism in the police.

Although she agreed with much of the analysis of the *Scarman Report*, Thatcher insisted that inner-city problems did not justify rioting, looting, and crime, especially if they were carried out under the guise of social protest. She was convinced that one reason for disorders was the belief among young hooligans of all races that they could get away with it. She was willing to support sensitivity training for police, but she was also determined to back them up with improved riot control equipment and increased powers to make arrests.

When unemployment was cited as the reason for riots, Norman Tebbit, a staunch Thatcherite, recalled his unemployed father in the 1930s. "He didn't riot," Tebbit said, "he got on his bike and looked for work."

Despite the prime minister's tough approach, the ministry did undertake some steps to deal with the economic and social disadvantages of the people living in the riot areas. Michael Heseltine was given responsibility for a task force charged with finding ways to improve living conditions in the Liverpool area. After a thorough investigation, Heseltime came to the conclusion that self-help, Tebbit style, was not enough. The Youth Training Program gave job training to young people who left school at sixteen, but the program was a drop in the bucket of youth unemployment. Despite tight budgets, funding for urban development programs in depressed areas was substantially increased.

In 1985, riots between black youths and the police took place in London, Birmingham, Liverpool, and elsewhere. The London riot was precipitated by a police attempt to make an arrest in Brixton in which shots were fired. A crowd attacked the local police station with Molotov cocktails, and an orgy of burning and looting followed. The police reported 724 crimes and 53 people injured (including 10 police officers). Two white women were raped, and 230 arrests were made.

Shortly thereafter another police raid led to riots in an impoverished housing estate in north London, where guns were used against police and reporters. One police officer was hacked to death with a knife and a machete while defending firefighters trying to control a blazing building. In Birmingham, the arrest of a black youth for drug offenses led to attacks by skinheads and black toughs on Asian shopkeepers, two of whom were burned to death defending a sub-post office.

This time the ministry made a harsh response. The riots were treated, not as race-relations issues but as "law and order" issues. Douglas Hurd, home secretary, remarked that the riot "was not a cry for help but a cry for loot." Norman Tebbit, now chairman of the Conservative Party, declared that unemployment could not explain "a hundred people falling on a single policeman and murdering him." Labour joined in the outcry. Roy Hattersly, a mature and moderate Labour MP, condemned the riot as criminal and different from the riots of 1981, which grew out of deprivation and despair. Labour accused the Conservatives of not being tough enough on crime. Others blamed the government for neglecting the inner city and the police for "insensitivity."

Thatcher's first response was that there was "no excuse, no justification whatever for the riots." At the party conference that autumn she stated angrily: "Those who take to the streets on the first available pretext, to fire, loot and plunder, will be subject to the full rigors of the criminal law." Hurd made it clear that there would not be another *Scarman Report*. The London Metropolitan Police were equipped with water cannons and other instruments for riot control.

Thatcher insisted that liberals and social workers had created "a culture of excuses" that had to be reversed by firm and certain punishment. The Criminal Justice Bill (1986) demonstrated the Thatcher ministry's commitment to "law and order." It provided for longer sentences, compensation to victims of crime, limitation on defense challenges to jurors, and privacy for children called to testify in child abuse cases. The Public Order Act of the same year gave the police new powers and resources for riot control. It reflected the view of many Conservatives that a strong hand was necessary to deal with the volatile populations of the central cities.

By itself, more legislation could not reduce crime, and the number of reported offenses increased from 3.1 million in 1980 to 4.4 million in 1990. More offenders were being caught, but the rate of detection declined. Prisons were jammed, and in 1990, Strangeways Prison in Manchester erupted in violence and destruction that lasted for twenty-five days.

Thatcher's tough "law and order" views met a surprising defeat in 1979, when a bill to restore the death penalty was defeated. Thatcher favored the death penalty, which had long been a part of Tory political rhetoric. When a free vote was taken in the House of Commons, opposition surfaced in both parties, and the bill failed by a large margin. A similar proposal was made annually for the next few years, but the death penalty was always defeated. Parliament also ended corporal punishment in schools by one vote, Thatcher voting against the proposal.

Another kind of rioting belied the reputation of he British people as polite and orderly. British football crowds were notoriously rowdy, and in 1985 ugly crowd behavior became a national embarrassment. British fans at the European Cup final in Belgium attacked Italian fans, leading to a stampede in which more than thirty spectators were killed.

When the governing body of European football barred British clubs from European Cup competition for five years, most Britons agreed that firm action was long overdue. Shortly thereafter, hooliganism broke out among British soccer fans at a match in Germany. Thatcher was furious, and legislation was passed requiring identity cards for admission to matches.

Britain's stadiums were old and poorly maintained; in 1985 a stadium fire killed fifty-five people and injured many more. British stadiums had large standing-room areas bordering the field where the hooligans gathered. The worst disaster in British football history took place at Sheffield in 1989: ninety-five people were killed when a stampede took place in the standing-room area and spectators were trapped against the fence. The answer to that problem was to have numbered seats and require every person attending to have a ticket for a specific seat, thus ending the standing-room area where disorders usually took place.

Northern Ireland

In 1921, the island of Ireland was divided between the independent Republic of Ireland and the six northern counties (Ulster), which chose to remain with the United Kingdom. Northern Ireland received Home Rule, which meant that it had its own ministry, civil service, police (the Royal Irish Constabulary), and parliament. It also sent MPs to the Parliament in Westminster. Its people participated fully in the benefits of the British welfare state.

Life in Northern Ireland was dominated by powerful communal attachments and antagonisms. The Protestants, who were in the majority, thought of themselves as British, and relied on their membership in the United Kingdom to guarantee that they would never be absorbed into the Republic. Confidently, they exercised leadership in government, the economy, and educational and cultural institutions. The Catholic minority was alienated and resentful at their inferior condition, and their sense of Irish nationalism was strong. They maintained ties with the Republic and thought of themselves as Irish.

In 1968, long-simmering conflicts led to Catholic civil rights marches demanding reform of the electoral system, which was rigged to favor the Protestants. The Catholics complained of discrimination in education, housing, and other public services. When concessions to the Catholics were proposed, the Protestants reacted in force and violent clashes broke out between the two communities. A paramilitary group calling itself the Irish Republican Army (IRA) was formed to protect the neighborhoods of West Belfast from Protestant hooligans. It became a terrorist organization seeking to end British authority in Northern Ireland.

In 1969, seeking a quick military solution to what was really a political and communal problem, Harold Wilson sent in units of the British Army to restore order. When Sir Edward Heath became prime minister, he strengthened the military presence, but strikes and violence continued. In 1971, 184 people were killed in clashes, British soldiers among them. The government of Northern Ireland began interning suspected terrorists without trial. By 1972, more than twenty thousand British troops were stationed in Northern Ireland, supported by much-expanded police forces.

In January 1972 ("Bloody Sunday"), British paratroops, trying to stop a civil rights march that had been banned, panicked and killed 13 marchers (another died later) at Londonderry. The IRA responded with "Bloody Friday" in July, when 9 people were killed and 130 injured by 22 IRA bombs in Belfast. The worst year was 1972, when there were almost fourteen hundred explosions and many more bomb scares. In that year, 146 security officers (army and police) were killed. A young activist named Gerry Adams was one of the leaders in these events. Heath suspended the Northern Ireland parliament and introduced direct rule from London.

In 1973, Heath attempted to resolve tensions by introducing a government with a parliament based on proportional representation, although British troops remained to preserve order. Neither side was satisfied with this compromise. The IRA declared that British troops were an army of occupation and legitimate targets for terrorist bombings. A strike of Protestant workers led Heath to suspend shared governance and resume direct rule from London.

Then the IRA extended the terror into Britain. Seven died and 120 were injured when two Birmingham pubs were bombed in 1974. In 1975, London was struck by a series of bombings at the Tower of London, Harrod's department store, the Hilton Hotel, and several underground stations. Parliament responded with the Prevention of Terrorism Act, which outlawed the IRA and prohibited suspected members of the IRA from entering Britain.

When the Thatcher government came to power, it had no declared policy concerning Northern Ireland apart from the promise in the election manifesto to "maintain the union." The main Protestant party in Northern Ireland was the Ulster Unionist Party (UUP), which had controlled the government prior to the establishment of direct rule. They attracted middle-class business and professional people. The Democratic Unionists were

Protestant and populist and appealed to the working class. They were hostile to any concessions to the Catholics.

The Social Democratic Labour Party (SDLP), led by John Hume, was a moderate Catholic party that worked to remove the disadvantages of the Catholics, but by peaceful, constitutional means. In the 1980s, Gerry Adams, leader of Sinn Fein (the political wing of the IRA), challenged the moderate approach of Hume. Thatcher's unionism put her on the side of the Protestants, but within the framework of the United Kingdom, she was willing to work to resolve the grievances of the Catholics of Northern Ireland.

Shortly after taking office, Thatcher received news that Lord Mountbatten, a member of the royal family and a man of distinguished public service, had been killed, along with three others, when the IRA planted a bomb on his boat. The same day eighteen British soldiers were killed by two IRA landmines detonated by remote control. The first mine killed a group of soldiers, and when other soldiers arrived to care for their injured comrades, a second mine exploded.

Thatcher met the president of Ireland at Lord Mountbatten's funeral where she initiated efforts to obtain cooperation in law enforcement between the British and the Irish authorities, an approach abhorrent to the unionists. Her main objective was joint action against terrorists, who moved freely across the border, but the idea soon gained wider ramifications.

The problem of public order was aggravated in October 1980, when a group of IRA prisoners in the Maze Prison led by Bobby Sands went on a hunger strike to assert their demand to be treated as "political prisoners." Thatcher firmly refused political status for men whom she regarded as common criminals.

During the hunger strike the prisoners were offered meals three times a day, which they refused, although they drank water. When a prisoner lost consciousness, members of the family were authorized to use intravenous feeding. As fate would have it, during the strike an MP for a Catholic constituency died and Sands was entered as a candidate for the seat. Sands was elected by a narrow margin over the unionist candidate.

In the meantime, the hunger strike had gained extensive media coverage, which is always responsive to human drama and usually sympathetic to underdogs. Sands died after sixty-six days of fasting and others followed until ten IRA hunger strikers had died. At this point the families of the remaining strikers agreed to intravenous feeding to prevent further deaths, and the IRA called off the strike.

Despite additional troops flown in from Britain, violent clashes broke out and seventy-three people were killed. Particularly outrageous was a random shooting into a small Protestant church during the service, killing three worshipers and wounding seven. The IRA also assassinated a Catholic judge as he was leaving church, on the grounds that by holding judicial office he was supporting British oppression. The effect of these events was to polarize further the people of Northern Ireland. British treatment of the prisoners also inflamed public opinion in the Republic and brought an end to Thatcher's early efforts at cooperation.

After the failure of the hunger strikes of 1981, the IRA decided to take its war of terrorism to the British mainland. In October 1981, a bomb filled with six-inch nails was exploded outside Chelsea Barracks in London, killing one bystander and injuring many soldiers. In July 1982, the IRA set off two bombs in London: one in Hyde Park directed at the Horse Guards, and the second under the bandstand in Regent's Park while a military band was playing. Eight people, soldiers and civilians, were killed and fifty-three people were injured. During the Christmas shopping period of 1983, an IRA bomb in a car parked at Harrod's department store in London killed five people, one of them an American, and injured ninety-one others, some of them seriously.

In 1984, terrorism almost brought the Thatcher ministry to a fatal end. In October of that year, the Conservative Party Conference met in Brighton. At 3:00 A.M., an IRA bomb exploded in the Grand Hotel where Thatcher and many leading Conservative politicians were staying. Five floors of the hotel, including Thatcher's suite, were wrecked and five people were killed, including a Conservative MP. Thatcher was unhurt. She appeared at the conference that morning as scheduled and received a great ovation.

Thatcher's response was to seek the help of the Republic of Ireland to satisfy nationalist aspirations and control terrorism. She remained committed to the principle that Northern Ireland should remain part of the United Kingdom as long as the majority wished it, but she was also ready to concede that the Republic of Ireland had "a legitimate interest in Northern Ireland, and a special part to play in the politics of the minority there."

The result was the Anglo-Irish Agreement, which was signed in November 1985. It provided for consultations between the British and Irish governments, joint consideration of problems and grievances, and a permanent secretariat in Belfast. To reassure the unionists, the Irish government recognized British sovereignty over Northern Ireland and agreed that no change would be made without the consent of the majority of the people of Northern Ireland.

The agreement was rejected by the unionists as giving the Republic a voice in the affairs of Northern Ireland. They suspected that once the camel got its nose in the tent it would not stop there. The leader of the Ulster Unionist Party (UUP) declared that Northern Ireland, "bound and trussed like a turkey for the oven," was going to be turned over to the Republic. Thereafter the unionists became even more defensive, fearing that the government in London would abandon them to the Republic.

The Social Democratic and Labour Party (SDLP) hailed the agreement. They assumed that further steps toward unity with the Republic would follow in due time. Sinn Fein rejected the agreement, as recognition of the separation of Northern Ireland from the rest of the island. The House of Commons ratified the agreement overwhelmingly, as did the Irish Dail, although the vote was closer.

Behind these institutional arrangements lay Thatcher's fierce determination to stop terrorism, and in that, she did not succeed. The violence of the IRA had given rise to a counterforce, swaggering bands of loyalist paramilitaries, who used intimidation to drive Catholics from their homes. On the first anniversary of the agreement, Protestant demonstrations took place in Belfast in which two people died, seventy were injured, and shops in the center of the city were damaged.

An incident in 1988 inflamed the situation. Three Irish terrorists preparing a bombing in Gibraltar were discovered by British troops and shot dead. Their funeral outside of Belfast drew a huge crowd of sympathizers, who regarded them as martyrs. At the funeral, a gunman fired on the mourners, killing three and wounding sixty-eight. When one of the dead mourners was buried, the infuriated crowd turned on two young soldiers in civilian clothes, pulled them from their car, and lynched them on the spot. When Thatcher went to console the relatives of the slain soldiers, Gerry Adams, leader of Sinn Fein, told her to expect many more.

The Commonwealth

For more than two decades, the Rhodesian issue had disturbed British politics. The white minority government, led by the wily and tenacious Ian Smith, had declared independence and was holding out against giving political power to the black African majority. The white settlers realized that little sympathy could be expected from Britain, and the rest of the world ostracized them. Their only active support came from the *apartheid* regime of the Union of South Africa. In 1976, South Africa, pressed by the United States, withdrew its support for the Smith regime. It was evident that the isolated position of the settlers could not be indefinitely sustained.

Rhodesia was a divisive issue within the Conservative Party, where "kith and kin" sentiments toward the settlers were strong. Thatcher was determined to remove this festering sore. Shortly after taking office, she stepped forward and called a constitutional conference in London. The contending leaders were presented with a constitution that gave power to the black majority but guaranteed the rights of the white minority for ten years. The document was presented on a "take it or leave it" basis. After the predictable protestations, the constitution was accepted.

In December 1979, British authority over Rhodesia was temporarily restored and a governor was sent to oversee the transition to the new constitution. Shortly thereafter the independent state of Zimbabwe came into existence. Thatcher was credited with a triumph that had removed an embarrassment for Britain, and that was her main concern.

South Africa had been part of the British Empire and Commonwealth for a century and a half until it left the Commonwealth in 1961. The white population was divided between the Afrikaners, descendants of the original Dutch settlers, and people of British background. The ruling Nationalist Party was primarily a party of the Afrikaners. South Africa also had a substantial population of mixed race and of Indian descent. The great majority of the people consisted of black Africans, who were denied political and civil rights and, under the policy of *apartheid*, were required to live in separate areas.

Thatcher's toughness was conspicuously displayed in the continuing dispute over the Union of South Africa, for the South African policy of *apartheid* aroused worldwide condemnation and demands for economic sanctions. While stating her own disapproval of *apartheid*, Thatcher wished to preserve constructive relations with that country.

At the Commonwealth conference in 1985, her refusal to impose sanctions infuriated the other members. Angry scenes took place at the Commonwealth conference in 1986. Thatcher continued to hold out against the denunciations of other Commonwealth members and the pressures of world opinion. The European Community, Canada, and the United States imposed economic sanctions on South Africa, leaving Britain isolated on this issue.

Eventually external and internal political pressures brought the South African economy to its knees. Within the ruling Nationalist Party there was growing recognition that it had become necessary to bring the black majority into the political process. In 1989, F. W. de Klerk became president. De Klerk realized that *apartheid* had to go, and courageously he took steps to get rid of an unsustainable system. The next year Nelson Mandela and other prominent black leaders were released from prison and the African National Congress, led by Mandela, was permitted to engage in political activity.

Despite bitter opposition from the Afrikaners and considerable apprehension by other whites, the South African government began preparations for a new constitution in which blacks would participate. Working together, De

Klerk and Mandela kept a volatile situation under control until the work was complete.

By the time Thatcher left office, the process of establishing a nonracial South Africa was well on its way. In 1993, the Nobel Peace Prize was awarded jointly to De Klerk and Mandela, and in 1994, Mandela was inaugurated as president of the new Union of South Africa.

In the Far East, it was essential to settle the status of Hong Kong, for the People's Republic of China was determined to take over the colony when the British lease ran out in 1997. Under British rule, Hong Kong had become a world center of finance, trade, and industry, and any workable settlement would have to preserve the distinctive characteristics of the colony.

In 1982, Thatcher visited China in an attempt to resolve disputes about Hong Kong. Although the people of Hong Kong wanted British rule to continue, the Chinese were determined to obtain sovereignty. Britain had no choice but to attempt to get the best deal possible for the colony. The Chinese recognized the value of Hong Kong to the their economy, which needed commercial ties with the industrialized world. Thatcher urged them to continue the existing system of government and the capitalistic economy. The main concern of the Chinese was that their sovereignty be recognized. Deng Xiaoping, the Chinese premier, proposed the formula "one country, two systems," which would allow Hong Kong to continue unchanged while becoming part of China.

Thatcher accepted the inevitable, and in 1984 she traveled to China to sign a joint agreement by which Britain agreed to relinquish Hong Kong in 1997. She also made it clear that, in the interim, Britain intended to move the government of Hong Kong toward greater democracy. The Chinese, in turn, agreed to give Hong Kong special status for fifty years as a financial center and free port, with civil liberties and an elected legislature. The agreement was the focal point when Queen Elizabeth II visited the colony in 1986.

The Hong Kong agreement raised again the issue of immigration. The non-British residents of Hong Kong were not entitled to settle in the United Kingdom. Despite widespread sympathy for their plight, both parties agreed that it would be impossible to accept the number of Hong Kong people that wanted to come. Eventually the decision was reached to grant British citizenship to some two hundred thousand administrators and officials, to encourage them to remain until the transition to Chinese rule was complete.

CHAPTER SIX

~

John Major and the Thatcher Legacy, 1990–1993

John Who?

John Major was relatively unknown to the public when he became prime minister, but he was well regarded by politicians and those whose business it was to follow politics closely. He was better qualified than most people realized. He was intelligent, articulate, hard working, and personable. His experience as a whip had taught him how to work with members of the House of Commons. His service as a minister at the Department of Health and Social Security had familiarized him with the problems of the welfare state. As chief secretary to the Treasury, he had developed an intimate knowledge of the workings of the government.

His surprising appointment as foreign secretary in July 1989, replacing Sir Geoffrey Howe, gave him a quick lesson in British foreign policy. He was already well acquainted with the Treasury when Margaret Thatcher suddenly moved him to the Exchequer. The opportunity to prepare a budget completed his preparation for the highest political office.

In November 1990, Major was probably as amazed as anyone to find that he was the prime minister. At age 47, he was the youngest prime minister of the twentieth century until Tony Blair (age 43) succeeded him. He was seen as a moderate, who would continue the fiscal and economic policies of Thatcher, but with more understanding of the needs of ordinary people and greater willingness to work within the European Community.

Major moved into No. 10 Downing Street with his usual earnestness and good nature. As prime minister, he continued to advance the substance of

Thatcherism but with gentler style. In his first New Year message, Major, alluding to his own personal background, stated that his goal was to make Britain an "opportunity society" where individuals would receive the education and other support needed to make their own way rather than becoming dependent on government.

"I want to bring into being a different kind of country," he said later, "to bury old differences in Britain between North and South, blue-collar and white-collar, polytechnic and university." He expressed special concern for low-income and unemployed people who had not benefited from Thatcherism. In his autobiography he commented wryly that many of the stock phrases of Tony Blair and New Labour were originally his: "A hand up, not a hand out; for the many, not the few; education, education, education."

Lacking Thatcher's prestige and dominating ways, Major consulted regularly with his Cabinet, formally and informally, and worked to repair the cracks in the Conservative Party. He showed his desire for reconciliation by bringing Michael Heseltine into the Cabinet as minister for the environment, which included local government and finding a replacement for the poll tax. The Cabinet included some of the "new men" who had risen to prominence under Thatcher: Douglas Hurd (foreign secretary), Norman Lamont (chancellor of the Exchequer), Kenneth Baker (home secretary), and Kenneth Clarke (Education).

There was no place suitable for Thatcher, who had been too powerful to fill a subordinate role and sat uncomfortably on the back benches, testily watching for any attempt to dilute her legacy. Strong leaders often resent their successors, and Thatcher was no exception.

The Poll Tax

Thatcher's stubborn insistence on the poll tax had been an important reason for her downfall, and the Major ministry knew that the tax had to go. In his first budget, Lamont included funds that enabled local governments to reduce the average poll tax by about a third, giving the ministry time to find a replacement. Lamont replaced the lost revenue with an increase in VAT from 15 percent to 17.5 percent.

The problem with repealing the poll tax was to find a replacement that would make councils responsible and would require every adult to pay something. Heseltine replaced the poll tax with the council tax, a tax on households based on the market value of the residence. Since most households consisted of one or two adults, the poll tax principle was maintained by a higher charge for households of two or more adults than for a single-person household. Low-income people would have their council tax paid for them by the welfare system. The uniform business rate was retained, and strict caps were placed on local spending, leaving local governments in the straitjacket devised for them by Thatcher. To provide time for transition, replacement of the poll tax by the council tax did not take place for two years, a situation that left masses of poll taxes uncollectable and angered those who paid.

To keep the council tax at a reasonable level, caps were placed on both the taxing and spending powers of local authorities. The government determined the amount needed to provide a standard level of service, with local government providing 20 percent of the cost and the Treasury the remainder. The expenditure of each local authority was fixed, and borrowing to evade these limits was prohibited. The centralizing thrust of Thatcherism in relation to local government had been taken about as far as possible.

Reforming Government

Thatcher introduced fundamental reforms in British public administration, and the principles of Thatcherism were widely extended under her successor. Major was genuinely devoted to good government, and he came from the kind of people who depended on the public services. The goals of the Major ministry were unveiled in a document entitled *The Citizen's Charter*. The key principle was to raise the quality of the public services by making government more responsive to ordinary citizens.

Government departments and agencies were expected to deal promptly and openly with the people whom they served. Each agency was required to post a statement of the standards of service it intended to maintain. Penalties would be imposed if those standards were not met, and individuals who experienced delays or poor service were entitled to compensation. It seems that the *Charter*, by putting agencies and public servants on the spot, raised the level of service.

Powerful departments were compelled to implement the principles of the *Charter*. In the National Health Service, doctors were required to provide information about the kinds of medical care they offered and make reasonable efforts to meet appointments on time. Hospitals were ranked on the facilities and care they provided, and the maximum waiting time for patients was posted. British Rail was required to post its standards of cleanliness and on-time performance; passengers would be entitled to financial compensation if the posted standards were not met. Every year British Rail paid out a considerable sum in compensation to passengers for late trains.

During the Major ministry, the *Next Steps* principle separating the policy role of departments from the delivery of services was widely extended by the creation of new executive agencies. In 1991 and 1992, the large revenue departments were organized into agencies. Customs and Excise were decentralized into thirty "executive units," and the Inland Revenue into thirty-four.

In the huge Department of Social Security, 98 percent of employees were in agencies, although it was discovered that some of them were transferred nominally to an agency while continuing to work in the department. By 1997, there were 137 agencies employing more than 60 percent of the civil service. The largest was the Benefits Agency, with more than seventy thousand employees.

An important feature of Thatcherism was contracting with private firms to perform services formerly performed by public employees. In 1991, the Treasury published a document entitled *Competing for Quality*, which proposed competitive bidding by private enterprises for professional, specialist, and clerical services. Competitive bidding would provide a realistic assessment of costs ("market testing"), and it was believed that private firms in a competitive situation would give better service at a reasonable price. It was expected that substantial savings would be achieved by eliminating the salaries, pensions, perks, and other overhead expenses of civil servants. Another kind of contracting out was the Private Finance Initiative, in which buildings were financed and built by private contractors and leased to the government, thus reducing capital expenditures.

The Deregulation and Contracting Out Act (1994) completed the process. By March 1995, more than £1 billion of government work had been transferred to private contractors, and twenty-six thousand civil service jobs had disappeared. These contracts included everything from keeping up the parks to data processing for government departments. Many of the redundant civil servants were employed by the private contractors who displaced them. Other civil servants formed private firms and bid for their own jobs, sometimes settling for less than they had earned before.

Local Government

Under Thatcher, local government, once an important element in the British constitution and in Conservative thought, had been emasculated. As with so many things, it was left to Major to advance and complete what Thatcher had begun. Under the direction of Heseltine, the Major ministry decided that Britain was too small to need two separate layers of local government (counties, districts), and committed itself to the principle of unitary local government.

Heseltine's plan provided that the counties would disappear and rural England would be divided into tidy units of moderate size. Towns would become distinct units independent of their rural surroundings. All would be supervised by the Department for the Environment and given well-ordered functions and budgets.

In 1992, a Local Government Commission under Sir John Banham was appointed and was expected to recommend a unitary structure. As he traveled about taking testimony, Banham discovered that people were attached to their counties and districts and that most people wanted to maintain a two-level system. He was impressed by the variety of arrangements that had developed between towns, suburbs, counties, and districts to meet local needs.

When the commission finally reported in 1995, the government was dismayed to find that Banham recommended that thirty-two of the thirty-nine counties should remain and that many towns should continue under their county councils. Larger towns, the commission agreed, should be independent local government units.

Neither political party was pleased with the report. The Conservatives were relieved that most counties were preserved, but they were unhappy with the proposal to remove some large towns from county control. Labour welcomed Banham's proposal to give some towns unitary government, but they objected to preserving the role of the counties and much of the two-level system.

John Major wanted to preserve his county of Huntingdonshire, whose council was controlled by Conservatives. Clarke advocated a unitary system to preserve his urban constituency from interference by a Labour-dominated county council. The Department of the Environment criticized the report because it failed to recommend the unitary system that the department preferred.

Banham and most members of the commission resigned. During the investigation, the existing two-tier local governments had made fervent promises of cooperation: "one-stop shops" for citizens, decentralization of services, and the like. In 1996, in its closing report, the commission stated that these promises, "obtained in the sight of the gallows," had not been kept.

As an example of efficient consolidation, the Banham Commission noted that the bucolic minicounty of Rutland (pop. 34,000) had been joined to Leicestershire in 1974. There was a great deal of local loyalty in Rutland, and the people had never accepted the change. In 1997, presumably with the election in view, the independence of Rutland was restored, although still dependent on Leicestershire for police, fire protection, and other services that it could not provide for itself.

Some progress was made. The English counties and their nonmetropolitan districts continued to share power, but forty-five English districts that were urban were made independent of county government. In 1994, eight government offices for the regions were established to coordinate the use of regional development grants. People began to think that these regions might become the foundation of democratically elected governments to supersede the counties.

The most remarkable example of Thatcherite mistrust of local government was the proliferation of quangos (quasi-autonomous nongovernmental organizations) established as a means of securing implementation of national policies on the local level. When Major left office, there were approximately forty-five hundred of these. They carried out functions entrusted to them by law, and presumably, they were accountable to ministers, but they often acted quite independently.

There were sixty-four thousand or more members of these boards, who served part-time and without pay. They usually were appointed on the recommendation of existing board members or some administrator and were far from representative of the local population. Their names and addresses were not published, nor did they meet regularly with interested individuals or groups. They were, in practice, accountable only to themselves and, perhaps, some sense of local wishes and needs.

The Gulf War

When he took office, Major was confronted with the Gulf War, to which Britain was already committed. He came out firmly on the need to reverse Iraqi aggression, and polls showed strong public support (60 percent) for the war. Just before Christmas, Major traveled to Washington, to meet President George Bush and agree on plans for the military buildup.

Early in January he went to the Gulf, where he met with Arab allies and visited the troops. In Parliament, the Conservative members in the House of Commons supported the war, although Sir Edward Heath thought that negotiation could bring a satisfactory settlement. The Liberal Democrats and about three-fourths of the Labour members supported the United Nations action. The large Muslim community in Britain was divided on the war.

On January 16, 1991, after a massive buildup, allied forces attacked Iraq by air, followed by a ground attack. Kuwait, badly damaged by Saddam Hussein, was liberated, but the allies had no authorization to move on to Baghdad and Saddam remained in power. The war had been conducted in the full glare of television, which provided exciting viewing, and Major was able to share in the plaudits that rained down on the victorious allied leaders. Bush's ratings in the political polls soared to 90 percent. Polls showed that Major had the highest rating of any prime minister since Winston Churchill. Bush and Major soon discovered how ephemeral such war-based ratings were.

Shaping a Post–Cold War Foreign Policy

In the meantime, British foreign policy was changed dramatically by the unification of Germany, the breakdown of the Soviet empire in Eastern Europe, and the collapse of the Soviet Union. With the Cold War consigned to the historians, Major had to define a new foreign policy. He handled his role smoothly, and few partisan differences emerged, apart from the endless wrangles about the European Community.

The Major ministry was firmly committed to NATO, which institutionalized a security role for the United States in Europe. British involvement in the Gulf War strengthened ties with the Bush administration. Both countries approached foreign policy from a global perspective, and with similar concerns for the free movement of people, money, goods, and ideas around the world. Close and mutually beneficial connections were maintained between their intelligence agencies and military services, especially their navies.

When President Bill Clinton was inaugurated in January 1993, British relations with the new administration were at first cool. During the presidential campaign of 1992, the Bush people had asked the Conservative Party Central Office to search the public records for evidence of any antiwar activities by Bill Clinton while he was a student in Britain during the Vietnam War. Nothing damaging was found. Clinton won the election, and the Conservative Central Office was duly embarrassed.

The main foreign policy issue of the Major ministry was the breakdown of Yugoslavia in 1991. The Serbs, led by Slobodan Milosevic, took over the Yugoslav government and army and undertook to create a "greater Serbia." Croatia declared its independence and began a ruthless "ethnic cleansing" of Serbs within its borders. Attempts by the European Union to arrange an orderly dismantling of Yugoslavia failed when Germany unilaterally recognized the independence of Croatia, and Milosevic invaded Serb-dominated areas in Croatia and Bosnia.

War broke out between the Serbs and Croats for the disputed territories. The center of attention was Bosnia-Herzegovina, which the European powers recognized in 1992 as an independent state. The population was mainly Croat and Serb, with an important Muslim minority. Serbia and Croatia each laid claim to parts of Bosnia, and they supported their own nationalities, who rose up against the Muslims centered in the capital city of Sarajevo. Bosnian

Serbs armed by Milosevic, who had all the resources of the former Yugoslav army at his disposal, occupied much of Bosnia and shelled Sarajevo, the capital, from the surrounding mountains. Horrifying accounts of concentration camps, atrocities, and "ethnic cleansing" were published in newspapers and broadcast on television.

These scenes were intolerable, and the United Nations launched an effort to alleviate the suffering by bringing humanitarian aid to the Bosnians. When the warring parties threatened aid workers and convoys, the United Nations called on its members to provide troops to protect the humanitarian effort.

Britain and France agreed to contribute troops and other resources for humanitarian purposes, although it was recognized that peacekeeping could not take place where there was no peace. The American view was that the European Union should accept responsibility for Bosnia, which was in its backyard. The Russians were pro-Serb, but the chaotic condition of Russia precluded their doing anything. Lacking power to impose a settlement, the United Nations involvement was ineffectual and the atrocities continued. Since British troops were an important part of the United Nations force and a British general was in command, the daily diet of unfavorable news from the former Bosnia was politically unsettling in Britain.

By 1995 the view had taken hold that only NATO, with American airpower and military infrastructure, had sufficient power to end the war. In May, NATO air strikes (mainly American) were launched against the Bosnian Serbs who were shelling Sarajevo. The Serbs retaliated with attacks on United Nations aid convoys and peacekeepers. A well-armed Croatian army entered Serb areas in Croatia and another "ethnic cleansing" took place, as more than half a million Serbs were expelled.

Responding to urgent British appeals, in October 1995 the Clinton administration, under the auspices of the United Nations, summoned the leaders of the warring parties to a U.S. Air Force base in Dayton, Ohio, where they were sequestered and subjected to unremitting negotiations. They accepted an agreement that created a united Bosnia, with separate sectors for the Croats, Muslims, and Serbs. NATO ground forces, including twenty thousand American and thirteen thousand British troops, entered Bosnia to maintain order and prevent further atrocities. Open warfare ended, but life in Bosnia was still disrupted, and the NATO mission continued indefinitely.

The Movement for European Unity

Major's main goal was to unite the Conservative Party. To satisfy the people who had led in the overthrow of Thatcher, he needed to reverse her contentious relationship with the European Community. On the other hand, he had to look "tough" to satisfy many members of his party whose attitude toward Europe was skeptical or negative.

When Major took office in November 1990, Jacques Delors's plans for closer European union were well advanced. In Germany in March 1991, Major stated effusively that for his generation "Europe was a cause of political inspiration." He added that his goal for Britain was to be "at the very heart of Europe." He hedged by adding that "Europe is made up of nation states," but this Thatcherite expression was overlooked. Commentators assumed that Major intended to signal a break with Thatcher's confrontational approach to Europe.

In December 1991, the Council of Ministers met at Maastricht in the Netherlands to approve a treaty that would convert the European Community into the European Union. Delors brought forth his proposals for a federal Europe with a common foreign policy and defense, a common currency, and a Social Chapter that called for uniform social policies and costs.

Major was well aware that resistance was building at home to closer involvement with Europe. He insisted on the principle of "subsidiarity," which meant that policy should remain as much as possible at the level of the member states. He declared that Britain could accept the treaty only if it could "opt into" the single currency at a time of its own choosing, leaving the other eleven members to proceed with the project. Without its own currency, he argued, Britain could not control the money supply, interest rates, and other elements crucial to the British economy. He flatly rejected the Social Chapter, which involved high labor costs that, Major insisted, Britain could not afford. Nor would he agree to a common foreign policy and defense.

The Maastricht conference was Major's first great foreign policy test, and he succeeded to the satisfaction of most of his countrymen. After intense negotiations, Major was given his "opt in" on the single currency. The Social Chapter was excluded from the treaty and converted into a separate agreement signed by the other members. Britain chose to "opt out." To the dismay of Jacques Delors, Major also succeeded in removing the word "federal" from the clause calling for a closer union.

When Major returned from Maastricht, his performance was hailed as a triumph. The House of Commons declared its approval, although seven Tories voted against the treaty and Thatcher abstained. Major had been pro-European enough to satisfy one wing of his party, and "tough" enough to satisfy the other. Britain signed the treaty in February 1992. With an election approaching in April, Major thought it best to keep Europe out of the campaign, and he deferred parliamentary action on the treaty until later in the year.

Economic Crisis

In the industrial world, the cheers of victory in the Gulf War were soon muted. The war aggravated inflation and other economic problems, and it created another spike in oil prices that precipitated a worldwide recession. Norman Lamont, chancellor of the Exchequer, decided that priority should be given to reducing inflation. Interest rates were raised to reduce borrowing and spending and to keep the pound in step with the ERM.

Lamont's anti-inflationary measures achieved their purpose, and price inflation fell from 9.3 percent in 1990 to 2.6 percent in 1992. Inflation had been whipped, but at the cost of a brutal recession in which unemployment rose from 1.75 million to 3 million, the highest since 1986. At the end of 1991, the recession hit bottom: business failures reached a record number, car sales were down, and more than seventy thousand mortgages had been foreclosed. The carnage was especially bad among small retailers and craftsmen whose skills were irreplaceable.

This time the recession hit the south of England hardest. Regionally, the misery index was almost equalized: unemployment in the north was 10.4 percent and in the south it was 9.5 percent. Job losses fell mainly on managerial and clerical workers as businesses cut employees in an effort to stay afloat.

Unemployment and high interest rates forced many homeowners to default on their mortgages, and house prices plummeted. In 1992, house prices fell 7.8 percent on average and 11.4 percent in London. More than 1.5 million homeowners were faced with negative equity—their house was worth less than the mortgage. In 1992, Canary Wharf, a huge property development in the former London dockyards, went bankrupt. Banks were left holding loans that could not be repaid. The building trades were devastated.

Britain's manufacturing base declined dramatically as inefficient firms went to the wall. British Steel announced a 20 percent cut in production and put workers on short time. Large firms in the auto industry and aerospace announced job cuts, especially in middle management and white-collar positions. Small businesses were devastated. The efforts of Thatcher to restore an enterprise culture to Britain went down the drain.

To soften the effects of the recession, Major and Lamont made generous pay settlements with teachers and doctors, expanded government programs for training unemployed workers, offered financial support to local governments to ease the transition from the poll tax to the council tax, and provided help to pensioners on Income Support. Unemployment benefits and other unavoidable costs due to the recession mounted. Borrowing rose from an anticipated £8 billion in 1991–1992 to £14 billion, and to £36 billion in 1992–1993. In

March 1992, Lamont presented a preelection budget with a new income tax band of 20 percent to help low-income taxpayers. Spending increases and heavy borrowing sowed the seeds of a financial crisis yet to come.

The Election of 1992

In a party democracy like Britain's, the ultimate test of a leader is the ability to win votes for his party in an election. Much of Thatcher's support in the Conservative Party rested on the fact that she had won three elections. Her leadership was overthrown when it was believed that she could not win the fourth. Many Conservatives saw Major as the sacrificial lamb who would lead the party in an election it was expected to lose.

They were wrong. With the departure of Thatcher, the fortunes of the Conservative Party rapidly improved. Before Thatcher's resignation, polls showed 34 percent favoring the Conservatives and 46 percent Labour. A few weeks after Major's accession, the numbers were reversed: Conservatives 45 percent; Labour 39 percent. The reason was not Major, who was virtually unknown; it was the absence of Thatcher.

Major enjoyed a surprisingly long honeymoon. He was most popular during his first two years, when Britain was wracked by inflation and recession. His main asset was his ability to unite the Conservative Party and minimize public squabbling. He was a consolidator, keeping Thatcher's agenda moving along, but giving Conservatives a breather from her relentless activism. As time passed, voters came to like Major and his low-keyed style. By installing a new prime minister and other fresh faces in the Cabinet, it seemed as if a change had taken place, although the essentials of the Conservative government remained as before.

Meanwhile, Neil Kinnock had strengthened the leadership and public image of the Labour Party. He undertook a policy review, which was the first step in changing the unpopular policies that had damned the Labour Party in the past. He brought forward promising young leaders: Tony Blair, who had become a star performer, and Gordon Brown, who impressed everyone by his keen intellect. Kinnock took steps to reduce the weight of union bloc votes in the selection of candidates for Parliament. He also proposed reducing the share of the union votes at the annual conference from 90 percent to 70 percent, but he backed off to avoid a fight with the unions, which did not seem desirable with an election in the offing.

Kinnock and his team realized that Labour could never win unless its policies and public image took into account the economic and social changes that had taken place during the Thatcher years. They struggled with their membership to bring "a new realism" to the party in the interest of electability. Renationalization of the nationalized industries, strongly supported by the public-sector unions, was abandoned. An effort was made to gain support from business by accepting the principle of a free-market economy and abandoning Labour's traditional commitment to regulation and economic planning.

Kinnock knew that he had to destroy the image of the Labour Party as the lapdog of the unions. As shadow employment secretary, Tony Blair led in a broad review of Labour's employment policies. The party's commitment to full employment was reaffirmed, but it was to be achieved, not by protecting jobs, but by support for industrial modernization and job training. Blair persuaded the party to abandon its commitment to the closed shop, arguing that it was an abridgment of individual rights. He promised "there will be no return to the trade union legislation of the 1970s" or to "flying pickets." In 1990, Kinnock stated that Labour's industrial policy would be justice for all, not favors to friends.

Labour's Achilles' heel was its policy on defense. The breakdown of the Soviet empire and the collapse of Soviet Union made it possible to drop policies that the voters had rejected in the past. After much indignation and hand wringing, membership in NATO was accepted. The pledge to unilateral nuclear disarmament, a cause with which Kinnock had been strongly identified, was quietly dropped.

Labour also abandoned its opposition to Britain's membership in the European Community. Labour intellectuals had concluded that the growth of international trade and multinational corporations made it impossible to maintain socialism on a national basis. The trade unions had also changed their views; they saw in the social policies of the EC a way to recoup the loss of power and benefits that they had suffered under Thatcherism. Acceptance of the ERM sealed Labour's commitment to Europe. Sensing a possible electoral victory, the members of the parliamentary party and the National Executive Committee, often the scene of intraparty disputes, fell into line.

The election took place in April 1992. The Conservative Party's manifesto promised a continuation of Thatcherism by privatizing British Coal and British Rail. Emphasis was placed on Major's favorite project: improving the quality of the public services. In Scotland, Major declared his opposition to devolution: "The United Kingdom is in danger," he declared. The Maastricht Treaty was not an important issue.

Labour approached the election with a sense of optimism, and the polls gave Labour a slight edge over the Conservatives. After years of struggle with the left wing and his own earlier ideas, Neil Kinnock had given the Labour Party strong leadership and a set of policies that would appeal to the changing electorate. Polls showed the Conservatives with one great advantage: despite the recession, more of the voters (40 percent) trusted them on the management of the economy than Labour (under 30 percent). Labour had been out of office for thirteen years, and voters questioned their ability to organize and conduct a competent government.

This was an election where the campaign probably made the difference. Television was an important factor. On the tube, Major appeared as an earnest, decent, well-informed, well-meaning leader who understood ordinary people and their needs. Accompanied by Norma, he traveled around the country in a bus, taking to the streets and mingling with the crowds. On several occasions he displayed his ability to talk to the voters while standing on a soapbox. He stressed his humble origins and his desire to provide opportunities through education and training. Heseltine played the role of pit bull, vigorously attacking Labour's leaders and policies.

Labour's campaign was disappointing. Peter Mandelson was busy running for a seat in Parliament, and his touch was sorely missed. Kinnock did not have widespread personal appeal. His campaign of photo-ops and controlled meetings with voters was intended to make him look prime ministerial, but at times, his flamboyance and verbosity made him appear egotistical and bombastic. His triumphalism at a rally in Sheffield, intended to encourage his supporters, was perhaps a turnoff for some undecided voters. The tabloids conducted a relentless campaign against him. *The Sun* topped them all with the headline: "IF KINNOCK WINS TODAY WILL THE LAST PERSON TO LEAVE BRITAIN PLEASE TURN OUT THE LIGHTS?"

The election of 1992 was the most embarrassing ever for the polls. A week before the election they gave Labour a slim lead, with the possibility of a hung Parliament. They missed a late swing to the Conservatives, as many uncommitted voters made up their minds in the last week or two. Ladbroke's, a chain of betting parlors, got it right. They had money at stake, and perhaps they were closer to the real world.

When the votes were counted, it was found that the electorate had decided to stay with the Conservatives. The Conservatives got their usual 43 percent of the votes. Although they received 14 million votes, the largest number ever polled by any party in any election, the distribution of seats was such that the Conservatives had to settle for a narrow margin of twenty-one seats in Parliament. Labour improved its share of the vote to 34 percent and did unexpectedly well in marginal seats. With 18 percent of the votes, the Liberal Democrats had declined from 23 percent in 1987. The next day the feisty tabloid with the huge circulation boasted: "IT'S THE SUN WOT WON IT."

The Scottish Nationalists won three seats, and the Welsh Nationalists (Plaid Cymru) four. Northern Ireland has its own political parties: the Ulster Unionists (UUP) won nine seats, the Democratic Unionists three, the Social Democratic and Labour Party (SDLP) four, and the Ulster Popular Unionist Party one. Thatcher, who did not seek reelection, received a peerage and entered the House of Lords. Betty Boothroyd, a Labour Party MP, was chosen Speaker of the House of Commons, the first woman to hold that office.

After the election, Neil Kinnock, who had done so much to develop New Labour, retired as leader of the Labour Party. John Smith, a sturdy, shrewd Scottish lawyer, was chosen as his successor. Smith accepted the principles that had been adopted under Kinnock and tried to steer a middle course between the modernizers and "Old Labour." He fought successfully to reduce the influence of the unions in Labour Party elections: unions still had a fixed share of the votes, but the members voted as individuals. Apart from that, Smith was not a modernizer. He committed himself to a "long game," seeking to wear down the Conservative majority gradually. His tough questioning in the House of Commons hammered home the ego conflicts and policy differences of the ministry.

Major had led his party in a successful election, but his slim majority left him on shaky ground. Seldom had a prime minister been so weak in his own party after an electoral victory. A quarter of the former Conservative MPs had retired or were defeated in the election, and many of the new members felt that they owed little to the prime minister. They tilted the Conservative Party in an anti-European direction, and they could become prickly when some local interest was threatened. Lacking an adequate base in the House of Commons, Major was vulnerable to pressures from dissident Conservatives or from the Ulster Unionists. For the moment, those in the Conservative Party who considered Major to be an ineffective leader had no likely alternative, but his support within the party was soft. At best, he had proven to be a survivor.

"Black Wednesday"

As chancellor of the Exchequer, Major had recommended membership in the ERM. As prime minister he stuck doggedly to that decision. Britain had joined the ERM at an awkward time, for Germany was engaged in vast expenditure and borrowing to finance German unification and had raised interest rates accordingly. British interest rates were already high when Britain joined the ERM, and Norman Lamont had raised them further to maintain the required exchange rate with the mark. Steps to stimulate the sagging economy were out of the question. Interest rates in other members of the European Union rose in step with the mark, stalling economic recovery. Major's desperate efforts to persuade the Germans to lower their interest rates foundered on the stubbornness of the Bundesbank, which was primarily concerned with preventing inflation at home.

Lamont declared his determination to remain within the ERM, raising interest rates to 12 percent and then 15 percent to keep the pound at the required exchange rate. All in vain. When the pound fell below the ERM floor, vast British reserves were dissipated to buy sterling at the required rate. The only answer was to leave the ERM and let the pound float downward to its market value.

On "Black Wednesday," September 16, 1992, the British public was shocked when a precipitous drop in the international value of the pound made it necessary to leave the ERM. Speculators made a killing. Other countries were in similar straits. Italy withdrew after the Bundesbank had spent large sums to support the lira, and France was able to continue only with massive support from Germany. Spain, Portugal, and Ireland also devalued their currencies. The debacle strengthened the arguments of those who held that efforts to remain in step with Europe monetarily would be damaging to Britain.

Major had persuaded Thatcher to enter the ERM. Now it was Major who took Britain out. Ministers were dazed by the debacle. The public was outraged. By the end of the month, Tory support in the polls had plummeted to 30 percent, and confidence in Tory management of the economy was never regained. The dominant newspapers, which had inclined toward the Tories, changed their tune and became increasingly negative. "NOW WE'VE ALL BEEN SCREWED BY THE CABINET," screamed *The Sun*.

In actuality, an event that seemed to be a disaster proved to be an economic benefit. Leaving the ERM turned the economic situation around for Britain. Instantly, imported goods became proportionately more expensive, and British exports cheaper. By December, inflation had fallen to 2.6 percent. No longer required to keep interest rates high, Lamont reduced interest rates to 7 percent. He promised a budget designed to stimulate industry, housing, and investment. If not exactly a "U-Turn," it certainly was more than a modest course correction.

Black Wednesday, which followed the election by five months, shattered the Tory reputation for economic competence and was a shock from which the Major ministry never recovered. People wondered why Britain had joined the ERM and had paid such a high price to remain in it. The fiasco intensified the growing division within the Conservative Party concerning relations with the EC. Critics of the movement for European unity called the day "White Wednesday," because they believed that it proved their case. Major's long honeymoon with the British public eroded as the recession dragged on. In 1993, a poll showed that only 16 percent of the people had confidence in the Major government, and 77 percent were dissatisfied.

The Budget Crisis

The Conservatives had won the election of 1992 on the grounds that they were the party of responsible public finance: holding the line on taxes and tight control of public spending. Immediately after the election, however, the Major ministry faced a financial crisis partially of its own making.

Major lacked Thatcher's authority and toughness. When he became prime minister, he agreed to spending increases that would be popular with the public and would establish a favorable climate for the approaching election. Unlike his predecessor, Major believed in an important role for government in improving the lives of ordinary people. He was willing to spend for education, training for the unemployed, the National Health Service (NHS), and social security.

Economic recovery came slowly, and unemployment rose to 3 million. The revenue held fairly steady, but from 1990 to 1994 spending increased by 36 percent, much of it unavoidable. The number of people claiming unemployment benefits climbed by 45 percent, which was a huge drain on the Treasury. Lamont made a determined effort to rein in spending while still providing increases for education and the NHS. The deficit for 1993 was 6.4 percent of the Gross Domestic Product: more than double that of 1992 and nine times greater than in 1991.

It was time to pay the piper. In March 1993, Lamont proposed sharp increases in taxes, including a two-step extension of VAT to domestic fuel and electric power, plus increased National Insurance contributions. These were increases that prosperous people could handle comfortably, but VAT on home heating would hit hard the poor, the unemployed, pensioners, and struggling young families.

Lamont's tax increases violated election promises and seemed to confirm the widespread idea that the Conservatives were the party of the well to do, lacking an understanding of those who were less well off. They outraged the base of the Thatcher coalition: employed people with modest incomes, first-time homeowners, small entrepreneurs, and the self-employed. A tax on home heating was almost as insensitive as the poll tax. Parliamentary and public outrage was so intense that two days later Major announced that funds would be provided to help 10 million low-income people pay the VAT on fuel.

Ever since "Black Wednesday," Lamont had been the scapegoat for the economic problems of the Major ministry. Major called him his "lightning rod." Lamont became one of the most unpopular politicians in Britain when he defiantly remarked, "Unemployment and recession were a price worth paying for getting inflation down." Major realized that Lamont had become a political liability and asked him to take a different office. Instead, Lamont angrily resigned and was replaced by the confident and thick-skinned Kenneth Clarke.

Lamont, once Major's friend, did not make a graceful exit. In his resignation speech, he criticized the politically driven short-term approach of the government and its responsiveness to media criticism and polls. "We give the impression of being in office but not in power," he charged.

The media, smelling blood, joined the chorus with angry interviews and touching human-interest stories. Tory backbenchers erupted in fury when Heseltine proposed to close thirty-one inefficient pits as a prelude to privatizing what was left of British Coal. The government bought peace by increasing the funding for compensation.

In April 1993, polls showed declining support for the Conservative Party, even in its strongholds in the south and west. Gallup polls in early 1993 showed public support for Conservatives at 31 percent, Labour at 48 percent, and the Liberal Democrats at 16 percent. By summer these numbers were 25 percent for the Conservatives, Labour 45 percent, and the Liberal Democrats 26 percent.

In the county elections of 1993, the Conservative vote plummeted to 31 percent, the party's lowest level in any twentieth-century election. Formerly impregnable Tory counties were lost, mainly to the Liberal Democrats. It was evident that the Tory political base was crumbling. When he was asked if he intended to resign, Major replied: "I'm fit, I'm well, I'm here, and I'm staying."

~

CHAPTER SEVEN

John Major: Continuing the Thatcher Revolution

Privatization

When Margaret Thatcher left office, privatization had gained a momentum of its own and powerful interests had gathered to support it: managers who wanted private-sector salaries and perks, workers who thought that privatization was the key to their future, investors who wanted to buy shares, and the Treasury, which needed the money.

John Major followed through on the privatizations that had been planned under Thatcher. The privatization of the electricity industry continued, and in 1991, 60 percent of the two generating companies were sold. The privatization was a success even before the shares were offered, with applications for almost twice the number of shares available. Most of the remaining shares were sold in 1995.

The twelve separate electricity distribution companies disappeared rapidly, as mergers and takeovers reshaped the electricity distribution industry. American firms began buying into the electric companies. They believed that the profits of these companies could be substantially improved by American management methods and technology.

The most difficult problem was disposal of the nuclear plants, which were unattractive investments and carried with them potentially heavy losses for environmental pollution. In 1995, they were organized as British Energy, and the next year they were privatized, although the sale did not go well. In order to sell British Energy, the government had to agree to pick up the cost of decommissioning obsolete nuclear plants. Questions were raised about the safety of Britain's nuclear waste reprocessing plant at Sellafield.

Despite some successes, privatization of public utilities was widely unpopular. A poll in September 1996 showed that the privatized utilities ranked high on the public hate list, and British Gas was the most despised of all. One reason was the disproportionate remuneration given to its officers and directors. Another was a chaotic billing system, in which people had their gas cut off for nonpayment when they had never received a bill. In a search for immediate profits, British Gas had engaged in an excess of downsizing and was unable to fulfill service contracts in the cold of winter or even answer the phone in a reasonable period of time.

The British public was never pleased with privatization of the water companies, and experience since then made them deeply dissatisfied. After privatization, water bills rose approximately 40 percent, primarily to fund capital improvements and environmental cleanup, but some of the additional revenue went into high executive salaries. During the dry summer of 1996, Yorkshire Water, one of the most criticized, lost one-third of its water through leakage. Watering of lawns and washing of cars were prohibited. Nevertheless, Yorkshire Water proposed a special dividend to its shareholders (already well rewarded) instead of spending more on improvement of its leaky water pipes.

In 1992, shortly after the ERM disaster, another political squall arose when the government brought forward its plan to privatize British Coal. The generating companies had switched to natural gas, and many mines had already closed. In the run-up to privatization, the Energy Department proposed to close more than half the remaining mines, with the loss of thirty thousand jobs at a time of high unemployment. The remaining mines would be privatized.

An outcry arose from the affected areas. In the House of Commons, Tory backbenchers led the protest, supported enthusiastically by Labour. With his slim majority, Major could not afford defections. To soften the blow, he provided generous redundancy payments to the miners, further straining a dangerously stretched budget.

The privatization plan divided the assets of British Coal into five regional packages that were to be put up for sale. British Coal held a great deal of land and property not used for mining. Some of this property was well located for industrial development. An informed estimate was that British Coal was worth about £135 million with property valued at £300 million.

In 1994, British Coal began selling off its collieries to private buyers. The miners union had no choice but to accept these changes, conceding that the number of miners would decline, but those who remained would have steady jobs. In 1995, the remaining property, mainly large areas of wasteland, was sold. The last employee turned out the lights, left the office, and British Coal was no more.

Another controversial proposal was the plan to privatize the Post Office, a project of Michael Heseltine, who had moved to the Department of Trade and Industry with the title President of the Board of Trade. The Post Office was eager for privatization, confident that it could operate a high-technology mail and parcel service that would be competitive throughout the world. Post Office executives knew that only private industry would make the kind of investment necessary to be competitive. As in other privatizations, they expected to receive private-sector salaries and bonuses.

The plan developed by the government would separate Post Office Counters, which dealt with the public, from Royal Mail, which processed and delivered mail. Privatization met clamorous resistance due to the possibility that convenient but unprofitable small post offices would be closed. The plan was abandoned in 1994 due to backbench opposition. With its slim majority and mounting political difficulties, the Major ministry was unwilling at that time to tackle the politically dangerous task of postal privatization.

In July 1992, the last of the great privatizations began when Major announced plans to privatize British Rail. There was need for new management, new technology, new equipment, new tracks, and new labor relations. It seemed that only private enterprise could provide the capital and incentives necessary to modernize the system. The political and social effects would be enormous: entire communities would be threatened and hundreds of thousands of jobs were at stake. The rail lines were essential to the movement of people and freight and were the safest and most economical alternative to Britain's crowded roads.

Privatizing British Rail meant splitting it up into almost one hundred companies that would be sold separately. The tracks, signaling, tunnels, and stations were put under a public corporation called Railtrack, which would manage ten thousand miles of track, four thousand stations, the signaling and safety systems, and numerous other railroad assets. The transportation services of British Rail would be franchised to twenty-five separate passenger lines and five freight lines that would operate the trains and pay fees to Railtrack for the use of the tracks and stations. Three companies would take over the rolling stock and lease it to the franchised rail lines. Nineteen maintenance companies would keep the trains rolling. These companies would contract with each other, but there was no central coordinator, apart from a regulator who would monitor rates and service.

The proposed privatization of British Rail aroused considerable resistance. Labour promised to renationalize, a threat that had to be taken seriously as the likelihood of a Labour victory in the next election increased. It was evident to the railroad unions that there would be heavy job losses as new methods and technology replaced the obsolete practices of the past.

Another source of resistance to the privatization of British Rail was public anxiety that the operating franchises would close down unprofitable small stations and feeder lines. Tory backbenchers from rural areas were sensitive to such concerns. The government stated that the new operating companies would be required to run a specified number of trains, and the minister of transport expressed hope that they would offer new and better service.

The main concern of the government was to avoid unpopular increases in fares—"a poll tax on wheels." The principle was adopted that fares would not be permitted to rise faster than inflation. The government promised substantial subsidies to the privatized companies, to get them off to a good start and help them begin the process of modernizing. They were guaranteed a predictable stream of capital for the next ten years.

The key to the privatization of British Rail was the sale of Railtrack, which possessed enormous assets of land and buildings, including huge stations and hotels at city centers. To make Railtrack marketable, the government invested substantial amounts in the improvement of the stations, tracks, and signaling, and wrote off Railtrack's debt. In May 1996, Major announced the sale of Railtrack to a group of investors. In the rush to privatize Railtrack before the expected Labour victory in the approaching election, assets of enormous value were virtually given away, accompanied by long-term commitments to large subsidies.

As the privatization plan unfolded, executives of British Rail began incorporating to make bids for the new franchises, bringing in capital from banks and other investors. Since Labour had promised to renationalize, there were few bidders, and valuable franchises with hefty subsidies were sold at fire sale prices. The new operators contracted with Railtrack and other service companies, but the low and ill-defined standards of British Rail, plus guesswork, were the basis for these contracts.

The last operating franchise was awarded in February 1997. The operators introduced new rail lines with new names and new schedules; the trains began running; and before Major left office, British Rail had ceased to exist.

The privatization of British Rail handed extravagant profits to entrepreneurs. British Rail sold its engines and cars to three companies that leased them to the franchised operators. The management and staff of one leasing company put up 20 percent of the money themselves and borrowed the rest from a merchant bank. They introduced innovative methods for managing rolling stock, and six months later, they sold out at a profit of 600 percent.

As a result of the sale, some fifty secretaries, clerks, and other administrative staff received £50,000 each, and the directors divided a pie of £34 million. The outcome of the privatization was a national disaster. The plan was hastily thrown together, as the government rushed to complete the privatization before the approaching election. Some franchised operators were inexperienced, and it was difficult to coordinate schedules for twenty-five different passenger lines. Featherbedding had been rampant on British Rail, and the franchised operators sometimes downsized hastily without allowing for the complexity of the railroad network.

Turbulent scenes took place at railway stations as trains were canceled or delayed. A national system established by twenty of the twenty-five operators to answer questions about schedules and fares broke down and had to be entirely reorganized. The regulator imposed heavy fines on Railtrack or the operators for failing to meet schedules. By March 1997, shares in the railroad operating companies had fallen 23 percent.

Under Thatcher, deregulation was extended to the bus lines. It soon appeared that excessive competition was the result. Many "cowboy" bus lines with low capitalization, ill-trained drivers, and old, poorly maintained buses appeared, clogging up town centers and spewing pollution. Liverpool, for example, had three bus lines in 1986, and in 1995 it had fifty-seven. Some towns decided to make their city center a pedestrian walkway to keep the buses out.

In 1996, the Major government announced a return to a modest regulation of buses, including engine emission standards, safety standards, and correlation of bus timetables. The largest bus companies welcomed the opportunity to eliminate the small, one-horse lines that had driven down fares but also had created chaos in the business.

A privatization that brought with it nostalgia for the ideals of former times was the sale of the new towns that had begun with Letchworth (north of London), which was founded in the early twentieth century. The Labour government had founded more new towns after World War II. These planned communities were based on ideas of that time concerning desirable features for urban living, including ownership of the property by a corporation responsible to the residents. Many of the new towns had proven to be attractive places to live, but their corporate structure had become unwelcome. People wanted to own their own houses and be the masters of their own small domains. Others, mainly in the north and west, suffered from poverty, dilapidation, and crime.

Under Thatcher, the process began of selling off the land, buildings, houses, and factories of the new-town corporations. In 1995, it was reported that the Commission for New Towns had nearly completed selling off the assets of those communities.

The Workforce

The Major government drove a stake into the heart of British trade unionism. Legislation was passed that refined strike procedures and gave workers the right to join the union of their choice or none at all. This legislation was justified on the grounds of "management's right to manage" and the need to protect workers against irresponsible unions. It was held that the global market required "labour flexibility." Employers were authorized to offer workers inducements to decertify their union, an additional blow to union membership. The legislation included some worthwhile provisions concerning pregnancy, maternity leave, and health and safety.

It was thought that this legislation would mark the end of the unions, but in many places they continued because they were a convenience to employers and employees as a medium for communication. In some cases shop stewards were taken into management and became intermediaries rather than exclusively spokesmen for the workers. In 1990, the proportion of workers covered by collective bargaining agreements was still 41 percent in the private sector and 78 percent in the public sector.

An example of the Major ministry's commitment to a free labor market was the abolition of the Wages Councils, which established minimum wages for 2.5 million workers in nonunionized sectors of the economy. The argument was made that the minimum wage priced unskilled workers out of jobs and that "low pay is better than no pay." The measure was strongly supported by hotels, restaurants, retailers, janitorial services, and other employers of low-paid workers, many of whom were women or immigrants. Thus ended an institution that had begun with the trade boards instituted by Winston Churchill under the Liberal government in 1908.

The changing job market altered the employment of men and women. Between 1979 and 1997, the number of employed women increased by 700,000 but the number of employed men decreased by 2.7 million. The deindustrialization of Britain destroyed many well-paid jobs for men while creating many low-paid jobs for women.

The number of part-time jobs increased notably, especially among women. Some people held two or more part-time jobs. Although these were often regarded as an inferior kind of employment, investigation showed that many of these jobs had considerable permanence and that many people holding them wanted them that way. Frequently, these jobs were not seen as sustaining the household but as adding welcome additional income.

The productivity of British workers remained lower than in other major industrial countries. One reason was deficiencies in training and education; another was the difficulty of moving from areas of high unemployment, where housing costs were low, to areas with jobs, where housing costs were high. Workers were unwilling to commute considerable distances to find jobs. Managements were slow to introduce technology that would improve productivity. The Thatcher effort to create an enterprise culture that would weed out inefficiencies had not penetrated very deeply into the British economy.

Britain continued to receive immigrants, most of them from India, Pakistan, Bangladesh, the Caribbean, and former colonies in Africa. The success rate of Britain's ethnic groups varied greatly. The Chinese, who came mainly from Hong Kong and Southeast Asia, were the most likely to be successful. The least successful were people of Afro-Caribbean ancestry, who were clustered in the inner cities or in high-rise estates.

Social Security

One of the consequences of Thatcherism was to increase significantly the disparity between the wealthiest and the poor. A study by the Rowntree Foundation showed that between 1979 and 1992 the real incomes of the richest 10 percent had risen by 55 percent, while the real incomes of the poorest 10 percent stayed the same. In the United Kingdom the top 1 percent of the population owned 19 percent of the wealth, and the top 10 percent owned 52 percent. The bottom 50 percent of the population owned only 8 percent of the wealth. For these people, their job or pension was almost all they had. When ill, disabled, elderly, or unemployed, they had nothing to fall back on but the benefits of the welfare state.

A report in November 1996 showed that "the poverty trap" was somewhat porous. Between 1991 and 1994, more than half of the people whose income was in the lowest 10 percent rose out of poverty. Although others were slipping into that category, there was movement within the poor that provided hope for borderline cases.

Fraud was an inevitable problem of the welfare state. The Department of Social Security found it difficult to monitor all claims. Some payments depended almost entirely on information supplied by the recipients. It was found that ten thousand public employees of Lambeth, a Labour-controlled low-income part of London, were receiving welfare payments, most of them unjustified. In January 1996, a report from the National Audit Office stated that almost 10 percent of welfare recipients had presented fraudulent claims and had received £1.4 billion in improper benefit payments.

There was general agreement that reform of the welfare system required insistence that able-bodied people of working age find employment or undergo training likely to lead to employment. The Major ministry abolished the unemployment benefit that went back to 1911 and replaced it with the "Job Seeker's Allowance," which required a systematic, monitored, thirteen-week search for a job. During that time, job seekers would get a "top-up" benefit of £10 per week in addition to benefit payments roughly equal to the former unemployment insurance. Another program, "Project Work," required thirteen weeks of job search or training, followed, if necessary, by thirteen weeks of work on community projects.

An important concern was the rising number of people on sickness or disability benefits, which were more generous than unemployment benefits. Although more expensive, this practice had the public relations effect of lowering the official number of people unemployed. In some instances, Disability Benefit became a kind of early retirement, until the pension age was reached. Housing Benefit also grew with unemployment.

The Major government established the Child Support Agency to reduce welfare costs by requiring fathers to pay for the support of their children, who almost always were in the care of the mother. The agency could take legal action to compel the father to pay at a set level, even if the father's obligations under a divorce settlement had been fulfilled. The money obtained from the father was deducted from the mother's benefits, so the mother was no better off than before. The agency, which was enormously unpopular, was badly managed and had little success in extracting money from fathers.

The Maastricht Treaty

Major's first two years were difficult, but there was general agreement that he was a reasonable, moderate man, who, unlike his predecessor, sought consensus rather than confrontation. He had restored confidence to the Conservative Party, gotten rid of the poll tax, continued the Thatcher privatizations and reforms, and led his country in a victorious war in the Gulf. His surprising victory in the election of 1992 seemed to signal acceptance by the public, and gave him a weak but unmistakable mandate to continue. The problem that he could not resolve, which destroyed his ministry and shattered the Conservative Party, was Britain's place in the European Community (EC), which in 1992 became the European Union (EU).

The Treaty of European Union, negotiated at Maastricht in December 1991, was well received at first. Major's hard-won concessions to "opt out" of the single currency and the Social Chapter seemed to satisfy Britain's concerns. The treaty was not an issue in the election of April 1992. Everyone assumed that it would pass during the summer.

Signs of trouble appeared in May 1992 when Thatcher attacked the treaty in a speech, and a group of Conservative MPs called for a referendum. In early June, the Danes rejected the treaty in a referendum, which put the treaty on hold and led to a wave of negative sentiments throughout Europe. Encouraged by the Danish referendum, eighty-four Conservative MPs signed a motion asking for a "fresh start" on relations with the EC. In her maiden speech in the House of Lords, Baroness Thatcher declared her intention to vote against the treaty.

It was clear that in Britain and the Conservative Party deep differences existed concerning the movement toward European unity. The ambitions of Jacques Delors had generated a growing reaction among many of the Conservative backbenchers. The leading Conservative newspapers, the *Telegraph* and the *Times* were hostile. The main purveyor of British xenophobia was Rupert Murdoch's tabloid, *The Sun*, with the largest circulation of any British newspaper. A poll showed that the British were the least favorable toward the European Union of any member country. *The Sun* expressed its opinion in a striking headline: "UP YOURS, DELORS."

The election of 1992 had given Major a slim margin in the House of Commons, and many of the new Conservative MPs, perhaps reflecting the views of their constituents, came with an anti-European bias. The Labour Party had become more sympathetic to the EC because the common social policy would give unions and workers benefits that Thatcherism had taken away. The Liberal Democrats were fully committed to participation in the movement for European unity. Business leaders welcomed access to the European market, but they did not want the flexibility that Thatcher had brought to the British economy to be lost in the rigidities and regulations of the proposed European Union. Polls showed that more than half the British people opposed closer union with Europe. The ERM and "Black Wednesday" confirmed negative views.

The Conservative Party conference in October 1992 was dominated by hostility to the Maastricht Treaty. Major believed that the British veto in the Council of Ministers, plus his "options," gave Britain all the security it needed. He sounded like Thatcher when he exclaimed: "I will never, come hell or high water, let our distinctive British identity be lost in a federal Europe."

When the treaty came before Parliament in November 1992, John Smith seized the opportunity to embarrass the government and widen the fissure in the Conservative Party. Although Labour favored the treaty, opposition at crucial points in the ratification process would give Tory rebels a chance to show their colors. The Paving Motion, which began the ratification process, aroused a fierce debate and was won by the government by a vote of 319 to 316, but only after intense pressure on Conservative MPs and with the support of the Liberal Democrats. Twenty-six Tories voted with Labour against the government and seven abstained.

The debate over Maastricht continued into 1993, consuming twenty-three days and over two hundred hours, and doing great damage to the public image of the Major government and the Conservative Party. With his slim majority riddled by defectors, Major's earlier experience as a whip was essential to his survival. Approximately fifty Conservative MPs, known as "Euroskeptics," showed varying degrees of hostility to the treaty, although not all were prepared to vote against the government. They were well organized, with their own whips.

When the Euroskeptics proposed that the treaty be submitted to the voters in a referendum, the government defeated the proposal by a comfortable margin, but fifty-one Tory rebels voted for it and another thirteen abstained. It was commonly believed that in a referendum the treaty would lose. In an unguarded moment, Major complained heatedly about "those bastards out there," whom he described as "the dispossessed and the never possessed." When the referendum was proposed in the House of Lords, Lady Thatcher voted for it—the first time that she had ever voted against a Conservative government.

Within the Conservative Party, the antagonisms spawned by Europe took on the features of a cultural conflict. Ever since the days of Lord Chesterfield and William Hogarth, two interwoven strands had coexisted in British culture: cosmopolitanism and insularity. Disputes about the European Union brought them into the open.

Finally, Major showed that he could crack the whip. In July 1993, the Maastricht Treaty had been before the House of Commons for a year and a half. Labour moved an amendment that the Social Chapter must be included in the treaty. Sensing the possibility that the government might be defeated and forced to call an election, the Liberal Democrats and Scottish Nationalists joined Labour in supporting the amendment. Although they opposed the Social Chapter, the Euroskeptics supported the amendment because it would unite the Conservatives against the amended treaty, which would be defeated when the main motion was voted on.

The Ulster Unionists agreed to vote against the amendment with the understanding that Major would lend a sympathetic ear to their special concerns. The amendment failed due to the tiebreaker vote of the Speaker, Betty Boothroyd, whose office obliged her to support the government in case of a tie.

At this point, Major called a halt to the wrangling. He demanded a vote of confidence, and the Conservative rebels, faced by the prospect of an election if the government was defeated, gave in. The vote the next day was an anticlimax. The treaty with the "options" was approved by a majority of thirty-eight votes. Major had shown that he could be tough when necessary, but he had not healed the rift in his own party concerning Britain's relations with the European Union.

Despite his narrow victory on the Maastricht Treaty—or perhaps because of it—Major found that the question of Europe would not go away. There were many differences between Britain and its partners in the European Union: they were heading toward a federal union, while Britain wished to maintain national sovereignty; they wanted a common currency, while Britain wished to preserve the pound and Britain's role as a world financial center; they wanted a European defense structure, while Britain wished to maintain NATO and the U.S. role. They wanted to harmonize taxation and social policy, while Britain had created a freer, more open and competitive model and did not wish to lose it.

An important consideration was Britain's close ties with the United States, Canada, Australia, and New Zealand. Another was the domination of the European Union by France and Germany, whose condominium had infuriated Thatcher and put up barriers that Major's conciliatory approach could not penetrate. Major's contention that Britain could be "at the heart of Europe" was an illusion.

Both sides constantly badgered him. Pro-Europeans, among them Sir Edward Heath, Michael Heseltine, and Kenneth Clarke defended the movement for European unity and wanted Britain to be an active participant. Much of the time, however, they prudently remained silent, allowing nonpolitical groups to make the argument. The Euroskeptics, who were strong on the Conservative back benches, demanded assurances that the government would accept no further integration with Europe. They insisted that the prime minister challenge the authority in Britain of the European Commission and the European Court of Justice.

Labour took a strong stand in favor of greater involvement in the European Union. They portrayed the Conservatives as the misfits of Europe. Although Labour, too, had its Euroskeptics, they maintained a low profile. The

Liberal Democratic Party continued its support for British participation in all aspects of the movement for European unity.

Major fought back by stating that he was "fighting Britain's corner hard." He charged that Labour would "sign away our votes, sign away our competitiveness, and sign away our money." He referred to John Smith as "Monsieur Oui, the poodle of Brussels." Polls showed that the majority of the British public regarded the Tories as the "patriotic party" in contrast to the pro-European views of Labour and the Liberal Democrats.

These divisions within the Conservative Party came to a head at the end of 1994 on a bill to increase Britain's financial contribution to the European Union. To forestall expected opposition from the Euroskeptics, Major staked the future of his government on passage of the bill. Unwilling to face the prospect of an election under unfavorable circumstances, the Conservatives supported the bill, which passed by a close vote. The Euroskeptics took advantage of the opportunity to express again their dissatisfaction with the European Union and Britain's place in it. Despite Major's threat, eight Conservative rebels abstained. The rebels were "denied the whip," that is, they were excluded from the Conservative parliamentary party.

Responding to pressures within his own party and the country, Major increasingly took a Euroskeptic line. In September 1993, he published an article in *The Economist* that echoed Thatcher's speech at Bruges in 1988. He stated that he sought "a different kind of Europe," which would be a "loose union of sovereign national states" including as many democracies as possible. The official Conservative statement on the European Union (April 1994) stood fast on the Maastricht Treaty and Britain's precious "options." It favored a "decentralized Europe" and accused the opposition parties of favoring a "centralized superstate in Europe." NATO should remain the basis of European defense.

In a television interview with David Frost in January 1995, Major said that he was opposed to constitutional changes in the European Union that would limit British sovereignty or weaken the British veto and that he would resist additional powers for the European Parliament. As to the single European currency, he continued to finesse the issue by refusing to make any commitment, adopting a "wait and see" policy. In February, Major stated: "Unless economic conditions were right, a single currency would tear the European Union apart."

In March 1995, the government survived another crucial vote on Europe by a narrow margin of 319 to 314. Given his slim majority, Major had no choice but to offer an olive branch to the eight rebels who had defied the party leadership. In April, the "whipless" Tories returned to the fold, unrepentant and unchanged in their views. By 1995, the Euroskeptics had won the battle within the Conservative Party. The rising new mantra was "Euro-realism," which recognized the importance of Britain's membership in the European Union, but advocated a looser community open to Eastern Europe and the wider world overseas.

John Major under Siege

When the Conservative Party conference met in October 1993, Major looked for a formula that would serve as a rallying cry. At the conference he used the slogan "back to basics," which he defined as excellence in the schools, the public services, and industry; commitment to sound money and free trade; and a fight against crime—all of these being long-established Conservative principles. He added concern for basic moral qualities: "Self-discipline and respect for law; consideration for others; accepting responsibility for yourself and your family." Many Conservatives responded positively to his remarks about personal morality, but the press jumped on "back to basics" as a call for a puritanical moral crusade.

The public response to back to basics grew out of increasing concern with the moral character of the young. In February 1993, two 10-year-old boys in a shopping mall lured a toddler away from his mother and killed him. Teenage crime was widespread, especially in the large public housing estates inhabited by low-income people. Data showed that one-third of all births were to unwed mothers, most of them young and living in poverty. The new slogan resonated with Conservatives, because it implied tightening the welfare system and re-straining the idle and disorderly lives that many Conservatives assumed were characteristic of those who depended on public assistance.

The opening months of 1994 were a comedy of mishaps. Back to basics became a source of mocking humor as the press, in one of its periodic fits of morality, made a game of uncovering Tory misdeeds. It was discovered that a married Conservative minister had fathered a child outside his marriage; a promising young Conservative MP died as a result of an autoerotic practice—fully explained in the media to the uninitiated; the wife of a Conservative peer and junior minister committed suicide in reaction to her husband's philandering; the chief of the defence staff decided to retire when a young woman with whom he was romantically involved sold her story to the tabloid press.

Under the circumstances, the best Major could do was to claim that back to basics referred to public policy, not personal morality. Nevertheless, the media flap contributed to the view that he was a political lightweight who did not belong at No. 10 Downing Street.

The financial crisis continued to plague the Major ministry. In October 1993, Kenneth Clarke, the new chancellor of the Exchequer, faced a mountain of debt. He began a rigorous review of spending, looking for cuts. Public sector salaries were frozen, and the universities were further squeezed.

In December 1994, Clarke announced that he would impose the second installment of Lamont's VAT increase on fuel. At this point, the Tory backbenchers erupted and the government was defeated, 319 to 311. Once again Major's slim majority had given the backbenchers an influence out of proportion to their numbers. Clarke hastily withdrew the VAT increase and replaced it with increased taxes on gasoline, tobacco, and alcohol.

Collectively, the Lamont-Clarke budgets of 1993–1994 were the largest peacetime tax increases in British history. The public reaction was predictable. Even friendly newspapers like the *Times* were outraged. One prominent Tory called the tax increases "a long walk to the scaffold." Clarke's last-minute efforts to cut spending were too little, too late. The Conservative reputation for sound public finance had been irreparably damaged, and public confidence in the election promises of political leaders reached a new low.

The papers were filled with columns declaring that a leadership change was imperative. A *Times* poll in March 1994 gave Major ratings of 20 percent for honesty, 17 percent for understanding the problems facing Britain, 11 percent for leadership, 51 percent on "out of touch with ordinary people," and 5 percent on "has a lot of personality." Only 20 percent of the voters thought he was doing a good job. By midsummer, Major's ratings were the lowest of any prime minister since 1940, when polling began.

The Conservative Party's political base was melting away. Conservative support was 28 percent and the Liberal Democrats were at 20 percent, their bedrock figure. In the polls, Labour was at 48 percent and making striking advances in the middle class, where support for Labour and the Conservatives had been equally divided. In May 1994, the Conservatives received only 27 percent of the vote in the local elections and lost more than two thousand seats. On a low turnout, Labour garnered 44 percent.

Heseltine, who had asserted his independence under Thatcher but accepted office under Major, was widely touted as Major's successor. His nickname was "Tarzan": it was said that he could "fill a room" with his powerful presence, in contrast to the modest overachiever who had become prime minister. Clarke also stated his desire to be prime minister when Major left. Faced with the prospect of a leadership contest, Heseltine did not pursue his chances further.

The Major ministry was further embarrassed by news stories about the Matrix Churchill deal with Iraq when Major was foreign secretary. Press reports indicated that there had been more to the Matrix Churchill deal than met the eye, and in November 1992, the Customs and Excise brought a prosecution against the Matrix Churchill executives. At their trial, the executives claimed that the ministers had known that they were shipping machine tools that could be used to manufacture weapons and had given their tacit consent.

On the basis of protecting the national security, the ministers concerned attempted to cover up their role by obtaining gag orders that denied the defense access to the relevant documents. Left twisting in the wind, the executives pleaded guilty. They were fined and received suspended sentences. On appeal, one of the ministers involved admitted that he had been less than candid when replying to parliamentary questions about the sale. A judge refused to agree to the gag orders and the sentences were quashed.

When the ministers were accused of letting innocent men be convicted to avoid political embarrassment, Major appointed Lord Justice Richard Scott, an esteemed judge, to investigate. The Scott report was published in February 1996. Thatcher and Major received light taps on the back of the hand on the grounds that they had been inadequately briefed.

The ministers involved were cleared of any intentional wrongdoing. But the damage had already been done in the press and in the parliamentary debates, where Labour took the lead in denouncing a "cover-up." When the Scott report was presented to Parliament, the government squeezed by, 320 to 319. Later in the year, the House of Commons laid down guidelines requiring ministers and heads of agencies to answer parliamentary questions fully and completely.

Additional embarrassments resulted from an investigation of the Pergau Dam affair, where it became quite clear that Margaret Thatcher had improperly used foreign aid to grease the skids for large sales of weaponry. John Major found that some of Thatcher's less attractive chickens were coming home to roost.

All these violations of proper conduct—major or minor—were wrapped up in the word "sleaze," which conveyed a general sense of a decadent party and a ministry out of control. In 1995, questions were raised concerning the outside income of MPs, many of whom were employed by law firms, businesses, and other organizations. This practice had long been accepted, but MPs were required to enter them in the Register of Member's Interests. The press reported that some members had been paid by special interests to raise questions in the House of Commons and had not declared the connection. There was a growing sense that MPs should not have outside employment that might influence their judgment, such as an association with an important law firm or a directorship of a large corporation.

Major, whose personal integrity was not in question, responded by establishing a committee led by Lord Nolan, a respected peer, to set standards of conduct in public life. When the Nolan committee reported in 1995, it stated that there was no evidence of "systematic corruption" but proposed a new code of conduct for MPs: self-regulation through a Standards and Privileges Committee, publication of outside earnings, and curtailment of their opportunities to earn outside income. The government opposed full disclosure, but was defeated when twenty-three Tories voted with the opposition.

As if his other problems were not enough, in March 1993 Major faced another crisis in public opinion, when long-simmering anxieties about "mad cow disease" (bovine spongiform encephalopathy/BSE) were intensified. Each week, three hundred new cases of BSE appeared, although the offal that carried the disease had been banned from cattle feed since 1989.

In 1996, scientists learned that BSE could pass to humans by eating infected beef, leading to a disease in humans that was invariably fatal. Although human instances were few, panic ensued in Britain; restaurants, led by McDonald's, removed British beef from their menus. Sales of beef in Britain plummeted, and the European Union banned exports of beef from Britain to protect their own people and herds from contamination. British agriculture had suffered a devastating blow.

Major fought back on two fronts. A massive culling of British herds, with compensation to farmers, began. "There goes our tax cut," Major lamented, as he contemplated the cost. The disposal of several million carcasses was a nightmare. The other front was the European Union, where farmers used Britain's problem to increase their own sales and exports. When Major thought he had negotiated a rational, orderly process for gradual relaxation of the ban as controls in Britain took effect, the European Union reneged, citing consumer resistance.

The political fallout was enormous. British agriculture, one of the foundation stones of the Conservative Party, was furious. The Euroskeptics were unsparing in their criticism of the prime minister's efforts to work with the EU. The Labour Party had a field day, as it criticized the government and the hapless minister for agriculture for their floundering efforts to understand, explain, and control the problem.

In June 1995, Major, tired of constant harassment from his own party, resigned as leader and called for a new leadership election. He told the Conservatives to "put up or shut up." John Redwood, an avid Thatcherite and a leading Euroskeptic, challenged him. Major was fully supported by Heseltine, thus depriving his opponents of the most credible alternative. He won the leadership election handily, but the eighty-nine votes for Redwood plus twenty-two abstainers comprised one-third of the Conservative MPs and indicated more trouble ahead. Heseltine was rewarded, and his ambitions were satisfied by his appointment as deputy prime minister and first secretary of state. In these offices he chaired Cabinet committees, served as a troubleshooter, undertook special projects, and occasionally replaced the prime minister at "Prime Minister's Questions."

Preserving the United Kingdom

Major described England as "the country of long shadows on county [cricket] grounds, warm beer, invincible green suburbs, and dog lovers." Although this romantic picture was far removed from the crumbling buildings and hard streets of his native Brixton, it reflected his essential Englishness. When he was able, Major moved to his rural constituency of Huntingdon, which corresponded more closely to his English dream.

Proud as he was of his England, Major was prime minister of a country with several other nationalities. Their differences had been accommodated by considerable administrative devolution: the secretaries of state for Scotland and Wales had minicapitals in Edinburgh and Cardiff, which exercised extensive responsibilities. Scottish and Welsh MPs formed committees of the House of Commons that dealt with legislation concerning those parts of the United Kingdom. Northern Ireland was a case unto itself.

Most of the population and wealth of the United Kingdom were concentrated in England, which had become the stronghold of the Conservative Party. Scotland was another matter. The Conservative Party had not gained a majority in Scotland since 1955; in the election of 1992, the Conservatives won only 25 percent of the Scottish vote.

The Conservative grip on power in Westminster led some in Scotland to return to the idea of devolution, presumably buried in the referendum of 1979. The Labour Party was dominant in Scotland, but its inability to win a majority in Parliament left Scotland on the outside looking in. Scots had the sense that they were ruled by the English, with little or no chance of asserting their own concerns.

The policies of Thatcher had been devastating to Scotland, with its large public sector, unionized and overmanned industries, and extensive welfare dependency. Thatcher's dismantling of nationalized industries, restrictions on local governments, and financial squeeze on the public services had left the industrial cities of Scotland prostrate. Unemployment in Scotland was 25 percent higher than in the United Kingdom as a whole. As in England, the poll tax had been seen as an outrage. One benefit of Thatcherism to

Scotland was the sale of council houses, leading to 58 percent home owner-ship by 1996.

Scottish nationalism gained confidence in the 1990s with the revival of the Scottish economy. The Scots had a fine school system and a strong work ethic. Foreign investors began building high-tech factories in parts of Scotland with cheap land, good workers, and easy access to Europe. Electronics was an important new industry, and "silicon glen" produced 30 percent of all computers manufactured in the European Union.

A factor in the revival of Scottish nationalism was North Sea oil, which came ashore in Scotland, although the revenues went to London. Scots had the feeling that the English were benefiting from their oil. An important in-fluence was the European Economic Community. When Britain had an em-pire and was the acknowledged economic leader of the world, there were great advantages to Scotland being part of the United Kingdom. When the empire faded away, British membership in the EC gave Scotland the eco-nomic outlets it needed.

In the 1980s the Scottish National Convention was formed, an anti-Thatcherite group comprised of representatives of the Labour and Liberal Democratic parties, the trade unions, and the churches. The Convention advocated a Scottish assembly elected under proportional representation with powers to tax and use the money to fund programs intended to mitigate the ravages of Thatcherism. The Scottish National Party did not join, pre-ferring full independence within the EC.

John Major, like Margaret Thatcher, was a strong unionist. He shared the Conservative Party's long-established commitment to the supremacy of Par-liament (i.e., the central government), although he was willing to make pragmatic adjustments to regional differences. He believed that devolution was merely a halfway house to independence. He charged that the proposed assembly would be a needless expense and would impose a "tartan tax" on Scotland. He expressed concern that devolution would encourage proposals for devolved regional governments in other parts of the United Kingdom. Scottish Conservatives reported that the pressure for some form of devolu-tion was growing, and they suggested that it would be best to make conces-sions before it was too late.

Eventually, Major agreed to a referendum on a devolved Parliament for Scotland, but he insisted that it must include a second question concerning the power of the new parliament to tax. Scottish advocates of devolution op-posed a referendum, especially if it included the taxing power, fearing a re-peat of the failure in 1979. Labour, seeking to hold the Scottish vote, sup-ported the concept of a Scottish Parliament. Without that pledge, Scottish voters would have bolted in large numbers from Labour to the Scottish National Party.

Tony Blair, now leader of the Labour Party, temporized, but eventually he came out in support of a two-part referendum and persuaded the Scottish Labour Party to accept it. Meanwhile, Alex Salmond, leader of the Scottish National Party, viewed devolution as a step toward an independent Scotland within the European Union.

Wales was always included in discussions of devolution, but there was little public interest. Wales did not have the strong political and cultural heritage of Scotland, and the industrial areas of southern Wales identified more closely with England. The Welsh nationalist party (Plaid Cymru) was weak and regarded by some as a party of backwoodsmen and eccentrics. Major attempted to satisfy Welsh aspirations with the Welsh Language Act (1993), which extended the use of the Welsh language by public and private bodies.

This modest concession was more than offset by the appointment of John Redwood to the post of secretary of state for Wales. Redwood used Wales as a launch pad for his own national ambitions, introducing Thatcherite reforms into Welsh government and using conditions in Wales to instigate a national debate on policy toward unmarried mothers. When Redwood resigned in 1995 to challenge Major in the leadership election, he was replaced by young William Hague, who was unable to repair the damage.

Northern Ireland

One of Major's principal goals was to establish a peaceful settlement in Northern Ireland, and he came close to achieving it. While keeping Northern Ireland within the United Kingdom, he was open to some form of power sharing within Northern Ireland and with the Republic of Ireland.

Meanwhile, he had to deal with the IRA, which continued its bombing attacks in Britain. The most daring took place in February 1991 during the Gulf War, when the War Cabinet was meeting. Three mortar shells were lobbed into the courtyard of No. 10 Downing Street from a parked van with an opening in the top. No one was hurt, but damage was done to the building and the windows were blown in.

In April 1992, a powerful IRA bomb went off in the City of London killing one person, injuring ninety-one, and causing damage estimated at £1 billion. A year later, another IRA bomb was exploded in the City, wreaking great damage and leaving one person dead and forty injured. The little stone church, St. Ethelburga, which had stood in the City for six hundred years, surviving both the Fire of London (1666) and the Blitz of World War II, was another victim. Bombings and beatings continued to afflict Northern Ireland. In October 1993, Loyalists retaliated by attacking a pub frequented by Catholics, killing six people and wounding nineteen.

In the meantime, secret negotiations were taking place to end the violence. Gerry Adams, leader of Sinn Fein, the political wing of the IRA, met with John Hume, leader of the moderate Social Democratic and Labour Party to probe the possibility of a political solution. In February 1993, Major received a secret message from the IRA, stating their desire for peace, as long as it was not interpreted as surrender. The Major ministry had ample reason to mistrust the IRA's intentions, but there was a possibility that the IRA had come to realize that their violent methods accomplished nothing.

Major decided to take a chance and pursue the olive branch beckoning in the distance. He knew that no settlement would succeed without the agreement of the unionists, and with that in mind he laid down two main conditions: Northern Ireland would remain part of the United Kingdom unless changed by the vote of the inhabitants, and all parties had to renounce violence and pursue constitutional and democratic processes.

The Irish prime minister, Albert Reynolds, was aware of intimations of peace issuing from Sinn Fein, and he proved willing to help. In December 1993, Major and Reynolds met at No. 10 and issued the *Downing Street Declaration*, which began a new series of negotiations intended to bring Sinn Fein into the process. The declaration called for an end to terrorism and violence and stated that political talks with all parties concerned, including Sinn Fein, could begin after three months of peace.

The people of Northern Ireland and the Republic of Ireland were assured that no changes would take place without popular support as shown in a referendum. To satisfy the nationalists, the declaration stated that some institutions might be created for the island as a whole, "including a united Ireland achieved by peaceful means." The unionists interpreted "peaceful means" as requiring IRA disarmament before the talks could begin.

The unionist population of Northern Ireland was outraged. They feared that someday Britain would abandon them to the Irish Republic. They were opposed to any steps that would involve the Republic in the affairs of Northern Ireland. They wanted no political involvement with Sinn Fein, and they were determined to fight IRA terrorism tooth and nail. The IRA intensified their concern by setting off bombs in Oxford Street (a major shopping street in London) during the Christmas shopping season and dropping mortar shells on Heathrow Airport.

The nine Ulster Unionist MPs, who normally supported the Major ministry, were upset at the idea of talking with IRA terrorists about anything, especially Northern Ireland. They resented seeing Adams making statements on television, his voice provided by an actor. They were appalled when President Bill Clinton permitted Adams, a front man for terrorists, to visit the United States and raise money for the cause. Major endeavored to reassure them by reaffirming his promise that any settlement would be subject to a referendum of the people of Northern Ireland. With his slim majority, he could not afford to lose their support.

Despite heated and tedious debates in the media, some progress was being made. Perhaps Adams enjoyed being vaulted into prominence and wanted to continue his role as a world statesman. In August 1994, the IRA declared a cease-fire, and the Protestant paramilitaries followed with a similar declaration in October. The refusal of the IRA to begin decommissioning their vast hoard of weapons was disturbing, but Major was cheered in Protestant and Catholic neighborhoods for bringing the nightmare to an end.

In February 1995, the British and Irish governments published the *Framework Document* for negotiations intended to lead to peace and reconciliation in Northern Ireland. The document assumed the continuance of Northern Ireland in the United Kingdom, called for increased cooperation between London and Dublin, proposed a cross-border assembly of representatives from both parts of the island, and promised a referendum in Northern Ireland to approve any changes. The Republic agreed to an amendment to remove from its constitution the claim to Northern Ireland. The British government began reducing the number of troops in Northern Ireland, and withdrawals were expected to continue as long as the cease-fire lasted.

Adams was rewarded with a trip to Washington, meeting with President Bill Clinton in the White House on St. Patrick's Day, 1995. The White House announced that the Adams' visit was in recognition of his willingness to discuss with the British government the reduction of IRA weaponry. Incredibly, Clinton announced that the American ban on IRA fund-raising would end, thus providing the IRA with the wherewithal to purchase more weapons.

Major hurried off to Washington to point out to the president that Adams was the spokesman for a terrorist group that was still heavily armed and dangerous and had made no agreement to disarm. Clinton then agreed in a press conference that IRA fund-raising in the United States must be for peaceful purposes and accompanied by a promise to reduce their arsenal.

As his paper-thin majority in the House of Commons crumbled, Major was increasingly dependent on the Ulster Unionists for support. Their new leader, David Trimble, was cautiously willing to continue the peace process, as was John Hume, leader of the Social Democratic Labour Party. To satisfy the Unionists, Major insisted that the IRA begin decommissioning its weapons, a condition implied but not explicitly included in the *Framework Document*. In the next several months, Major made several trips to Northern Ireland, where he announced the lifting of restrictions and promised a referendum on any final settlement. In November 1995, Clinton was enthusiastically received when he made a visit to Northern Ireland to congratulate the people on the steps that had been taken to end the violence.

In January 1996, American involvement continued when former Senator George Mitchell went to Northern Ireland as leader of a three-man commission (the others were a Canadian and a Finn) sent to act as impartial mediators. Sinn Fein declared that the IRA would not give up its weapons until a full agreement had been reached. The Ulster Unionists refused to accept any settlement extracted at the point of a gun; they insisted that the IRA give up their weapons before they would begin any negotiations.

Patiently, Major played this tedious game, inching the contentious politicians of Northern Ireland forward. Departing from the *Framework Document*, he proposed a special election in Northern Ireland to choose a conference body of eighty-two members that might possibly break the impasse. The IRA showed what it thought of this idea by setting off a huge bomb in the London docklands, close to the new financial and newspaper offices. Adams seemed to be isolated, even in the Clinton White House. He said he was "saddened" by the blast.

Despite bombings in Britain, the cease-fire was maintained in Northern Ireland, which justified continuing the peace process. In the elections for the all-party peace conference held in June 1996, the voters showed their approval of the cease-fire by giving Sinn Fein 15 percent of the vote. The IRA showed its colors by setting off a huge bomb that devastated central Manchester and injured more than two hundred people.

The all-party peace talks for Northern Ireland went ahead without Sinn Fein, which refused to disavow the return to violence by the IRA and the bomb in Manchester. In July, a march of angry Protestants through a Catholic neighborhood of Belfast led to new disorders. In September, London police raided an IRA center in London, where they seized a large quantity of weapons and explosives. The next month the IRA exploded two car bombs in British Army headquarters near Belfast. In Northern Ireland, killings and bombings declined, but beatings and church burnings continued to be everyday occurrences. Major's determined effort to resolve the problems of Northern Ireland through negotiation was left to Tony Blair to complete.

CHAPTER EIGHT

~

The Triumph of "New Labour," 1994–1997

The Challenge of New Labour

The weakening of the Major ministry and the Conservative Party was due, in part, to the emergence of a Labour Party and leader with a credible claim to being an alternative government. By 1994, the troubles of "the winter of discontent" had become a fading memory. The nationalized industries had been privatized, and the unions had been tamed. Margaret Thatcher's legislation had made possible the rebirth of the Labour Party.

Although John Smith was recognized as a man of strong character and reasonable policies, his age and Scottishness made him seem like a relic of the Labour Party's past. He did not offer a new vision of Labour but excelled at pointing out the divisions and inconsistencies of the Tories. He appealed to the British sense of community and collective responsibility, taking advantage of the growing undercurrent of resistance to Thatcherite individualism. Smith was steadily gaining public respect when the "long game" ended with his sudden death from a heart attack in 1994.

For his successor, the party turned to Tony Blair, age forty-one, who advocated a transformed Labour Party—New Labour. In addition to his youthful energy and personal charm, Blair was a clear and dynamic speaker and an enthusiastic advocate of his cause. He had worked closely with Gordon Brown, Peter Mandelson, and a few others on their "project": to transform the Labour Party into a party that would appeal to middle-class voters who were employed in the growing white-collar, white-jacket, and service industries.

Blair and his colleagues knew that Labour had to move from its strong-holds in the industrial cities of northern England and Scotland to the prospering regions of the south, where most of Britain's population and economic growth was located. They recognized that Labour's historic con-stituency—the industrial working class, employed in factories, organized in unions, and living in close-knit neighborhoods—was a declining ele-ment in the national life.

In 1992, Blair and Brown had gone to the United States to observe the Clinton campaign for the presidency. From that visit they derived two prin-ciples: that elections are won by appealing to the center of the political spec-trum, and that voters in the center are primarily concerned about social is-sues such as education, health care, pensions, public disorders, and crime.

The selection of Blair as leader was an intraparty coup, skillfully organized by the small group of "modernizers." It was justified by the "unelectability" of Labour, demonstrated by three losses to Thatcher and, most dramatically, by the defeat of Neil Kinnock in 1992, an election that Labour should have won. Blair's rival for the leadership, Brown, stepped aside to avoid splitting the modernizers, although resentment lingered. Despite grumbling that Blair was "the most un-Labour politician in the party," the constituency organiza-tions and the unions fell into line. In July 1994, Blair became leader of the Labour Party. "Electability" was the watchword.

Peter Mandelson, Blair's principal electoral adviser, was responsible for the public relations aspects of "the project." He knew that it was essential to change the public image of Labour as the party of the unions, unemployed and unemployable, social security recipients, and ethnic minorities. Influ-enced by Clinton's efforts to broaden the electoral base of the Democratic Party, Blair and Mandelson undertook to sell New Labour to the public as the party of fiscal responsibility, free enterprise, and social reform.

Blair and Mandelson aimed their policies and rhetoric at the lower mid-dle class and aspiring workers, whose support had been essential to Thatcher's three electoral victories. They advocated good public services—transportation, health care, and schools—that were historically identified with Labour and seemed threatened by Thatcherism. In an age of rapid eco-nomic change, lower-middle-class people faced job insecurity, neighborhood degradation, and crime. While Thatcherism offered opportunity, Labour was the party identified with the safety net. These voters could be won over to Labour, but only if the left wing was silenced and Labour was seen as a party of moderation and consensus.

At the Labour Party conference in October 1994, Blair announced that he intended to create a "new Labour Party" that was committed to the future, not the past. He advocated a "middle way" between individual responsibility and social provision. The great symbol of Old Labour was Clause IV of the party constitution, which advocated nationalization of industry.

Blair knew that changing Clause IV would be a dramatic signal that New Labour had abandoned socialism. He proposed a new Clause IV that advocated free enterprise and a market economy leading to "a thriving private sector and high-quality public services." He toured the country, meeting party leaders to persuade them of the need for fundamental change in the policies of the party. Socialism, he argued, "is not about class, or trades unions, or capitalism versus socialism. It is about belief in working together to get things done" (Rentoul). The new Clause IV was adopted at a special party conference in April 1995.

With an election close at hand, Tony Blair knew that strong leadership and party unity were essential. He proposed reforms of the Labour Party's National Executive Council (NEC) that would strengthen his grip and prevent the NEC from providing a forum for dissident views. He changed the annual conference from a meeting where issues were debated, sometimes heatedly, to a showplace where the ideas of the party leadership were presented in a controlled format. He used a referendum of party members to win grassroots support for Labour's election manifesto. Many of Labour's constituency organizations were small, closed organizations controlled by Labour activists. Blair imposed "one member, one vote," on these building blocks of the party to broaden Labour's electoral base.

Under Blair's leadership, the Labour Party abandoned virtually all that it had once stood for. The principles of New Labour proved to be much like those of the Conservatives: a capitalist economy within a free market, tight control of taxation and expenditure, low inflation, commitment to improvements in education, law enforcement, and health care, containment of welfare costs, and a vigorous attack on unemployment and other social ills. Blair declared that his policy toward the unions would be "fairness, not favours." He adopted the Thatcherite "law and order" agenda: "Tough on crime, tough on the causes of crime."

New Labour accepted the overriding power of global financial markets and abandoned the Keynesian principle that the state should intervene in the economy with fiscal and monetary policies that would stimulate growth and maintain full employment. Old Labour, Blair said to a group of businessmen, "thought that the role of government was to interfere with the market. New Labour believes the task of government is to make the market more dynamic, to provide people and businesses with the means of success."

Gordon Brown, shadow chancellor of the Exchequer, accepted the mone-tarist doctrine that gave priority to balanced budgets, low inflation, and a strong pound. He would encourage economic development by providing a positive environment for investment and trade. For that reason, he opposed raising income taxes on the wealthy. The Old Labour principle that the state should pursue economic justice by redistribution of resources through taxa-tion and social spending had come to an end. Thatcherism, globalism, and electoral politics had triumphed.

In January 1996, a *Times* poll showed that Labour held a commanding lead. Labour was at 55 percent, the Conservatives at 29 percent, and the Liberal Democrats at 13 percent. The poll revealed that 76 percent of those interviewed were dissatisfied with the existing government. The popularity of Blair was an important factor: 54 percent of those interviewed thought that Blair was ready to be prime minister. In another poll, 62 percent thought that Blair had changed the Labour Party for the better, while only 21 percent thought that Labour "has not changed very much, despite what Blair says."

"A Voteless Recovery"

Economically Britain was doing rather well. Thatcherism had worked: Britain was no longer declining in relation to its European peers, and since 1993 had been doing somewhat better. A study of international competi-tiveness put Britain behind only the United States and Japan among the large advanced nations, and ahead of Germany and France. The study rated Britain highly in financial services and in attractiveness for inward investment.

A sense of optimism led Major to propose London as the world center for observance of the millennium on New Year's Eve, 1999, with a vast dome as the centerpiece of the celebration. The Millennium Dome was a pet project of Michael Heseltine, who saw it as a means to revive deserted industrial land in the east of London.

In 1995, Kenneth Clarke's Thatcherite fiscal discipline began to pay off. The public finances were improving, and Clarke came under considerable pressure from backbenchers for tax cuts, which they hoped would restore the Tory reputation for competent, economical government. With an election approaching, Clarke cut the base rate of the income tax by one percentage point in 1995 and another in 1996, increased taxes on consumption, and squeezed the public sector even more.

Clarke's income tax reductions had little effect on public opinion; people remembered the increases in consumption taxes, which went out of their pockets every day. More important was the public perception that Clarke's penny-pinching meant falling standards in schools and in the National Health Service (NHS), while crime and disorders continued to rise. The priorities of the electorate were shifting from tax cuts to better public services.

The economy was growing at a 2.5 percent rate, interest rates were 6 percent, and inflation was low at 3 percent. Exports had risen 42 percent since leaving the ERM. The deficit for 1996 was 4.4 percent of the Gross Domestic Product (GDP), too high to meet the Maastricht standard for monetary union, but going down. Solid prospects for the future were underpinned by strong savings, which had increased to 13 percent of GDP, compared to 6 percent in the free-spending 1980s. Led by invisible exports such as financial services and tourism, the balance of payments was virtually balanced for the first time since 1985.

During the Thatcher–Major years, important changes had taken place in the labor market. Between 1979 and 1997 employment in manufacturing industry fell from 32 percent to 18 percent of the workforce, while service industries increased from 58 percent to 75 percent. The rise of "a knowledge economy" spelled doom for manual workers and offered new opportunities for women. Studies indicated that the average take-home pay of British workers was greater than in the European Union, with the exception of Germany. One reason was lower taxes, which took 38 percent of earnings in Britain, but an average of 46 percent in other European Union countries. In 1996, unemployment at 6.7 percent was lower than any other European country and gradually falling.

One sign of economic improvement was a rise in house prices, which in 1996 rose by 10 percent in greater London and the southeast, and somewhat less elsewhere. The result was a decline in negative equity, which was cut in half, falling from 1.7 million houses in 1993 to 800,000 at the end of 1996, a bit of good news for the Conservatives in an election year. The dark side of an improving economy was the persistence of an underclass, estimated by one author as one-quarter of the population, which did not share the standard of living expected in an advanced country.

Britain had become the most attractive advanced country in the world (with the exception of the United States) for investment from other countries. The United States was the largest investor in Britain, while Britain returned the favor by investing almost as much in the United States. After the United States, the largest outside investors in the United Kingdom were Germany, France, and Sweden. A Treasury report concluded that the British economy had become one of the most globally integrated of comparable countries.

Britain's economic revival had resulted in a strong pound, a point of national pride but actually a mixed blessing. The strong pound gave a signal to the rest of the world that Britain was back, but it was a burden on exports and made Britain more expensive for tourism. It was beneficial to financial services but damaging to manufacturing, which needed all the help it could get.

What was missing was "the feel-good factor." Major's best hope in the election was the revival of the economy, but he was disappointed. One Conservative remarked sadly that it was "a voteless recovery."

The European Union

In 1996, the main thrust of the European Union was toward a single currency (the euro), a goal strongly supported by Chancellor Kohl of Germany, the crucial player in the process. The plan was for the member countries (or some of them) to qualify financially for the single currency in 1999, then enter a three-year transition period, and fully adopt the euro in 2002. Since Britain had left the ERM in 1992 and the influence of the Euroskeptics was growing, the Major government was left looking on from the sidelines.

The intergovernmental conference called to advance European unity met in Florence in June 1996. It was concerned primarily with the strict guidelines required for introduction of the single currency. The main requirements for participation in the single currency were an annual national deficit of 3 percent or less of GDP and that the country's total debt be no more than 60 percent of its GDP.

Britain qualified in terms of its public debt (54 percent of GDP), but did not meet the deficit criterion with a 1996 deficit of 4.4 percent of GDP. The British deficit in 1997 was predicted to be 3.7 percent, a considerable improvement. Countries far from meeting the debt requirement in 1995 were Belgium (134 percent of GDP), Italy (125 percent of GDP), Greece (112 percent of GDP), and Ireland (82 percent of GDP). Even Germany with a deficit of 3.5 percent and France (4.8 percent) did not meet the convergence requirements. They imposed strict financial discipline to achieve the goal and were expected to "fudge" the rest of the requirements.

British business held mixed views on the common currency. Trade with the European Union would be simplified, but the euro might complicate the 40 percent of British trade conducted with other countries. London had 520 foreign banks from seventy-six countries and conducted more foreign-exchange transactions than any city in the world. Some analysts believed that this position would continue outside the single currency; some worried that it might not. The single currency was expected to encourage inward investment, because it would continue Britain's status as the best place for access to Europe. However, the memory of "Black Wednesday" was still fresh and dictated caution before committing the pound sterling to a perpetual ERM.

The dispute with the European Union concerning the ban on exports of British beef was especially disturbing to the Conservative Party, the party of agriculture. Major fought back by declaring that he would veto every European Union decision that required agreement by Britain. At the Florence summit in June, he changed his tune and agreed to a selective cull of 120,000 beef cattle. In turn, the EU stated that it would consider lifting the embargo when British beef was believed to be safe.

Under pressure from the Euroskeptics, supported by the farmers, Major reversed himself in September. He announced that the plan to slaughter great numbers of beef cattle would be dropped. He claimed that the latest scientific evidence showed that BSE would die out naturally in five years. Brussels was unmoved, and eventually Britain gave in.

In December 1996, Douglas Hogg, minister of agriculture, fisheries, and food, admitted that the EU would not lift the ban on British exports of beef until the culling was completed, as agreed at Florence. Beaten, the department prepared to resume culling. Eventually more than 1 million cattle were destroyed in a massive effort to eradicate the disease.

In the meantime, it was revealed that Hogg had failed to follow up on a report prepared in his own department that showed low standards of sanitation in Britain's slaughterhouses. Some questioned whether a department dedicated to the interests of producers should be the regulator of food safety. With BSE also in mind, the Vegetarian Society awarded Hogg a certificate for his contributions to their cause.

Major's handling of the "beef war" injured him in a variety of ways. It strengthened the public judgment of the Major ministry as incompetent; it deepened the fissure in his party concerning Europe; and it diminished his support among the most loyal constituency of the Conservative Party—agriculture and related industries. The ministry's meek climb-down was in striking contrast to Thatcher's forceful "hand bagging."

Inexorably, the European Union moved forward toward monetary unity. In December 1996, the Council of Ministers agreed to abandon the rigid convergence guidelines for adoption of the single currency, which included fines on countries that exceeded the limit on deficits. The French insisted such decisions should be "political" rather than economic, which made it more likely that the common currency would be established as planned.

Major, hamstrung by the Euroskeptics and his slim majority, looked on helplessly. The inability of the Major government to come to a binding decision on the single currency led to proposals to refer the issue to the people in the form of a referendum. The Euroskeptics demanded a referendum, which they were confident they would win. Sir James Goldsmith, an elderly billionaire, organized the Referendum Party to put forward candidates pledged to a referendum. Norman Lamont, seeking to return to the main stage, gave his support, and Lady Thatcher expressed sympathy with the objective. While Major resisted a referendum, claiming that the Cabinet and Parliament should make the decision, Blair promised that any decision in favor of a monetary union would be referred to the people for their approval.

An Election Approaches

By 1996, Major was locked into a political situation that gave him virtually no freedom of action. His slim majority exaggerated the influence of dissidents within his own party, especially the Euroskeptics. The growing popularity of Blair and New Labour eliminated the possibility of a snap election.

The local government elections in May 1996 were a disaster for the Conservatives: it appeared that Labour and Liberal Democrat voters had ganged up to oppose Conservative candidates. The formerly Tory press poured scorn on the Major ministry. In contrast, Blair was presented as dynamic, purposeful, fresh, and interesting.

As public support for Major faded and the Conservative Party crumbled, Blair seemed to have found the formula for success. A *Times* poll in September 1996 showed how the electoral landscape had changed in the previous two years. Labour was at 52 percent, the Tories at 29 percent, and the Liberal Democrats at 14 percent. Labour held the lead on the standard poll questions: most likely to keep promises, understanding Britain's problems, advocacy of sensible policies, concerned about people, not out of touch, and party unity. The approaching election was Blair's to lose, and he was determined not to make the mistakes that had doomed Labour in the past.

In December 1996, Major fought back with a strong television interview in which the best qualities of "Honest John" were evident: forthrightness, knowledge, and experience. He stated that he would stand by his "wait and see" policy on the single currency and would oppose further unification of the European Union. He defended the transformation of Britain that had taken place in the previous seventeen years.

In any case, the coming election would not be a referendum on Thatcherism. The Thatcher Revolution had become part of a new consensus, and the main policies of Thatcherism had been implemented. The economy had been through two recessions and a wrenching restructuring, but it had revived in a new and modern form. Thatcherism and the dragons that it had slain were no longer a party advantage to the Conservatives.

Political leaders and parties were coming to terms with a changing electorate. The growth of the middle class and the emergence of the "contented voter" meant that ideology and class-consciousness, the bases of the pre-Thatcher political parties, had decreased. Each of the two major parties could count on the support of about 30 percent of the population, and the other parties roughly 15 percent. The remaining quartile of the electorate held the balance, and the parties had to appeal to them.

These middle-class swing voters were not ideological, nor were they inclined to join political parties or engage in political action. To the extent that they maintained an interest in national and international politics, they relied on newspapers and television. They wanted capable management of the central government and the public services. They were absorbed in their careers, families, homes, communities, and recreations. They were worried about crime and "the dependency culture."

Changes in the electorate and the decline of partisanship forced political parties to find new methods of campaigning. The political parties of the past had been parties of politicians, led by members of Parliament, and supported in the constituencies by a few paid staff and a modest number of dedicated members.

In the new circumstances, parties had to mobilize a mass electorate, taking care to hold their core constituencies, but broadening their appeal to nonpolitical voters by avoiding ideological positions and controversial issues. Campaigning had been changed by television, which focused attention on the party leaders and dramatized (while simplifying) what the broadcasters (and hence, the politicians) thought were the issues of the moment.

The new generation of Labour Party leaders had perfected the art of campaigning through the mass media. Campaign headquarters was located near the news and media outlets, in a new building fully equipped with the latest means of mass communication. Tony Blair, as party leader, took center stage, focus groups were used to test reactions to proposals and slogans, constituencies and voters were targeted to achieve the maximum electoral result, and politicians, national and local, were kept "on message" by modern means of communication. In 1996, Blair brought party members into the process when he polled them on his proposed election manifesto.

New sources of funding were needed to sustain mass campaigns. The Conservatives could anticipate adequate funds. Blair was determined to end

Labour's financial dependence on the unions. Professional methods of fund-raising involved contributions from membership dues, individual donations, and fund-raising dinners for likely big contributors. The Liberal Democrats did not have enough members or money to match the two major parties and relied on their core constituencies supplemented by unhappy Conservatives.

In January 1997, Ladbrokes, the chain of betting shops that had predicted the outcome of the 1992 election, was taking bets at odds of 7–2 against a Conservative win and 1–6 in favor of Labour. A *Sunday Times* poll at the end of February showed that Labour was holding its own: Labour was at 52 percent, the Conservatives were at 31 percent, and the Liberal Democrats at 11 percent.

As Labour soared in the polls, Major seemed to be on the ropes. While the British public recognized his good qualities, the opinion grew that, try as he might, for whatever reason, things just did not go his way. It seemed that one Tory mess followed another: the ERM, negative equity, "Black Wednesday," the Maastricht debates, the tax increases of 1993, "back to basics," and "mad cow" disease. Blair displayed the killer instinct when he shredded Major's floundering ministry: "Weak, weak, weak," he cried. "Weak, weak!" He even had nice things to say about the zeal and toughness with which Thatcher had driven her agenda.

Public disdain for the Conservatives was enhanced by continuing incidents of sleaze: the chairman of the Scottish Conservative Party resigned because of an "indiscretion," believed to be a homosexual affair with an aide; another MP resigned due to alcoholism and an affair with a mother of four; another resigned when *The Sun* alleged that he had engaged in "nights of passion" with a seventeen-year-old nightclub hostess; another withdrew as a candidate after admitting that he took payments to ask questions in Parliament; two others were under pressure to step down for receiving unreported cash from a lobbyist. A distinguished retired military officer commented: "This government lives on a permanent banana skin."

With an electoral victory close at hand, Blair knew that he still had to prove the fitness of himself and the Labour Party for government. He traveled throughout Britain, meeting owners of small businesses as well as heads and directors of large corporations. He claimed to have met ten thousand business people. His main purpose was to reassure business about the intentions of New Labour. He promised again and again that the changes of the 1980s in business and labor relations would not be reversed.

Blair also realized that a Labour victory would require closing the gender gap. In 1992, the Conservatives led Labour among women by 15 percent, whereas among men the two parties were virtually even. Among women over fifty-five, only 25 percent had voted Labour. To win favor with women voters, Blair required some constituencies to choose a woman candidate, a policy that later was overruled by a court as gender discrimination. Nevertheless, until it was outlawed the policy seems to have worked. In the election Labour fielded 158 woman candidates.

Glenda Jackson, a distinguished actress with two Oscars, who was also a Labour MP, toured the country bringing Labour's message to women and young people. Labour placed ads in women's magazines, the first political party to do so. A poll of women in March 1997 showed Labour leading the Tories 52 percent to 32 percent, with the Liberal Democrats at 14 percent. Blair was also winning the youth vote. Among those between 18 and 27, Labour was at 62 percent, the Conservatives at 22 percent, and the Liberal Democrats attracted a mere 9 percent.

The Liberal Democrats were determined to maintain their own identity. They had to differ from Labour enough to keep their members from defecting and to attract disgruntled Conservatives. At the same time they wanted to keep close enough to Labour to be part of a coalition should Labour need their support in the new Parliament. Paddy Ashdown's nightmare was a Labour landslide that would make his party irrelevant.

The End of an Era

The completion of the Thatcher Revolution was evident in the large number of issues where the differences between the two major parties were minimal to nonexistent. The economic principles of Thatcherism had become conventional wisdom; the Thatcher civil service reforms, privatizations, and limitations on trade union power had been generally accepted. Blair abandoned his threat to renationalize British Rail, on the grounds that money would not be available.

The polls showed that the most important issue was job insecurity, followed by crime, health care, and education. On these, Labour overwhelmingly was regarded as the party with the best policies. Relations with Europe were rated as of secondary importance.

The Conservative campaign attempted to revive public mistrust of Labour with the slogan "New Labour, New Danger." Blair was depicted wearing a black mask with red demon eyes. Billboards proclaimed, "Britain is Booming. Don't Let Labour Blow It." On taxation, Conservative efforts to paint Labour as the high-tax party were negated by the tax increases of Norman Lamont and Kenneth Clarke. Gordon Brown promised that Labour would not increase personal income tax rates and would cut VAT on domestic fuel.

The only new tax proposed by Labour was a "windfall profits" tax on the profits of the privatized public utilities, to be dedicated to reducing youth unemployment. Much to the dismay of some in his party, Brown promised a two-year freeze on spending at the level set in Clarke's tight budget for 1997. After the Labour victory, this promise was kept, and Clarke's tax increases and spending cuts were important in the success of Brown's financial policies.

Thatcherism ended the political and economic powers of the unions. To erase memories of the past, Blair made it clear that the unions would not control a Labour government. "It's our job to govern for the entire country," he said. Blair declared that he would not seek to change the trade union legislation of the 1980s. During the summer of 1996, Blair had been upset by intermittent strikes in the Post Office and London Underground. He was determined that Labour's electoral prospects would not be destroyed by public-sector strikes, as in 1979. One union leader complained that Blair "has kicked us in the teeth."

One of Labour's strong points with the public was its support for the National Health Service. Labour had no important proposals for reform, apart from promising to reduce administrative overhead and modify Thatcher's internal market. The tight Conservative budget for the next two years included negligible increases for the NHS. But Blair's claim that Labour had founded the NHS and Labour would improve it carried conviction with the public.

Blair gave education a high profile, as the key to the modern, high-performance, world-leading Britain that he had set out to achieve. At the Labour Party conference in October 1996 he declaimed: "Ask me my three priorities for government, and I tell you—education, education, education." He declared that his main thrust would be to improve education, not by trying to squeeze schools into a single pattern but by making all schools better. Like the Conservatives, he would adopt national standards and enforce them.

Labour presented ambitious plans for constitutional change: devolution for Scotland, Wales, and the English regions if they wished it; metropolitan government for Greater London with an elected mayor; a Freedom of Information Act; incorporation of the European Declaration of Human Rights into British law; and reform of the House of Lords by eliminating the hereditary members and eventually making it a partially elected body. Blair stated that he was "not persuaded" of the need for some kind of proportional representation, but he promised to hold a referendum.

Major declared his opposition to proposals for reform of the House of Lords, electoral reform, and devolution for Scotland and Wales. He appealed for preservation of the United Kingdom as a sovereign entity within the European Union. He claimed that Labour's devolution plan would lead to the breakup of the United Kingdom, a possibility that some Scots welcomed. Constitutional reform had gained wide public acceptance. A poll conducted for *The Economist* the week before the election showed that the voters favored a bill of rights (7–1), a Scottish parliament (2–1), reform of the House of Lords and elected mayors (9–1), and reform of the voting system including proportional representation (2–1).

Electorally, devolution for Scotland was an important issue for Labour, which had to compete with the Scottish National Party. Within the Scottish Labour Party devolution was popular, not only as a reaction against Thatcherism, but because Scottish Labour was not Blairite, retaining much of the social democratic heritage of "Old Labour." Polls in Scotland showed Labour at 46 percent, the Scottish National Party at 26 percent, the Conservatives at 16 percent, and the Liberal Democrats at 10 percent. Scottish voters favored devolution (44 percent), but there was surprisingly strong support for independence within the European Union (34 percent). Only 18 percent favored the status quo.

There was no appreciable difference between the Conservatives and Labour on Northern Ireland. Blair accepted the *Downing Street Declaration*, the *Framework Document*, and the efforts of the Mitchell Commission to make headway on decommissioning weapons. The IRA participated in the election campaign in its own special way, setting off bombs both in Northern Ireland and in Britain and disrupting transportation with bomb scares, one of which forced delay of the Grand National steeplechase at Aintree. The press reported that sixty thousand people attending the race were affected. As many as five thousand people were taken into homes by local families. Major called the bombings "an insult to democracy," and Blair stated that he had "an iron determination to stand up to outrages of this kind."

Relations with the European Union, and especially the movement toward a single currency, was the great issue that Major and Blair, aware of differences within their own parties, preferred not to discuss from the hustings. Major attempted to maintain the "wait and see" policy against a rising tide of Euroskepticism. Almost 100 Tory MPs, including Sir Edward Heath, Michael Heseltine, and other former ministers, issued a statement supporting Britain's adoption of the single currency. Another 120 MPs issued a statement opposing monetary union. Polls showed that 60 percent of the voters were opposed to joining the single currency. This was the only issue where the Tories could have been in tune with the public, but they neutered it by their own internal divisions.

Blair was friendly to the European Union, an attitude welcome to many businessmen. He continued to advocate acceptance of the Social Chapter, but he promised that Labour would consult with business and the unions first. Brown pointed out important economic disparities between Britain and the continent, which would make it difficult to join the single currency within the next several years. In so doing, he laid down the principle that economic convergence would be the determining factor.

Major called the election in mid-March 1997, with voting to take place on May 1. A campaign lasting six weeks was unusually long (British election campaigns are normally four weeks), but Major hoped to find chinks in Labour's armor or exploit opportunities that might arise.

Blair's main concern was that some unforeseen controversy or unguarded remark might deprive him of the victory that seemed to be in the bag. Seeking to exploit voter uncertainty about the newness of New Labour, the Conservative slogan was "You Can Only Be Sure with the Conservatives." Labour showed its commitment to incrementalism by claiming that "Britain Can Be Better."

The newspapers were less partisan than in previous elections. *The Sun* endorsed Labour, the *Sunday Times* endorsed the Conservatives, and the *Times* made no party endorsement, urging voters to support Euroskeptics of all parties. An analysis of two thousand newspaper articles showed that the press was tilted toward Labour, which had 26 percent positive articles and 31 percent negative. Articles about the Tories were 17 percent positive and 40 percent negative.

Mainly the campaign was conducted on and for television. The candidates appeared in frequent press conferences and interviews and exposed themselves to questions from ordinary citizens on radio call-in shows. In Britain, purchase of television time for political purposes is prohibited. Instead, the parties are given free television time for political broadcasts. Prepared by advertising agencies, these slick presentations were perhaps more entertaining than the talking heads of the past, but their effectiveness was questionable.

Missing from the mix was American-style prime-ministerial debates, an idea supported by the leaders of both major parties and welcomed by the public. Major believed that he would do better than Blair in a face-to-face confrontation. When Blair raised questions about the format, the Conservatives claimed he was "chicken" and sent an actor dressed as a chicken to follow him around the country.

The main obstacle to debates was Paddy Ashdown, who insisted on equal participation for the Liberal Democrats. The television producers believed that Ashdown's presence would disrupt the cut and thrust expected from Major and Blair, and neither major party wanted to give additional attention to the Liberal Democrats. So the debates did not take place.

Both party leaders toured the country in buses while their central offices coordinated campaign rallies, press conferences, and television interviews. Other party luminaries also held rallies and press conferences, but the public showed little interest or involvement in the campaign. Election rallies, once the core of political campaigns, were poorly attended. In the constituencies, efforts of the candidates to meet the voters on the streets or on the doorstep were usually met with polite disinterest. Foreign Secretary Jeremy Rifkind was seen in a supermarket parking lot, helping shoppers load grocery bags into their cars, as a means of meeting his constituents.

The determining factor was the desire of the voters to get rid of the Tories, not enthusiasm for Labour. Voters still liked Major, but they thought he was too weak to lead his party or the government. They were willing to give Blair a chance to show what he and Labour could do. The voters had decided that it was "time for a change," and nothing the politicians or their spin doctors could do would influence that.

The election was held on Thursday, May 1. The polls closed at 10:00 P.M., and the nation was stunned at the size of the Labour landslide. Labour won 418 seats with 45 percent of the vote, which translated into an overall majority of 177 members. The Conservatives gained 31 percent of the vote and 165 seats, which reduced them to one-fourth of the House of Commons. Seven Cabinet members were not reelected, including the foreign secretary, whose helpfulness with shopping bags could not overcome the unpopularity of his party. Compared to the election of 1992, the Liberal Democrats doubled their number of seats (46), but their 17 percent of the vote was slightly lower. With the result a foregone conclusion, many people did not bother to vote. The turnout was 71 percent, an all-time low for postwar elections.

Labour made huge gains in London and the surrounding counties. The Tories won no seats in the large cities and were reduced to a party of the small towns, the suburbs, and rural England. They were wiped out in Scotland and Wales. Conservative moderates were hardest hit, leaving the party even more divided than before. The Scottish National Party won 22 percent of the vote and 6 seats. In Northern Ireland, Sinn Fein drew 16 percent of the vote and Gerry Adams and Martin McGuiness were elected. Betty Boothroyd, the Speaker, denied them access to the House of Commons because they refused to take the usual oath.

On Friday morning, Major went to Buckingham Palace and resigned as prime minister. Earlier he had announced his resignation as leader of the Conservative Party. Perhaps recalling that his parents were entertainers, he remarked: "When the curtain falls it is time to get off the stage."

Later that day Blair met with the queen and was authorized to form a government. At forty-three, he became the youngest prime minister since Lord Liverpool in 1812. Announcements of the principal Cabinet officers followed quickly, and other appointments were made over the weekend. By Monday morning the Blair ministry was in business.

Unlike American elections, there was no elaborate inauguration. On election night, as the results came in, Labour Party workers held an ecstatic rally at the Royal Festival Hall. The next morning, an enthusiastic crowd of supporters and tourists gathered at Downing Street to greet Tony Blair and his wife, Cherie, as they entered No. 10. That was it!

The Labour victory in the election was anticipated, but it was astonishing in its completeness. Like the election of 1906, which ushered in "the New Liberalism," the Labour landslide in 1945, and the triumph of Thatcher and the Conservatives in 1979, the election of 1997 utterly changed the political landscape.

An important source of Labour and Liberal Democratic gains was their strength in local government. Most local councillors are elected on the basis of their affiliation with the national parties, but it is still important for them to win the approval and support of the local voters. In the previous few years, the Conservatives had been virtually shut out of local government offices. As the Labour and Liberal parties gained strength and experience in local government, they developed a pool of attractive candidates for Parliament. Of 181 new MPs (most of them Labour or Liberal Democrat), 120 had been councillors.

Labour's landslide brought important changes to the social makeup of the House of Commons. Labour elected 102 women ("Blair's Babes," the tabloid press called them) out of 158 candidates. One of them was twenty-four. The average age of the new Labour MPs was forty-three, the same age as their leader. They were public-sector employees, local officials, union workers (17), lawyers (29), social workers (21), teachers (54), lecturers in higher education (35), journalists, one was a firefighter, and one was a taxi driver. Eight of them were under thirty. There were five Asians and four blacks.

Tactical voting contributed to the outcome. There was a widespread desire to get rid of the Tory government. In constituencies where a close vote was expected, voters marked their ballots for the candidate most likely to defeat the Conservative. The Conservatives lost heavily in marginal seats, sometimes to Labour, sometimes to the Liberal Democrats. The resurgence of Paddy Ashdown and the Liberal Democrats was primarily attributable to tactical voting, but not entirely. Some Conservatives, who could not bring themselves to vote for Labour, saw the Liberal Democrats as an acceptable alternative.

Blair's claim that Labour had become the "one nation" party was con-firmed. Labour's support among men and women was approximately equal. The Conservatives held their support among voters over sixty-five, but Labour's vote among young people was up 57 percent over 1992. White-collar workers defected from the Tories in large numbers, giving 47 percent of their votes to Labour, compared to 28 percent in 1992.

Without minimizing the contributions of Neil Kinnock and John Smith, the Labour sweep was primarily due to the leadership, personal attractive-ness, energy, and realism of Blair. His determination to build a new Labour Party was vindicated by the election, although his claim that he had done so while preserving the values of the old was suspect. Blair made Labour elec-table by accepting the changes brought into British government by Margaret Thatcher and John Major. His victory rested on his promise to bring compe-tence, moderation, and concern for ordinary people to the challenges of the post-Thatcher era.

Looking to the future, the Conservatives were down but by no means could they be counted out. Although they gained only 25 percent of the seats, they received 31 percent of the votes. In 1992, with a larger turnout, Major had received more votes (14 million) than Blair received in 1997 (13.5 million). Many of the Tory voters of 1992 were presumably among those who stayed home in 1997. With strong leadership and a clear message, the Conservative Party could revive, especially if the Blair government made serious mistakes or Labour became divided along the fault line of "Old" ver-sus "New."

The election was not a repudiation of Thatcherism, for Labour and the public had accepted the Thatcher Revolution. Nor was it a repudiation of Major personally. The British people continued to like and respect him. But they felt that he had failed to give his party the strong leadership that they expect in a prime minister. The electorate repudiated the Conservative Party, and Major had to accept some responsibility for a party that had dis-integrated on his watch.

As the extent of Labour's victory became clear, there was a sense of relief that the election campaign was over. The Sun took a sentimental view of the Labour victory with a front page that showed Cherie Blair kissing her hus-band and the headline: "SEALED WITH A X."

CHAPTER NINE

~

Tony Blair: Getting Going, 1997–1998

Political Parties and Leaders

Tony Blair and "New Labour" came into power in May 1997 with an over-whelming majority in Parliament and a mandate from the country to carry out the ambitious agenda of reform stated in their election manifesto. After eighteen years in opposition, the British Labour Party, transformed by Blair, would have a chance to show that it could govern and "make Britain better."

Blair was an enthusiast, with grandiose aspirations and the eloquence to communicate them. His goal was to "modernize" Britain: develop a flexible and technologically advanced economy that would be competitive in the global marketplace, manage fiscal and monetary policy to achieve long-term economic growth with low inflation, fight chronic unemployment by strengthening the work ethic and by providing training in marketable skills, create an efficient and up-to-date welfare state with positive incentives to-ward personal responsibility ("compassion with a hard edge"), reform the constitution of the United Kingdom to bring government closer to the peo-ple, and identify roles for Britain in Europe and the world. With the excep-tion of his willingness to accept constitutional change, his agenda could be described as Thatcherism with a smiling face.

Blair wished to project an image of Britain as a young, dynamic, entrepre-neurial country with a vibrant, creative spirit: an international "hub" of fi-nance, communications, transportation, and travel; a modern, stylish center of advanced ideas in science, design, entertainment, and the arts; and a di-verse nation known for tolerance and fair play. He wanted to get rid of

Britain's reputation as a fuddy-duddy country in decline. "It is time to show the world that we are not only a country with a glorious past," he exclaimed, "we are a country with a glorious future."

Blair was an advocate of the millennium celebrations, especially the vast Millennium Dome that was already rising on deserted industrial land in Greenwich. He saw the millennium celebration as the opportunity to showcase "new Britain." He was confident that British talent would create attractions to put in the Dome that were original, educational, and fun for everyone. A new Underground station was being built to serve the area. Millennium celebrations and projects were also being planned for other parts of the United Kingdom, funded by money from the lottery.

The new prime minister was widely perceived as a leader who knew what he wanted to accomplish and who would act vigorously to achieve his goals. "What we have promised to do, we will do," he repeatedly declared. He was recognized as honest, even prim, in his personal and political life. After the election his popularity, as reflected in the polls, rose to the highest ever recorded for a prime minister, and these high numbers continued throughout his first two years. The British public was convinced that Blair's heart was in the right place, and that he would do nothing drastic or threatening.

As prime minister, Blair continued the campaign practice of keeping public attention on the leader. He was criticized for his "presidential style." He was highly visible on television and took frequent trips abroad, which also attracted media attention. He rarely appeared in the House of Commons, apart from the obligatory "Prime Minister's Questions" on Wednesday afternoons. His brilliant wife, Cherie, continued her high-profile career in the law.

After eighteen years in the wilderness, the Blair government was the most inexperienced of the twentieth century. The last Labour prime minister, James Callaghan, was now in the House of Lords, where his daughter, Baroness Jay of Paddington, became leader of the Labour contingent and joined the Cabinet as minister for women. The Cabinet was chosen from figures who had been active in the rise of New Labour. It contained five women, the highest number ever. Gordon Brown became chancellor of the Exchequer and responsible for fiscal and economic policy. Robin Cook, a hard-hitting political street fighter, was named secretary of state for foreign and commonwealth affairs. Jack Straw, known for his stern approach to crime and social disorder, became secretary of state for the home department. Genial John Prescott, Blair's closest link with "Old Labour" and the unions, was made deputy prime minister and secretary of state for the reconstituted and unwieldy Department of the Environment, Transport and the Regions. As deputy prime minister, Prescott occasionally substituted for Blair at question time, where his awkward rhetoric generated amusement on both sides of the aisle. Blair's closest political adviser was Peter Mandelson, minister without portfolio, who had been a major figure in the development of New Labour, and had managed the campaign.

The Conservative Party conducted a leadership struggle that displayed all the pettiness, careerism, and lack of principle that had contributed to their defeat. John Major was reelected as member for Huntingdon, but he was discredited by the electoral debacle. Michael Heseltine removed himself from consideration due to ill health. Kenneth Clarke was the most experienced candidate and popular among the rank and file, but his pro-European views made him unacceptable to the Euroskeptics. Clarke led on the first ballot, but he did not have the required majority plus 15 percent. William Hague, a thirty-six-year-old Yorkshireman with minimal experience and John Redwood, a principled Thatcherite and Euroskeptic, shared most of the remaining votes. Hague was thought to have the broad acceptability and administrative skills needed to reorganize the Conservative Party and calm its dissensions, while Clarke and Redwood represented distinct wings. A cry of disgust arose when Clarke and Redwood, despite their differences on Europe and other issues, joined to stop Hague.

With the support of Margaret Thatcher, Hague was chosen party leader by the Conservative MPs, a choice confirmed by a ballot of the party membership. He had to rebuild his party from an incredibly low base. In local government, the foundation of any political party, the Conservatives had become the third party. Hague began with a comprehensive reform of party organization, including stronger central control of political campaigns and democratization of the local constituency organizations.

He found it difficult to define a distinctive constituency for the Conservative Party. He could hope to restore Thatcher's support in the professional and white-collar workers of the suburbs, lost in 1997 to the youth and "lifestyle" politics of Blair. Many elderly people still felt loyalty to the Conservative Party; they did not welcome Blair's emphasis on "cool Britannia." In the election, women had given strong support to Labour, and Hague took steps to increase the number of women candidates for Parliament and local offices.

Rural and small-town England was unhappy with the urban focus of Labour, and agriculture was depressed. When a massive "Countryside March" took place in London in February 1998, Hague and other Conservative leaders were prominent participants. It looked possible to revive the former base of the Conservative Party in the suburbs, the small towns, and the villages of England. Scotland and Wales had to be written off.

Hague also had to develop distinctive Tory policies. In adopting Thatcherism, Blair had deprived the Tories of the issues by which they had been defined for eighteen years. In the process, Blair had also defined Labour as the "one nation" party, an image that the Conservative Party had lost under Thatcher. Traditionally, the Conservative Party had been the unionist party, but that position had been shaken by parliamentary and public support for Blair's proposals for constitutional change. Hague had no choice but to accept devolution for Scotland and Wales.

The one clear-cut issue that remained for the Conservative Party was relations with the European Union, and especially British acceptance of the single currency. Preservation of the pound sterling and keeping Brussels at arm's length were themes that resonated with the public and could lead to a revival of the Conservatives as the "patriotic" party. In October 1998, a ballot of party members showed 84 percent were opposed to adopting the euro. Hague announced that in the next election the Conservatives would oppose joining the single currency and would establish strict criteria for British membership after that. "In Europe, not run by Europe" became his slogan.

In many ways, Blair's ideas harked back to the Liberal Party of Gladstone and Asquith, updated to meet late-twentieth-century needs and expectations. As such, New Labour had much in common with the Liberal Democrats. They were both nonsocialist parties of the left devoted to free enterprise within a market economy, fiscal responsibility, and an inclusive welfare state with a wide range of public services. The main differences were the Liberal Democrats' insistence on proportional representation in elections to the House of Commons and adoption of the single European currency.

Labour's landslide left Paddy Ashdown and the Liberal Democratic Party in an anomalous position. Although the party had gained seats, Labour's overwhelming majority in the House of Commons deprived them of any leverage. Blair and Ashdown were personal friends and held similar views on many issues. There was reason to think that Blair's long-term objective was to absorb the Liberal Democrats into a broad party of the moderate left. As a step in that direction, Blair created a Cabinet committee that gave some Liberal Democrats an opportunity to share their views on issues of the day.

Many Liberal Democrats viewed this process with suspicion. They wished to retain the distinctive characteristics of their party. At a party conference in March 1998, party activists were firm in opposing any kind of coalition with Labour. Their concerns arose out of local politics, where the Liberal Democrats had most of their strength. In 1999, Ashdown resigned as leader. Since proportional representation seemed to be delayed indefinitely, he realized that the future of the Liberal Democrats as a national force was dim.

The first hitch in Blair's honeymoon came in November 1997, with a Clintonesque fund-raising scandal that damaged his image as Mr. Kleen. In his campaign Blair had given much attention to reassuring business that New Labour was not a threat. He had solicited contributions from businessmen to decrease his dependence on the unions for funds. Not all of these businessmen, it turned out, were starched-shirt officers of prestigious corporations. One was Bernie Ecclestone, an entertainment entrepreneur, who had made Formula One the dominant force in car racing. Formula One needed television, and television needed tobacco advertisements to make Formula One telecasts profitable.

But Labour had promised to remove tobacco advertisements from British television, and had supported a similar movement throughout the European Union. Suddenly the government announced that Britain would seek an exemption from the ban on tobacco advertisements in Formula One telecasts. There were too many jobs at stake, it was said, for Britain was the world leader in the design and manufacture of high-speed racing cars. Furthermore, the people who watched Formula One on television were more likely to smoke than viewers of other sports, and banning tobacco advertisements would not change that.

Then it was revealed that Ecclestone had given the Labour Party £1 million during the campaign and was offering another million. Blair, who had left many of the details of the campaign to Mandelson, was shocked at the appearance of corrupt influence, and so was the general public. The antitobacco enthusiasts, who thought they had won their battle, were appalled. The Conservatives were delighted to put the sleaze label on the other guys for a change.

Eventually a compromise was arranged with the European Union to phase out tobacco advertisements gradually, but the Blair ministry had been momentarily embarrassed. Blair appeared on television to apologize, and the Labour Party stated that it would return the donation. Another controversy arose when it was revealed that Geoffrey Robinson, a wealthy entrepreneur and generous contributor, maintained an offshore trust to avoid taxes while holding an office in the Treasury.

Some columnists and commentators complained that Labour ministers seemed too fond of their limousines, grace-and-favor flats, and other perks of office. Lord Irvine, the tactless lord chancellor (and legal mentor of Tony and Cherie Blair), spent £650,000 redecorating his office, including £65,000 for wallpaper, which he justified as historical restoration. Some thought he had gone too far when he commandeered over one hundred works of art from various national collections for his office, but he explained that these works would also be open to viewing by the public. The last straw was to cover large chunks of his expensive wallpaper with six 9-foot mirrors in the style of Pugin.

Once in office, Blair and Mandelson continued the political practices learned from Bill Clinton. "The permanent campaign" meant presenting policies and personalities in a way that would continue to hold the support and interest of the electorate. Focus groups were used to make soundings of the public mood in general and obtain reactions to specific proposals.

Another American import was the "spin doctor." In the campaign, Blair and Mandelson had emphasized management of the media and keeping everyone "on message." Labour MPs, many of whom had no previous parliamentary experience, were equipped with pagers that informed them of the current party line on upcoming matters in the House of Commons. Betty Boothroyd, Speaker of the House of Commons, complained that important policy statements were leaked to the press, with the government's spin before being presented to Parliament. No previous government had ever shown such skill and persistence in creating the public image it wanted. Blair was charged with being a control freak.

The most sensational scandal involved the master spin doctor himself, Peter Mandelson, recently named secretary of state for trade and industry. A newspaper revealed that in 1996 Geoffrey Robinson had given Mandelson a loan of £373,000 to enable him to purchase an expensive house in London. This cozy relationship appeared to be a crass attempt to purchase political influence. Mandelson did not report the loan when he joined the Cabinet in 1997. His responses to journalists were evasive. As the outcry rose higher, Blair referred to the episode as a "misjudgment," but Mandelson resigned anyway, much to the satisfaction of the Tories, whose sleaze had become a campaign issue. Robinson resigned shortly thereafter. Gordon Brown's press secretary, who was accused of leaking the information, also resigned.

The Constitution of the United Kingdom

During the election campaign, reform of the government of the United Kingdom, stimulated by eighteen years of Conservative rule, had become an issue, and Blair had been swept along by the tide. From its inception, the Labour Party had resented the hereditary privilege embodied in the House of Lords, and in 1999, an attempt was made to reform it. The role of the Lords in scrutinizing legislation was generally agreed to be useful, but its power to delay a bill for one year was challenged by many Labour MPs. Labour was determined to remove the voting rights of the hereditary peers, who were 790 out of 1,295 members. The rest were approximately 600 life peers, appointed by various governments, 26 archbishops and bishops of the Church of England, and 12 law lords, judges in the courts. Although few of the hereditary peers attended with any regularity, they were overwhelmingly Conservative.

The sticking point was finding an alternative. Introducing elected members would strengthen the House, an outcome that political leaders did not want. Relying on life peers appointed by ministries would leave the Lords a body of has-beens and politically connected dignitaries. In short, there was no agreement as to the shape of the new House of Lords. Blair decided that the best way to get the issue off his back was to make an interim settlement and refer plans for a permanent resolution to a commission.

Viscount Cranborne, the Tory leader in the Lords, seized the opportunity to strike a deal that would save some of the hereditary peers. He took matters into his own hands and negotiated a temporary settlement that left 75 hereditary peers plus the holders of 17 offices of dignity, making a total of 92. In the next several years, additional creations of life peers by Blair redressed the party balance in the Lords somewhat, but the House continued to reject legislation that ran counter to the views of its Conservative and aristocratic majority.

The movement for constitutional reform included widespread dissatisfaction with the House of Commons, especially its subservience to a prime minister with a strong majority. The most obvious reform, to reduce the size of the House from its unwieldy 659 members was objectionable to politicians, for obvious reasons. Another proposal, development of a strong committee system, would create a threat to ministers and their departments. The Treasury was determined to maintain control of finance. The resources of secretarial help, office space, and research assistance provided to MPs were well below accepted standards in other countries, but the additional cost could be absorbed only by reducing the number of members, which brought the debate back to square one.

Most proposals for reform of the House of Commons concerned the electoral system, which exaggerated the number of seats won by the party with the largest popular vote. Margaret Thatcher's parliamentary dictatorship, with never more than 44 percent of the electoral vote, had revived proposals for proportional representation. Blair, anticipating a Labour majority for ten years under the old system, was understandably reluctant to embrace any proposed change.

As a concession to the Liberal Democrats, he appointed a commission to recommend a "broadly proportional" alternative to the existing electoral system, with a referendum on the issue to come in the year 2000. When the commission reported, its recommendations were everything that the Liberal Democrats could have desired, but Blair's friendship with Paddy Ashdown did not extend that far. The report fell victim to more pressing matters.

A constitutional step of potentially great importance was the Human Rights Act (2000), which incorporated the European Convention on Human Rights into British law and made those rights enforceable in British courts. The Convention, which had been drawn up after World War II, was already law in the European Union, but Britons had to go to the European Court in Strasbourg and engage in an expensive process to claim their rights. Blair argued that the Human Rights Act was a mere convenience, but it was more than that, for it made the Convention a practicable option for litigants in the United Kingdom.

The Human Rights Act provided legal recourse in British courts for individuals who claimed that their rights had been violated by a "public authority," a term subject to a wide range of interpretation. The act protected fundamental rights such as life, liberty, expression, assembly, and conscience, and prohibited arbitrary and unreasonable treatment of individuals by the state or its agents, including the right to a fair trial.

The sovereignty of Parliament was preserved in the provision that judicial interpretations of the act could not override any existing or future act of Parliament. Where the Human Rights Act conflicted with British law, the court could issue a "declaration of incompatibility," and submit the matter to Parliament for adjustment.

Fears were expressed that the British judges would expand vague human rights into new areas of law that had previously not been subject to their jurisdiction. The Convention had gone into effect in Scotland with devolution, and had already generated controversy. Cherie Blair, a specialist in employment law and women's rights, doubtless saw the potential of the act for her clients.

Blair fulfilled his promise to provide municipal government for the sprawling megalopolis called London, with its runaway growth, enormous public services, and vast problems of congestion, poverty, crime, pollution, and decay. Early in 1998, the government came forward with proposals for a Greater London Authority (GLA) with a popularly elected mayor and an Assembly of twenty-five members elected by proportional representation. The proposal was approved by London voters in a low turnout.

The powers of the GLA are less than one might expect, and the powers of the mayor are by no means comparable to the mayors of Paris, New York, or Chicago. The mayor's main responsibility is to coordinate the public services, including the environment, traffic and public transport, health, culture, sports, and economic development. The mayor has considerable authority over Transport for London, fire protection, and the Metropolitan Police Authority. Most of the government of London is conducted by the thirty-three boroughs, which have responsibility for education, street cleaning, trash collection, and many other essential services. For public relations purposes, the Lord Mayor of London, the centuries-old leader of the City, continued to represent the financial community.

The Assembly does not have taxing authority, receiving its £3.3 billion budget from Treasury grants and a share of the boroughs' council tax. It can amend the budget, but a two-thirds majority is required. Its powers are mainly consultative. The most divisive issue was finding capital to rebuild the Underground: the Blair government favored partial privatization, but most Londoners wanted to keep it under public ownership and management.

An important part of Blair's program to "bring government closer to the people" was to strengthen local government, weakened over many years by the growing role of central authority and brought to its knees by Thatcher. Blair charged "there are just too many councils failing to deliver acceptable standards of service to their citizens." He was taking a short-term political risk, because it was obvious that many of the worst local governments were one-party rotten boroughs controlled by "Old Labour."

Blair faced the same dilemma as Thatcher: the only way to improve local government was through the use of central authority. His proposed reforms in employment, social services, and education required effective local governments to implement them. In 1998, John Prescott, deputy prime minister, presented proposals for extensive reform of local government by an injection of democracy: direct election of mayors, local initiatives and referenda, and supervision of expenditures by regional boards empowered to weed out corruption in appointments and contracts. These proposals were implemented, in part, in the Local Government Act of 2000.

Devolution

The election made it evident that devolution for Scotland should take place promptly, although its consequences for the United Kingdom were murky and its advantages for Scotland were questionable. Scotland already had considerable independence, with a mini-capital in Edinburgh under the secretary of state for Scotland, and separate electoral, administrative, educational, and legal institutions. A generous funding formula introduced by Labour in the 1970s gave Scotland 22 percent more per person than England, an arrangement that led some English critics to complain that Scotland wanted to have its cake and eat it too.

Economically and otherwise, Scotland was experiencing renewed confidence. New industries such as electronics were replacing the heavy industries of the past. Nevertheless, the grievances created during the Thatcher–Major years still rankled. While eastern Scotland thrived with brainpower industries, the Highlands and the old industrial centers of western Scotland were among the most impoverished areas in Europe. Furthermore, the Scottish Labour Party was unhappy with Blair's "Thatcherite" approach to the public services.

Donald Dewar, secretary of state for Scotland, assumed responsibility for the Devolution Bill and its passage through Parliament, which took place in 1998. The referendum passed overwhelmingly (74 percent "Yes"), and 64 percent approved giving the devolved government limited power to tax. The act established a Scottish Parliament of 129 members, with each voter having two votes: one for a named constituency member, and one for a party list. The Scottish Executive was based on a majority in the Parliament.

In the election, which took place in May 1999, the Scottish Labour Party gained the largest number of seats, but lacked a majority. Labour formed a coalition with the Liberal Democrats, and Dewar was chosen to lead the Executive. The Scottish National Party, which had accepted devolution as a step toward independence, did well, weakening the argument that devolution would reduce its appeal. The decision was made to construct a new building for the Parliament, and an architect was hired to draw up plans, which proved to be controversial architecturally and enormously expensive.

The Parliament controls the budget, although most of the funding for Scotland, as in the past, comes from London. The Parliament has extensive powers to deal with local government, economic development, transportation, health, education, law, police, and other domestic concerns. The United Kingdom remains responsible for foreign affairs, enforcement of treaties and European Union regulations, money and monetary policy, defense, employment legislation, and social security.

The dependence of Labour on the Liberal Democrats enabled that party to punch above its weight. Shortly after taking office, the Blair government required university students throughout the United Kingdom to pay tuition fees for higher education if they could afford them. This policy created resentment in Scotland, which was proud of its educational system that was free at all levels.

During the campaign, the Liberal Democrats had promised to restore free university education, a policy that many in the Labour Party regarded as a handout to the middle class. The coalition with Labour led to a compromise: the government paid the fees as a loan, to be repaid by the students through the income tax after graduation. The Liberal Democrats also got their way on provision of free personal care for infirm elderly people.

The Welsh referendum passed by a narrow margin in a low turnout and with little popular enthusiasm. The industrial areas of Wales were closely tied to England, and the main support for devolution came from Welsh-speaking rural areas. The implementing legislation established an Assembly of sixty members that assumed responsibility for the powers formerly exercised by the secretary of state for Wales. The Assembly has no taxing powers, receiving its funding in a grant from the national government. Its legislative powers are limited to the level of administrative regulations. There is no Welsh Executive, as in Scotland. The secretary of state for Wales continues to exercise administrative responsibilities from his office in Cardiff.

The establishment of distinct governments for Scotland and Wales led to proposals for further devolutions. In northern England, which had many of the same needs as Scotland, people argued that they should have devolution too, or at least public funding equal to that given to Scotland and Wales.

Building on the regional offices established by John Major, the Blair government established eight Regional Development Agencies (RDAs) for England. These were partnership organizations to promote economic development and competitiveness. They included people from local government, business, trade unions, and educational and cultural organizations. The RDAs could be seen as a stage toward devolved regional governments, with an executive, an elected assembly, and possibly powers to tax.

In the Northeast, a group calling themselves the Constitutional Convention, chaired by the Bishop of Durham, called for devolution to that region. A similar group appeared in Cornwall, which had many of the same problems as Wales. Blair was reluctant to see further unraveling of the United Kingdom, but Deputy Prime Minister John Prescott embraced the idea enthusiastically. He began planning for regional devolution in a second Blair ministry.

The Public Finances

The most pressing challenge facing the Blair ministry was to establish fiscal and monetary policies that would convince British businessmen and the global money markets that Labour would be fiscally responsible. Once in office, Blair confirmed his election promise: no increase in the income tax and adherence for the first two years to the spending limits imposed by the previous Conservative government. The Conservative increase of VAT on fuel, an emotional campaign issue, would be repealed.

Blair's fiscal conservatism was bad news for many important Labour constituencies. Public-sector employees—civil servants, teachers, nurses, and others—would have to wait for long overdue raises. Many Labour MPs were committed to improving and expanding the services of the welfare state. Blair assured them that prudent budgets would eventually pay off in economic growth and make possible the improvements that they wanted. Additional spending for health and education, Blair's immediate priorities, would have to be obtained by squeezing money out of other programs.

Management of the finances was entrusted to the chancellor of the Exchequer, Gordon Brown, whose fiscal policies followed the trail blazed by Thatcher. His long-term goal was to achieve steady economic growth without inflation, and to do that it was necessary to balance the budget and keep interest rates low. His close relations with Blair and his own abilities made him an economic czar, shaping the government's economic policies through his control of the public purse and exerting a powerful influence over all departments of government.

Brown had an immediate surprise up his sleeve. He moved quickly to implement a policy that had been discussed for some time: giving the Bank of England control over short-term interest rates on the model of the Federal Reserve Board in the United States. Under the new system, the chancellor the Exchequer would establish an inflation target (set at 2.5 percent maximum), and the Bank would manage interest rates and the money supply to achieve it. A committee, appointed by the chancellor, would supervise and report on the Bank's performance. The chancellor retained a reserve power to intervene, if necessary.

This change was intended to take monetary policy out of politics and to convince financial markets that Labour stood for sound money. Monetarism had triumphed. Brown also announced formation of a Financial Services Agency that would supervise banks and other financial institutions.

Adoption of Kenneth Clarke's spending plan for the first two years of the Blair ministry reassured the markets that Labour was no longer a "tax and spend" party, but it created a straitjacket that limited the pace at which Labour could pursue its other goals. In the campaign Labour had promised no tax increases, but Brown cheated a bit by finding a few sources of additional revenue ("stealth taxes"): a windfall profits tax on some privatized utilities, making dividends received by pension funds taxable, and raising the motor fuel tax. The windfall profits tax was earmarked to fund the new welfare-to-work program. In a pre-budget report in July 1997, Brown included extra money for health and education, but not for welfare reform, then floundering in the House of Commons.

Brown's big day came on March 17, 1998, when he presented his budget for the next three years. After a variety of leaks and conjectures had promised an attack on middle-class privileges and benefits, the budget revealed a kinder, gentler Gordon Brown, who carefully avoided alienating the wide spectrum of voters that had supported Labour in the 1997 election. The income tax base rate (23 percent) was unchanged, and taxes on cigarettes, petrol, and beer were raised.

Brown resisted the temptation to introduce flashy new spending programs, which disappointed many of the Labour faithful, who had waited eighteen years to enter the Promised Land. He conducted a careful review of the needs and expenditures of the various departments and agencies of the government.

In July 1998, he presented a spending plan for the next three years that proposed increased expenditure on health, education, public transport, and welfare benefits. New initiatives were announced for preschool child care and to combat drugs. Borrowing was down, and a modest surplus was predicted for the year 2000. Brown planned to accumulate a war chest to be prepared for contingencies; the Tories claimed it was to engage in a spending spree as the next election approached.

The Economy

The British economy was doing well, strengthened by the booming world economy, where Britain was a center of investment and financial services. There was reason to think that the changes in productivity and labor-force flexibility introduced by Thatcherism were having an effect. The principal problems were the consequences of success: a high pound that penalized exports, and a boom in house prices and consumer spending that threatened a return to inflation. The global recession of 2000–2001 took some of the steam out of the boom, but the economy weathered the storm reasonably well. The era of crises and devaluations, which had plagued Britain for half a century, had passed. After twenty years of Thatcherism, with its ups and downs, the British economy had finally achieved stable prosperity.

More than ever before, the economy was dominated by knowledge-based industries: financial and business services, pharmaceuticals, computer software, publishing, television, radio, and music. Manufacturing continued its long decline, although it was still an important part of the British economy. Retailing, travel, and tourism were important contributors.

Three-quarters of the labor force was in service industries. The number of women employees was virtually equal to the men. Workers in service industries are usually not receptive to trade unions, and union membership continued to fall. The British economy, once tormented by strikes, was now virtually strike-free, except for brief stoppages to make a point.

Unemployment and Welfare

Blair's major project was to reform the welfare state, which he presented as a moral crusade: offering people encouragement and opportunities to take responsibility for their own lives. Like Thatcher, he believed that the benefits system contributed to unemployment by reducing the motivation to work. He was determined to attack the "poverty trap" by combining inducements with discipline. His proposals ran counter to the deepest instincts of the Labour Party, which had not come to power to crack the whip over the poor.

In January 1998, unemployment was at 5 percent (1,400,000), the lowest for eighteen years. Nevertheless, there were pockets of long-term unemployment that showed no signs of improvement. Many young people had never been employed and showed no signs of getting jobs. They lacked the skills needed to fill the jobs available, and industrial demoralization had weakened the work ethic. Blair's own constituency, Sedgefield, was a decayed mining area where he had seen this problem firsthand. Blair was committed to a "welfare to work" policy, with special attention to youth unemployment.

He proposed a program that he called his "New Deal," which was a variant of Major's "Job-Seeker's Allowance." The program was funded by the windfall profits tax on the privatized utilities. The program required young people aged eighteen to twenty-four who were receiving unemployment benefits to enter into jobs, full-time education or training, or public service activities. If they refused to participate, they would lose their benefits. The pay would exceed the benefits received on the dole, and employers would be subsidized to provide jobs.

When the program was introduced, it was found that real jobs in areas of high youth unemployment were in short supply. Many of the participants (especially young men) entered the program reluctantly or were unlikely to develop the skills that were needed to obtain employment. Actors and musicians, who were often unemployed ("resting"), customarily lived on the dole between engagements. They complained bitterly about the requirement that they take a job or enter a training program. At the end of the year, the government claimed that fifty-two thousand graduates of the program had found jobs. Some participants regarded their training as just another way to keep the money flowing a while longer.

The centerpiece of Blair's agenda was welfare reform, but that would cost money, and Labour had locked itself into the Tory spending plan for the first two years. Blair's objective was to replace benefits with opportunities and to discourage welfare dependency by removing disincentives to work. One of the problems of welfare reform was that so many people benefited from the welfare state. The poorest 20 percent of the population received 30 percent of all social security spending, and the wealthiest 40 percent got almost as much (25 percent). Many of the programs were beneficial to the middle class, newly to support the Labour Party.

Proposals were floated that Child Benefit and Maternity Benefit should be taxed or based on need only. The large number of women MPs in the Labour majority meant that close scrutiny was given to proposals that affected women. Maternity Benefit made it easier for women to take time off from their jobs to have a child, and Child Benefit helped the career woman pay for child care. Labour's women MPs did not want to see women pay the price for welfare reform. They argued that deprival of these benefits might affect employment opportunities for women.

The fastest growing group of welfare dependents was single mothers, who received a somewhat higher Child Benefit than married mothers, on the grounds that they had greater need. More than 20 percent of British children lived in one-parent homes, some with a divorced parent but many of them with mothers who had never been married. Controversy erupted when a proposal was made to end the extra benefit for single mothers, which was seen as a disincentive to marriage. The result was the first open rebellion against the Blair government, as forty-seven Labour MPs voted against the proposal and another thirty-nine did not vote. The dispute was resolved the next year when Brown found the money to raise Child Benefit for all mothers.

A larger problem was the benefits paid to people who were unable to work because of disability (Incapacity Benefit). It was believed that there were many cases where fraud or administrative laxity had led to awards that were excessive or unjustified. Under the Conservatives, some of the unemployed were classified as disabled to keep down the number of people recorded as unemployed. Considerable anxiety was aroused when the Department of Social Security began making extensive reviews of recipients of Incapacity Benefit. The pensions minister justified this step by saying: "We know that perhaps £500 million a year may be going to people who don't have a legal entitlement to it."

A proposal to tighten requirements and flush out recipients who were capable of working incurred great resentment on the Labour back benches and in the House of Lords. Powerful protests came from organizations representing the

disabled, and pathetic television pictures of their clients became a public relations disaster for the government. In any case, the Orwellian "benefit integrity
inspectors" uncovered few cases of false claims.

After these unsightly wrangles, leadership in welfare reform passed to
Brown and the Treasury. Brown's approach to the welfare trap was to make
certain that "work always pays." One step was to restore the national minimum wage. To encourage people to get off the dole, the budget included a
Working Families Tax Credit, a subsidy intended to encourage parents to
take low-paid jobs by bringing their income up to a decent level.

Increases in Child Credit and a tax credit for child care were intended to
enable mothers to take jobs. These increases made no distinction between
married and unmarried mothers. It was discovered that many poor people
were unable to understand or claim these tax-based benefits or simply did not
respond to their supposed incentives. Useful as they were, Brown's measures
still left 14 million people in acute poverty.

Northern Ireland

During the campaign, Blair had promised to continue the efforts of Major to
bring the contending parties in Northern Ireland to an agreement that would
make possible a return to Home Rule. Former United States Senator John
Mitchell continued as principal negotiator. Blair faced difficulties in getting
the Ulster Unionists to sit down with Sinn Fein, but he gave them some satisfaction when he confirmed Major's promise that no changes would be made
in Northern Ireland without the consent of the people in a referendum. The
Republic of Ireland continued to offer positive support to the peace process.
Blair's friendly relations with Clinton meant that the American president
put his influence behind the British effort.

The goal of the Blair government was to bring all parties to the table to
negotiate a political settlement. The main sticking point was the requirement that the parties abandon violence and pursue their goals by democratic means. In July 1997, Sinn Fein agreed to these terms and reentered
the peace talks, although the militants of the IRA refused to surrender
their weapons. Unionists were not satisfied with the cease-fire and insisted
that the IRA give up its arsenals ("decommissioning") before talks could
begin.

In September 1997, David Trimble, leader of the Ulster Unionists, courageously decided to continue participation in the talks without decommissioning, despite severe criticism from his own party. He agreed to refer the
question of weapons to an independent commission.

Negotiations began in October and, as usual in Northern Ireland politics, were filled with bitterness and mistrust, punctuated by violence. In the meantime, ordinary people were working together in business, industry, and local government. It was evident that they were ready for peace. Whatever solution might be reached in the political discussions, strong police work would be necessary to control the violent men, some of them members of criminal gangs, who had made terrorism a way of life.

In April 1998, intensive talks between Blair and Bertie Ahern, prime minister of Ireland, produced a plan that eventually became the basis of a settlement. The contending parties gave their consent later that month, on Good Friday, which gave its name to the agreement. The Republic of Ireland agreed to give up its claim to Northern Ireland (a paper claim that would never be exercised anyway), but a bitter pill for Sinn Fein and the IRA. The Protestants received a promise that they could never be joined to the Republic without a referendum (a promise that had been made many times before).

The main feature of the plan was a devolved government with an Assembly of 108 members elected by proportional representation. The Assembly was not given tax-raising powers, and the government would continue to receive its funds from London. It could legislate on a variety of domestic matters. The government would be conducted by an Executive of twelve members chosen by the Assembly and led by a prime minister and a deputy prime minister. Proportional representation virtually guaranteed that power sharing would extend to the Executive and would require unionists and nationalists to work together.

Two coordinating councils were proposed that were expected to cushion the deep-seated antagonisms of the unionists and nationalists. A North–South Council would coordinate affairs between Northern Ireland and the Republic (the nationalists liked that); an East–West Council that combined representatives of the Assembly with their counterparts in Scotland, Wales, and the Isle of Man would also serve a moderating role (the unionists liked that). Steps would be taken to "harmonize" legislation and administrative procedures in both parts of Ireland. The United Kingdom would have a voice in Northern Ireland through the secretary of state for Northern Ireland. Extensive provisions were included to protect human rights.

Of more importance to most people were unspecified commitments to wide-ranging reforms of the police and criminal justice system. The Royal Ulster Constabulary (RUC) was regarded by the Catholics as an instrument of oppression and abuse. Chris Patten, former governor of Hong Kong and a prominent Conservative, was named to head a commission to reform the RUC. The agreement also called for a review of the criminal justice system and changes in the appointment of judges and prosecutors. Strong emotions were aroused by provisions for the release of prisoners who had been convicted of terrorist acts.

The main stumbling block was the requirement that the IRA give up its vast hoard of weaponry and explosives. Blair promised that parties linked to terrorists (presumably Sinn Fein) would not be permitted to sit in the Assembly or hold office unless they had genuinely renounced violence.

As the date of the referendum approached, nationalist support was strong, but polls showed that many unionists were doubtful or bitterly opposed. David Trimble, leader of the Ulster Unionist Party, was an active advocate of the agreement, although six of the ten members of his Ulster Unionist Party in Parliament opposed it. John Hume, leader of the Social Democratic Labour Party, a moderate nationalist group, had favored the agreement all along. Gerry Adams, leader of Sinn Fein, supported it as a "tactical advance" toward a united Ireland.

The campaign for approval of the Good Friday Agreement was intense. Blair made three visits to Northern Ireland to urge support; on one of them Major accompanied him. Brown promised a £300 million package of financial aid, plus tax breaks for investors in the province. The agreement received strong endorsements from Clinton and Ahern. The pop group U2 joined the chorus, and the queen promised a visit if the agreement passed.

A disturbing event took place shortly before the referendum, when Sinn Fein held its party conference in Dublin. The British government, as a concession to Sinn Fein, had transferred custody of some convicted IRA terrorists to the Republic of Ireland, which authorized them to appear at the conference where Adams triumphantly introduced them. The prisoners were serving multiple life sentences for bombings and murders in Britain in the 1970s. The sight of convicted terrorists raising their fists in triumph and being hailed as heroes angered many people in Britain and Northern Ireland.

In May 1998, the Good Friday Agreement was approved in referenda held in Northern Ireland and the Republic. In Northern Ireland, 71 percent of the voters approved it, but this figure was less overwhelming than it seemed. Nationalists approved the agreement by 98 percent; the unionists divided by approximately 55 percent for and 45 percent against. Since the unionists were 60 percent of the population and dominant in business and the professions, their defections were a warning of pitfalls ahead. In the Republic of Ireland the referendum passed by 94 percent. The agreement became law later that year.

People of good will, who were told by "the great and the good" that it was the last chance to end the troubles, overlooked the ambiguities in the document. Approval of the agreement grew out of the weariness of the people of Northern Ireland with unending conflict and violence. This widely shared mood, more than the specific provisions, was the main reason for its approval. Reporters noted that there were no celebrations in Belfast when the announcement was made that the referendum had passed. A hopeful sign was news that Trimble and Hume planned to form a coalition of the moderate parties that would squeeze out the extremists. For their achievement, they were jointly awarded the Nobel Peace Prize.

The peace process was interrupted in August 1998, when an IRA bomb went off in the central shopping area of Omagh when it was thronged with shoppers. The explosion killed twenty-nine people, injured two hundred or more, and destroyed the center of the town. It was the handiwork of an IRA splinter group that had access to the weapons dumps. This crime led to intensified Protestant demands for decommissioning of the IRA's weaponry. Trimble, under constant pressure from his Ulster Unionist Party, refused to constitute the Cabinet until the IRA took steps to decommission its arsenals.

The election for the Assembly took place in September. Trimble's Ulster Unionists won twenty-eight seats, followed by Hume's Social Democratic and Labor Party with twenty-four. Sinn Fein took eighteen seats and 17 percent of the vote. Trimble became prime minister.

The deadline to establish the Cabinet was March 1999, but continuing disputes concerning decommissioning of weapons delayed the process of organizing a government. When Trimble and Adams visited the White House on St. Patrick's Day, 1999, Adams stated bluntly that he could not deliver on decommissioning. Blair set an "absolute deadline" of June 30 to establish the Executive, but nothing happened, and he agreed to another extension. Senator George Mitchell was asked to resume his role as negotiator.

Summer passed and the standoff continued. In October 1999, Blair showed his determination to complete the peace process by appointing his close friend, Peter Mandelson, as secretary of state for Northern Ireland. Trimble knew that Sinn Fein was eager to see the new government established, but he knew that the Ulster Unionist Party would not support him if decommissioning had not begun.

In November 1999, Mitchell announced that he had cut a deal. The IRA agreed to accept an international commission to inspect the dumps and verify that the weapons had been put out of use. Trimble and the Ulster Unionist Party agreed to accept that promise as sufficient to enter the devolved government with Sinn Fein.

On December 2, 1999, the Executive, led by David Trimble, and the power-sharing Northern Ireland Assembly were officially constituted. Trimble promised the Ulster Unionist Party that he would resign and dissolve the government if the IRA failed to disarm. The North–South Council and the East–West Council had their first meetings later that month. The government of the Republic announced that it had renounced its long-dormant claim to Northern Ireland. It seemed that Northern Ireland would enter the new millennium with a democratically elected assembly and Executive.

As usual, the disarmament commission set up under the Good Friday Agreement received no cooperation from the IRA, who insisted on keeping their weapons. Mandelson, fed up with continuing delays, announced that decommissioning must begin within two days or direct rule would be restored. When the IRA again rejected decommissioning, the House of Commons promptly passed legislation to suspend the Assembly and reimpose direct rule. An IRA splinter group responded by setting off a bomb in a hotel in County Fermanagh.

In May 2000, Blair went to Northern Ireland to try to restore the devolved government. Blair and Ahern set a deadline of May 22 for decommissioning to begin and devolved government to be restored. Finally, the IRA agreed to allow inspection of dumps and "put their weapons completely and verifiably beyond use." That step put pressure on Trimble, whose Ulster Unionist Party had used decommissioning as a reason not to cooperate with the nationalists in the new government. They were dubious about IRA promises that had never been kept before. Once again, Trimble prevailed, and the Ulster Unionists agreed to return to the new government.

Thus fortified, Mandelson restored the Executive and Assembly. Trimble resumed his office as prime minister, along with ministers from the other parties, including Sinn Fein. The inspectors entered the weapons dumps and reported that they were secure. It seemed that the troubles were over. To indicate an end to hostilities, scores of prisoners, some of them convicted of vicious crimes, were released. Despite Mandelson's lenience—or perhaps because of it—bombings and shootings continued.

While the fragile peace agreement held, disorders continued as rival paramilitary groups fought each other for control of turf and the drug trade. In August 2000, when the police could not control the situation, Mandelson brought in British troops, for the first time in two years. The IRA interpreted this step as another reason not to give up their weapons. Trimble was savagely criticized by a large minority in his Ulster Unionist Party for continuing in the shared government, and in October, he narrowly repelled a challenge to his leadership.

In the meantime, the Patten Commission on reform of the RUC had published its report. In November, Parliament passed legislation based on the report, although the question of the name of the reformed police force—an emotional issue—was left for Mandelson to decide. More incidents of IRA terrorism showed the importance of destroying weapons, not just inspecting the dumps. In September, an IRA rocket hit MI6 headquarters in London, and in March 2001, a car bomb was detonated outside the headquarters of the BBC.

Although the devolved government headed by Trimble remained in office, continuing violence contributed to victories by the extremist parties in the general election of June 2001. In July, Trimble resigned as prime minister and leader of the Ulster Unionist Party, leaving a caretaker government in charge. His courage and firmness had brought Northern Ireland to the brink of peace, but the violent men, many of them members of criminal gangs masquerading as patriots, continued to disturb the province.

By that time, Mandelson was gone. His tenure as Northern Ireland secretary had been troubled, but he could claim that a workable settlement had been made that would gradually lead to peace. Once again he resigned his office because of a personal scandal. In January 2001, he admitted that, in 1998, he had improperly intervened with the Home Office to obtain British citizenship for two Indian businessmen who had contributed £1,000,000 to the Millennium Dome. An investigation cleared Mandelson of improper conduct, but his career as a Cabinet minister was finished.

~

CHAPTER TEN

Toward a New Mandate, 1999–2001

Foreign Policy

From the beginning of his ministry, Tony Blair showed great interest in foreign affairs. Like most leaders of important states, he was attracted to the drama of foreign policy, with its media coverage of conferences in attractive locations, meetings with distinguished world leaders, and opportunities for grandiose utterances.

Blair was determined that Britain would remain a power with a global reach, although in most cases under the umbrella of the United Nations and in tandem with the United States and the Commonwealth. He became increasingly interested in playing a role in Europe. He saw Britain serving as a bridge between Europe and the United States, where significant differences were developing, fostered mainly by the long-standing French resentment of American influence. He took the global view of foreign policy: "Our task is to build a new doctrine of international community," he declared, "defined by common rights and shared responsibilities."

The foreign and commonwealth secretary, Robin Cook, was acting in accord with Blair's views, in May 1997, when he declared, "Our foreign policy must have an ethical dimension." He advocated stronger measures by the international community to promote human rights, disarmament, and a ban on the use of land mines.

As an example of his "ethical dimension," Cook made international control of arms sales a major objective. In so doing, he created tension with the

Ministry of Defence, which was determined to protect Britain's defense industries, and powerful elements in the Labour Party concerned with protecting jobs. *The Economist* pointed out (August 2, 1997) that Britain was the world's second largest exporter of weapons; it was estimated that ninety thousand jobs depended on arms exports. These were important considerations for a Labour government, as they had been for Margaret Thatcher and John Major. Despite Cook's pronouncements, the government decided to continue arms sales to Indonesia, a major purchaser, which had been embargoed by other countries because of its bad human rights record.

The most remarkable aspect of the "ethical dimension" in Blair's foreign policy was his willingness to intervene militarily in places where democracy and human rights were being violated. The defense budget for 1998 included a proposal to establish a British rapid-reaction force of fifteen thousand well-trained and well-equipped troops, including "air cavalry" using helicopters. The air arm would be strengthened with additional fighter planes and the navy would receive two new, state-of-the-art carriers to replace three smaller, aging ones. The nuclear deterrent would be preserved, although reduced.

One intervention that created some political fallout was in Sierra Leone, a former British colony in West Africa, where a military dictator had seized power. The United Nations acted by imposing an embargo on sales of weapons and oil. Neighboring Nigeria intervened militarily, as hundreds of Westerners fled to avoid the fighting. The Foreign Office quietly gave permission to a British firm to supply arms to mercenary forces fighting to restore the legitimate government. When the press exposed the operation, the company stated that it was acting with the full support of the British government.

Blair and Cook, who had not been fully informed, denied any British role in supplying the mercenaries. They were contradicted by the Department of Customs and Excise, which stated that the shipment of weapons had indeed been approved by the Foreign Office. The company that sold the weapons revealed the names of the British diplomats who were involved. As usually happens when things are done with a wink and a nod, an official on the spot was held responsible. When a similar crisis arose in April 2000, Britain did the sensible thing: sent its own troops to free three hundred United Nations peacekeepers who were held prisoner and bring the country back under UN supervision.

Blair's desire to play an important role in world affairs contributed to British participation in American plans for a bombing campaign against Saddam Hussein, who was stealthily rebuilding his forces after his defeat in the Gulf War. The bombing was intended to force Saddam to destroy his stockpile of chemical and biological weapons and permit verification by UN inspectors. In November 1997, Saddam blocked the inspections, and the inspectors were withdrawn. The United Nations retaliated with an embargo on Iraqi exports of oil, except for limited shipments that could be used only to purchase food and medicine.

In February, Blair went to Washington for a three-day visit to discuss a variety of issues, especially the need for action against Saddam. Britain's military forces were modern, mobile, and accustomed to working with the Americans, who had state-of-the-art resources for satellite observations and communications. Britain's involvement was overwhelmingly approved in the House of Commons, 493 to 25. Major, recalling the Gulf War, spoke strongly in its support. Canada and Australia remained true to their Anglo-Saxon heritage and joined the alliance.

After nine months of fruitless threats and negotiations, the eventual outcome was an embarrassing climb-down. Kofi Annan, secretary-general of the United Nations, went to Baghdad to negotiate a last-minute deal, which turned into a reprieve for Saddam. Annan returned to New York with an agreement that supposedly opened Iraq to unimpeded inspections, and the United States and Britain suspended their planned attack. They continued to utter threats, but having backed off once, they were not taken seriously.

Despite the agreement, Saddam continued to frustrate the inspectors. In December 1998, the United States and Britain unleashed four nights of all-out bombing against Iraq. The allies declared that they had taught Saddam a lesson and had suffered no casualties, ignoring the death and destruction inflicted on Iraq. As usual, bombing proved insufficient to change the behavior of Saddam. Although Saddam was a brutal dictator and dangerous to his neighbors, the bombing had little support elsewhere, even among those countries that were most threatened.

The Russians, who were strengthening their ties with Iraq, were strongly opposed. Predictably, the European Union (EU) was divided: Germany offered limited support, while France joined Russia in opposing the operation. In December 1998, the UN inspectors, frustrated by Saddam's resistance, left Iraq, and Saddam was free to continue his efforts to develop deadly weapons.

In the meantime, Blair was concerned with another long-standing issue: violence in the former Yugoslavia, where Slobodan Milosevic continued to be a disruptive force. Milosevic attempted, unsuccessfully, to occupy Serb-dominated areas occupied by Croatia during the breakup of the country. He violated the Dayton Agreement by intervening in Bosnia, where British troops continued to be involved as part of the UN peacekeeping force.

While the old problems of Bosnia festered, a new problem flared in the province of Kosovo, where the Serb population was threatened by an influx of Muslim Albanians. In March 1998, Milosevic sent troops into the province to protect the Serbs and begin another episode of ethnic cleansing. Entire villages were burned in the Albanian parts of Kosovo. The Albanians fought back with a ragtag force called the Kosovo Liberation Army.

The United Nations made its usual weak response, imposing an arms embargo on Yugoslavia, although Milosevic had ample supplies of weapons and ammunition. In June, he defied the United Nations and escalated his scorched earth attacks on Albanians in Kosovo. A flood of Albanian refugees poured into Albania, Macedonia, and other countries. Calls arose for NATO air strikes against Serbia, which could be carried out only by using American airpower.

Once again, Blair's combination of morality and militancy came into play. Blair called for a "new internationalism where the brutal repression of whole ethnic groups will no longer be tolerated." As one atrocity after another appeared on television, Blair declaimed: "This is happening on our doorstep, and we simply cannot stand by and let it happen." Blair urged a reluctant President Bill Clinton to send American ground troops. He was seen as the Western leader most determined to destroy the Milosevic regime and end the ethnic cleansing of Kosovo. His willingness to commit ground troops was not shared elsewhere.

The Clinton administration, already involved in Bosnia, had no inclination to enter farther into the Balkan bog. Nevertheless, scenes of violence and refugees on American television finally persuaded Clinton that something had to be done. The president agreed that NATO should be the instrument for intervention, with the United States providing airpower.

In March 1999, NATO planes (mainly American) began seventy-eight days of bomb and missile attacks against Serbia and Serb forces in Kosovo, and NATO began mobilizing ground troops in the area. As Milosevic continued his war with the Kosovo Albanians, refugees by the hundreds of thousands poured into neighboring countries. In April, Clinton agreed to the use of NATO forces (including American ground troops) to expel Milosevic from Kosovo and return the refugees to their homes. In May, NATO approved the dispatch of fifty thousand ground troops to the area, and Milosevic threw in the towel. In Britain, Blair was hailed as a bold and courageous war leader, but there was no "Falklands effect." The British public was lukewarm about wars in remote places to promote human rights.

In June, a peace agreement was reached. Serbian troops in Kosovo withdrew in good order, little damaged by the air attacks. NATO and Russian forces entered Kosovo and took responsibility for peacekeeping. Albanians flooded into Kosovo and conducted an ethnic cleansing of Serbs. A year later, Milosevic was defeated in an election and was forced by mass protests to give up the presidency.

These commitments raised the question of overreach. Was Britain involved in too many places? With an army of 100,000, Britain had forces stationed in Belize, Gibraltar, the Falklands, Northern Ireland (15,000), Germany (17,000), Bosnia (4,500), Kosovo (10,500), Cyprus (2,300), and Brunei (1,000). The Ministry of Defence wanted to keep 10,000 troops available for emergencies. Long overseas deployments were damaging to morale and disruptive to families. The army had difficulty recruiting or retaining the number of troops that were authorized. The situation seemed unsustainable. Either Britain would have to retrench or receive help somewhere.

Britain still had global interests, but it could not afford a global reach. In September 1997, it was announced that Britain could not be a "world policeman," but that it intended to maintain armed forces that could "make a difference." Henceforth, Britain's major commitments would be NATO, the Gulf, and the Middle East.

The European Union

Within the European Union Britain was seen as an important country but an outsider in many respects. Blair offered mixed messages. Sometimes he said he wanted Britain to be a leader in Europe; on another occasion he declared, "Britain throughout its history has looked outward to the world." Ever since World War II and the Cold War, British foreign policy and defense had been closely bound to the NATO alliance, the United States, the United Nations, and a network of international organizations and agreements. The United States maintained a global intelligence and communications system based on satellites that was indispensable, especially at sea. American assistance had made possible Thatcher's victory in the Falklands. The comment was made that the U.S. and British navies acted as one.

The growing strength, unity, and confidence of the European Union led to a reevaluation of Britain's role in Europe. Within the European Union, the victory of New Labour was seen as a fresh start, after years of "hand bagging" by Thatcher, followed by Major's struggles with the Euroskeptics. By the 1990s, the European Union was a success, rivaling the United States economically. The United States was increasingly involved in other parts of the world, and NATO—although still useful—seemed less necessary after the fall of the Iron Curtain.

Blair saw Britain's membership in the European Union as a matter of "influence," which he expected to exercise by working within the EU as a full participant and not as a marginal member, which Britain still was. The British public was less enthusiastic. A study of the fifteen member states by the European Commission showed that the British were the least aware of European institutions, the most distrustful of the European Commission, the most opposed to the single currency, and the least able (19 percent) to hold a conversation in a foreign language. In national pride, they were exceeded only by Greece and Ireland. Germany ranked last in that respect.

In June 1997, the Council of Ministers signed the Treaty of Amsterdam, which moved the EU closer toward a political union. It strengthened the powers of the Commission and its president over the member states and pledged the member governments to closer cooperation in foreign policy and defense. Provisions for common police and immigration policies were established. Britain signed the treaty, but with exemptions giving it a veto on matters concerning defense, justice, and control of immigration and asylum.

Blair urged economic reforms that would increase internal competition, make labor markets more flexible, and reduce the level of taxation. He continued Thatcher's resistance to closer political union, the objective of most of the other member states. "The EU," he declared, "should be a superpower, not a superstate"; power should rest with "national parliaments and governments."

The immediate challenge facing the European Union was the process of establishing a European currency, the euro. By February 1998, all members except Greece had met the financial criteria, sometimes by creative accounting. Despite earlier doubts it seemed clear that the euro would come into existence as planned. The euro would begin as an electronic medium of exchange for banks and other financial institutions in January 1999, followed by three years to complete the transition to currency and coins for everyday use.

British policy toward the single currency was the first difficult decision that Blair had to make. Politically, he did not want his domestic goals to be threatened by a divisive referendum on the euro that would play into the strength of the Conservative Party. He knew that a great majority of the British people were dubious about the euro or flatly opposed. Furthermore, he did not want to threaten British prosperity by making the fiscal and monetary adjustments that would be necessary to adopt the single currency.

On the other hand, the trade unions were generally sympathetic to the European Union, and many British businessmen, whom Blair had courted assiduously during the election campaign, believed that remaining outside the euro would be a setback to exports and inward investment. As time went on, it became clear that Blair had strong European sympathies and wanted to play a major role in Europe, an objective that was impossible until Britain adopted the euro. In February 1999, Blair announced that the government would begin preparations for adoption of the euro by spending large sums to convert accounting and computer systems. He hedged his bet by adding that adoption of the euro was not "inevitable."

Blair's decision to delay enabled the Conservatives to gloat that Blair had adopted Major's "wait and see" policy. Blair punted the issue to Gordon Brown, who identified five criteria that had to be met before the referendum could be held: these were whether the euro would be good for jobs, investment, and financial services; whether the euro would preserve the flexibility of the British economy; and British convergence with Europe on inflation, interest rates, deficits, and debt. Since Brown would decide if the criteria had been met, he would determine whether the referendum would take place. Blair would decide the timing.

The Sun responded with a picture of Blair wearing a mask, accompanied by a blaring headline: IS THIS MAN THE MOST DANGEROUS MAN IN BRITAIN? To close the debate, Blair announced that he had decided to wait until after the next election before holding a referendum. In February 2001, he stated that an assessment of Brown's economic criteria would be held within two years after the approaching election.

In January 1998, it was Britain's turn to assume the six-month presidency of the European Union's Council of Ministers, the supreme decision-making body. Blair's tenure illustrated the contradictions in Britain's relations with Europe. When his chairmanship began, Blair, with his usual gusto, went into a pro-Europe mode, inviting Community leaders to London to observe "cool Britannia." A month later, he was in Washington, emphasizing the "special relationship" with the United States. British support of the United States in the Iraq crisis confirmed the European view that Britain would always be closer to the United States. A poll of the British public reported in the *Times* (February 11, 1998) showed strong public support for the statement that "Britain has more in common with America than with Europe."

Blair's presidency of the Council of Ministers was far from successful. His participation was halfhearted, and at times he seemed ill prepared. In March, the Council of Ministers met in London to discuss enlargement. They met with the representatives of eleven countries seeking admission. They recognized that Poland, Czechoslovakia, and Hungary were the closest to meeting the requirements. Enlargement was a policy that Britain supported, although some member states feared that low-wage workers and cheap agricultural products would threaten their economies.

Inexorably, the movement of the European Union toward integration and expansion continued. At a European summit at Nice in December 2000, plans were made to expand the Commission to include twenty-seven countries, with the larger countries (including Britain) having proportionately weighted votes. Integration also took another step forward. The powers of the president of the European Commission were strengthened, offering the prospect of a strong executive. For most decisions, the national veto was replaced by majority voting, but Blair was able to protect the national veto on taxation and social security.

It was in this context that Blair made a surprising proposal that ran counter to Britain's fifty-year reliance on the Atlantic alliance. Irritated by America's reluctance to become involved in Kosovo, he proposed that the European Union establish a rapid-reaction force that would respond quickly to international crises. This proposal was especially attractive to the French, who had long resented American influence in Europe, as exercised through NATO. With the end of the Cold War, the French were eager to develop a distinct European foreign policy, backed up by a military capability. With an unstable settlement in the Balkans, the other members accepted the idea, and in June 1999, they agreed to establish a force of sixty thousand troops, independent of NATO.

The idea was unwelcome to the Americans, who saw Blair's proposal as a betrayal of the long-standing "special relationship." Blair denied that Britain had to choose between an Atlanticist and a European foreign policy: "We have deluded ourselves for too long," he said, "with the false choice between the US and Europe." While Blair described the European defense force as limited to "crisis management, peacekeeping, and humanitarian tasks," the French made it clear that they had something more substantial in mind. The European force was established on paper, but it seemed unlikely to come together as a coherent European army for some time.

Politics and Political Parties

By 1999, the honeymoon period was over, and the Blair ministry, with its huge majority, was expected to show some results. The economy was doing well, with inflation and interest rates the lowest in thirty years, and unemployment at 4.5 percent. The public revenue was flourishing, and Brown was paying off debt at an unimaginable rate. Inward investment was strong.

Brown was the star of Labour's domestic program in 1999. In his budget, presented in March, corporate income taxes were cut to the lowest level of any industrial nation. To encourage hiring the unemployed, employers' contributions to the National Insurance system were reduced for low-wage workers, and they were required to pay more for high-wage employees. Brown reduced the basic rate of personal income tax from 23 percent to 22 percent, and introduced a new 10 percent rate for low-income taxpayers. The deductibility of mortgage interest, long resented by Labour as a benefit to the middle class, was eliminated. Later in the year, Brown presented himself as an advocate of "the entrepreneurial spirit" by proposing a reduction of the capital gains tax and giving tax breaks to encourage companies to extend share ownership to their employees. Almost everyone took a hit with another increase in the motor fuel tax.

The "welfare to work" program was strengthened by a new Working Families' Tax Credit to guarantee an income of £208 per week to people who were employed full time, plus a new tax credit for the first child. Complaints were made that this policy left out 20 percent of British families, mainly single parents, where no one was employed. Brown's Thatcherite response was that one or both parents should find a job.

Brown also proposed changes in the pension system, with a minimum-income guarantee for the poorest pensioners and a second state pension (replacing SERPS) to encourage lower-income people to save for retirement. The guarantee and the pension were somewhat contradictory, because the people who had contributed to the second pension would not qualify for the minimum income when they retired, while those who had spent everything as they went along, would receive the minimum income and have a retirement income almost equal to those who had scrimped and saved. While looking to a future where retired people were less dependent on public provision, Brown ignored existing pensioners, who received a derisory increase.

Despite success in management of the economy, the Blair ministry found itself in a mid-term slump. "Blair fatigue" began to set in, as the high hopes generated by the election failed to materialize. Polls in January showed that support for Labour had fallen below 50 percent. Rural people were upset by Blair's inability to resolve the European Union's ban on exports of British beef, which was devastating to cattlemen. Many were upset by a private members' bill to ban fox hunting, a time-honored part of rural life and a source of additional income to many people. Landowners opposed "right to roam" legislation that would permit city dwellers to hike in rural areas. Villagers feared reduction of bus services and closure of small post offices.

The Economist (July 31, 1999) pointed out the lack of substantial progress on the issues most important to the public. Waiting lists for operations, a widely used benchmark for the National Health Service, continued to be high; the number of people waiting more than twelve months for an operation was higher than in 1996. Class sizes, a measure of school reform, were as high as ever. Welfare reform had been stymied by the Labour majority in the

House of Commons, as well as by the general public, and welfare spending continued to rise.

Blair's large majority had not emboldened him. Rather, he had concentrated on maintaining his majority rather than using it to ram through Parliament legislation that he wanted—assuming that he knew what he wanted. In the year 2001, electoral considerations would take precedence over reform. It appeared that Blair, despite his majority, had failed to fulfill his promise to lead "one of the great radical reforming governments of our history."

At the Labour Party conference in September 1999, the prime minister attempted to regain lost momentum. He attacked the forces of conservatism in his own party and elsewhere, which he identified as "the old class divisions, old structures, old prejudices, old ways of working and of doing things that will not do in this world of changes." The government came forward with an ambitious agenda, which included elected mayors, a Financial Services Agency to regulate markets, a Strategic Rail Authority to deal with the unsatisfactory performance of the privatized rail system, commercial freedom for the Post Office, an Asylum and Immigration Bill to restrict abuse of the welfare system by immigrants, and continuation of reforms in the areas of education, health, welfare, pensions, and crime. Many of these proposals had been included in the election manifesto and were now emerging from the planning stage.

As usual, Brown led the charge. In March 2000, he presented his budget message, which was the culmination of three years of "prudent" economic management. At last, Brown was ready to begin the long-term "investment" needed to achieve the goals stated by New Labour. The Treasury had a surplus of £12 billion, and it continued to grow. Brown kept income tax levels about the same, but prosperity meant that most households paid about 5 percent more. Another increase in the motor fuel tax was made more acceptable by the (temporarily) low price of petroleum. Brown continued the policy of strengthening private enterprise with another reduction in the capital gains tax and established an Enterprise Fund to encourage small businesses.

When he presented a three-year spending plan in July 2000, Brown announced that his surplus was 50 percent larger than expected, which would allow an increase in spending of 30 percent over the next three years. The biggest increase (20 percent) went to rescue the floundering railroads and reduce traffic congestion. Spending on schools would increase by 5.4 percent a year, health by 5.6 percent, and criminal justice by an annual 6 percent. Increases were also planned for defense, neighborhood renewal, child poverty, and Regional Development Agencies.

Brown expanded the New Deal programs to move the unemployed "from welfare to work," increased the Working Families' Tax Credit and the Child Tax Credit, and continued to pay off debt. Many of these spending increases were accompanied by intimidating demands for "targets" and "performance reviews," as Brown extended the Thatcherite dictatorship of the Treasury over the public services. Brown's main political mistake was a modest increase to pensioners, who complained indignantly that they should share more in the good times.

One of the signs of prosperity was a shortage of housing in the Southeast, where prices were rising rapidly, threatening a rerun of the booms that had been so damaging to Sir Edward Heath and Nigel Lawson. Prices rose most dramatically in prestigious neighborhoods of London, driven to a considerable degree by wealthy foreigners, who could afford to live there.

Demand was greatest for houses on "green-field" sites in the suburbs or the country, but environmental pressures to preserve green space were powerful. John Prescott, secretary for the environment, transport and the regions, proposed increasing the number of permits for new houses, with the proviso that 60 percent of them be built on abandoned urban land called "brown-field" sites. Encouraging building on these sites would help improve run-down urban communities, a matter of considerable interest to the Labour Party.

Prescott unveiled ambitious plans for urban renewal in selected northern cities, where large areas had become dilapidated or abandoned. "Urban action zones" were proposed, which would receive funding to improve streets, schools, hospitals, parks, and other public facilities. The plan would encourage people to live in inner-city flats rather than the Englishman's preference—a suburban house with a patch of garden. There were many obstacles to making these sites attractive, one of them being their proximity to low-income neighborhoods that were rife with crime and other social ills.

Transportation was another responsibility of Prescott, who announced a ten-year program, using both public and private funding, to upgrade the entire transportation system. Major efforts would be made to improve the roads and railroads. The plan was criticized for not doing enough to reduce the use of cars, which clogged roads and streets and polluted the air in city centers.

The most serious problem was the breakdown of the railway system, due in part to the hasty and ill-planned privatization of British Rail, but also a result of years of bad management, underinvestment, and railway union recalcitrance. A system with twenty-five separate operators was a nightmare to people trying to obtain information or buy tickets. Many of the operators were inexperienced, but they were willing to learn and invest if the system would assure them a profit, which could happen only if they could provide faster, more reliable, and more attractive trains.

Almost one-third of all trains were late. The stumbling block was Railtrack, which was slow to improve the tracks and signaling to accommodate up-to-date rolling stock. When Railtrack did attempt improvements, the outcome was frustrating delays and cost overruns.

Spectacular train wrecks at Southall in 1997 and near Paddington station in 1999 led many to question the dedication of Railtrack to safety. A year later four people were killed and thirty-four injured in a crash at Hatfield. Railtrack admitted that the faulty track had been identified earlier, but repairs had been delayed. Some accidents were the result of trains running through red stop signals, and massive investment would be needed to establish a fail-safe signaling system. Public confidence in the railroads was further undermined in February 2001, when a passenger train collided with a freight train. Ten passengers were killed and seventy injured.

The main reason for these accidents seemed to be poorly maintained tracks, for which Railtrack was responsible. *The Economist* (July 23, 1999) pointed out that "some of Railtrack's contractors decided, in effect, which parts of the track needed renewal. Naturally, they appeared concerned less with passenger safety than with their own profits. Because they are paid by the mile, they have understandably tended to choose sections that are easy to renew than those that involve the most work."

To avoid more disasters, train speeds were greatly reduced on many lines, disrupting schedules and causing intolerable delays. Some trains were running without schedules, an invitation to accidents. Journeys by rail seemed to take forever. A cold, rainy winter brought spring floods that washed out rail lines and hampered repairs. Passenger traffic fell by 30 percent, as people abandoned the trains and traveled by car, which made Britain's crowded roads even more dangerous. A Strategic Rail Authority was established to take responsibility for performance and safety. In 2002 Railtrack was declared bankrupt and put into receivership.

Mounting complaints made it evident that the National Health Service needed to be expanded and modernized. Studies showed that Britain spent less on health care than other advanced countries, which made greater use of private medicine and health insurance. Britain had the lowest per capita proportion of doctors of any advanced country. Nurses were scarce, and many were leaving the profession. The number of hospital beds fell by 40 percent from 1988 to 1998 as a result of Thatcherite reforms that eliminated smaller hospitals. Fewer beds were needed, because changes in medical treatment reduced or eliminated hospital stays. Consequently, there never were enough doctors, nurses, or beds to deal with the flu and other ailments that came with a bad winter.

The yardstick adopted by the media (and therefore, the politicians) was the length of hospital waiting lists. To avoid criticism, hospitals were tempted to perform the easiest operations first, because they took less time and reduced the waiting list most rapidly. Time-consuming, difficult, non-emergency operations were delayed, because they did little to reduce the waiting list.

Blair realized the importance of the NHS to the British people, and he became personally involved in planning an extensive program of reform. Brown committed some of his flush finances, and spending on health was increased by 5.6 percent a year for the next three years. In July 2001, the government announced a ten-year plan to improve the NHS.

The most serious embarrassment came in the election for the new mayor of London. In October 1999, preparations began to establish the Greater London Authority (GLA) and elect the mayor and the members of the Assembly. Since Labour dominated London, Blair assumed that the Labour Party would accept his choice, Frank Dobson, a longtime Labour stalwart who was serving as minister for health. Blair's plans were upset when "Red Ken" Livingstone, the wisecracking radical who had tormented Thatcher, announced that he was a candidate. He promised to oppose privatization of the Underground, a position held by most Londoners.

Blair was shocked at the prospect of the return of "the loony left" to the pages of the tabloids. He was determined to maintain control of London, the great heart of the United Kingdom. Desperately he maneuvered to obtain the nomination of Dobson, including rigging the selection process to get what he wanted. In March 2000, Livingstone was rebuked by the Commons Standards committee for failing to declare his business interests and was charged with taking loans from phony business firms to finance his campaign.

Always a maverick, Livingstone announced that he would run as an independent and was expelled from the Labour Party. In May 2000, Livingstone was elected mayor with 58 percent of the vote. The Tory candidate received 42 percent, and Blair's handpicked candidate, Frank Dobson, was in third place. The prime minister had suffered an embarrassing political defeat. The seats in the assembly were divided among Labour, Conservatives, Liberal Democrats, and Greens. The Labour members agreed to support Livingstone's administration, and they received some offices.

To be on the safe side, the Blair government had given the London mayor few powers and modest funding. There was no need to worry. Livingstone had been tamed by years and experience. "Now I've got a position where I have to deliver a real improvement in services," he said in an interview. "I have to dump the street theatre and concentrate on my day job."

The main challenges facing the new mayor were the decay of London Underground, traffic congestion, and crime. The immediate issue was the government's plan to privatize the Tube. Beyond that, the vast metropolitan area governed itself through its thirty-three boroughs, some of which were efficient and others corrupt. There was not much that Livingstone or Blair could do about that.

Regional disparities and complaints continued. The Northeast, where Labour held thirty-one out of thirty-five seats (including Sedgefield) continued in a long-term recession. Unemployment was almost double the national average. With the decline of manufacturing, only 67 percent of the working-age population had jobs, while in the Southeast the figure was 80 percent. Complaints were made that government grants to Scotland were higher per person than in the Northeast, which also needed help. The Northwest, Midlands, and Southwest had similar complaints. Brown proposed additional funding for the Regional Development Agencies (RDAs), but these were far from enough to achieve some kind of regional balance. The movement for regional devolution continued to gain strength.

A problem that received much public attention was an influx of asylum seekers from Eastern Europe, the Middle East, Afghanistan, and China. Britain was a favored destination for refugees, for its regulations were slackly administered and its welfare programs were generous. Applications for asylum increased by 50 percent between 1998 and 1999. Countless other immigrants entered illegally and disappeared into the general population, aided by countrymen or relatives.

Italy, Spain, France, and Germany pushed these refugees to the Channel coast, where they found ways—costly, difficult, and dangerous—to cross to the southeast of Britain. Smuggling refugees into Britain became a huge and profitable criminal enterprise. When customs officers in Dover opened the back of a truck from Belgium, they found fifty-eight bodies of Chinese men and women suffocated under a load of tomatoes. Similar incidents happened elsewhere. No one knows how many immigrants disappeared along the way.

Increased immigration led to racial tensions. The National Front of the 1970s revived in the depressed industrial towns of the north and gained a militant following among white residents, whose neighborhoods were being taken over by immigrants. Riots broke out, as unemployed youths of both races battled each other—and the police—in the streets. The tabloids sensationalized these problems, which were serious enough when viewed calmly.

Public complaints, as well as mounting costs, led the Home Office to impose stricter controls on refugees. They were concentrated in London and the Southeast, where they became a burden to local governments and an annoyance to the residents. Legislation in 1999 attempted to relieve the problems of the Southeast by dispersing asylum seekers to other parts of the United Kingdom. The Immigration and Asylum Act (2000) changed welfare benefits from cash to vouchers and established detention centers for refugees where they were held until their applications for asylum had been decided. Heavy fines were imposed on drivers caught with stowaways.

Later that year, the home secretary acknowledged that it was difficult to enforce the deportation of rejected asylum seekers. He conceded that hundreds of thousands of illegal immigrants were secretly living and working in Britain. Efforts to get tough with refugees foundered because Britain was a free and humane country. Few would want it otherwise.

Despite a few bumps and bruises, a *Times* poll at the end of July 2000 showed Labour at 49 percent, the Conservatives at 33 percent, and the Liberal Democrats at 12 percent. On a satisfaction index, the public was slightly dissatisfied with Blair and Labour, but put them well ahead of Hague and the Tories. Unless something unusual intervened, Blair and Labour looked set to win another mandate in the election that was expected to take place in May 2001.

Suddenly the mood of the country changed. As summer drew to a close, the government slipped on a series of banana skins. Pensioners complained that their increases had been so low as to be insulting. Rural protests and "countryside marches" continued. People who traveled to America discovered that prices were unusually high at home, and a chorus of complaints arose about "rip-off Britain." An upward spike in oil prices led to complaints by farmers and truckers, who demanded a cut in the motor fuel tax as an offset. They picketed refineries and panic buying set in as petrol pumps ran dry. Government intervention was not feasible, because most people agreed with the pickets. By the end of the week the pickets backed off, satisfied that they had made their point.

For the first time, Blair seemed to "wobble." He was flummoxed by the crisis—a minor one at that. Polls showed that the government's disapproval rate had risen to 56 percent, and Blair's personal rating had fallen to 45 percent satisfied and 52 percent dissatisfied. Labour's electoral support had fallen to 37 percent as compared to 35 percent for the Tories and 21 percent for the Liberal Democrats. Pundits began to suggest a Tory comeback. A few months later oil prices began to fall, Blair's ratings went back up, and the crisis was seen as a momentary squall that could indicate stormier weather ahead.

At the Labour Party conference in September 2000, Blair faced complaints that Brown's policy of "prudence" had been continued too long: it was past time for the public sector to share in the benefits of Britain's prosperity.

Blair replied that the establishment of long-term economic growth, without inflation, had been the first priority. Brown satisfied the delegates by promising increased pensions, although he refused to give way on the motor fuel tax: "Tax policy," he said, "should not be decided by those who shout the loudest or push the hardest."

Nevertheless, in November Brown presented a pre-budget report that showed he was not unresponsive to public protests. Modest cuts were made in motor fuel taxes, and substantial reductions were made in the registration fees for trucks and smaller cars. A tax on foreign trucks using British roads would ease the competition faced by domestic truckers and help repair some of the damage that giant trucks ("juggernauts") did to the roads. Pensioners were promised substantial increases. VAT regulations on smaller businesses were eased, and tax breaks were offered to encourage the improvement of run-down commercial areas. NHS nurses were given substantial raises.

Another banana skin was the Millennium Dome, which Blair had hailed as the symbolic representation of the thriving Britain that he envisaged. A project of the Major ministry, and especially Michael Heseltine, the huge dome seemed the ideal showcase for Blair's image of a with-it, cool Britannia. Since a millennium is a measurement of time, locating the Dome at Greenwich, from which time and longitude are calculated throughout the world, seemed appropriate. An extension of the Underground and a splendid new station were undertaken to serve the Dome and help develop the neglected right bank of the Thames. The world's largest Ferris wheel loomed across the Thames from the Houses of Parliament, and a modernistic footbridge was built across the river to the cultural attractions on the south bank. The largest fireworks display in British history would be set off from sixteen barges on the Thames.

Festivities, which would include the queen, were planned to usher in the millennium on New Year's Eve, 1999–2000. The world would look to London as the flagship of millennium celebrations, and Blair would be at the center of it! It was a spin-doctor's dream.

The result was a fiasco of major dimensions. Access to the Dome was difficult. Construction of the Underground extension was beset by maddening delays, which were resolved by bringing in an American engineer. The pedestrian suspension bridge had a pronounced sway that frightened some pedestrians and sickened others. The Ferris wheel was declared open but was not yet safe to operate. On New Year's Eve, 1999, thousands of sponsors and celebrity guests failed to get their tickets in time and had to stand in line for hours in a cold Underground station to buy them. Bars were jammed, as guests struggled to get champagne in time to offer a toast to the New Year.

Worst of all, the exhibits were preachy and boring. When the Dome was opened to the paying public, it was a flop. Desperate management changes made things worse. On December 31, 2000, it was closed—the symbol of a ministry that had failed to live up to expectations.

Preparing to Face the Voters

By the year 2001, the Labour Party was no longer new. New Labour had been given four years to prove itself and was now established as the dominant political party. As the year 2001 opened, Blair intended to confirm Labour's role in the new millennium by calling an election, probably in May—the fourth anniversary of the great electoral victory of 1997.

Despite the widely held view that Labour had fallen short, Blair found himself in the enviable position of leading a party that held the support, if not the loyalty and affection, of the broad political center. A *Times* poll in January 2001 gave Labour 48 percent of the likely voters, the Conservatives 33 percent, and the Liberal Democrats 14 percent. These figures held up through the electoral period.

Labour had the upper hand on the issues. A BBC poll in February showed that Labour was well ahead of the Conservatives on the issues that the voters thought were the most important: education (43 percent to 25 percent), health (41 percent to 24 percent), and transport (32 percent to 14 percent). People were upset about antisocial behavior, and Labour came forward with legislation against "the yob culture" of public drunkenness and misconduct. By 44 percent to 26 percent, people trusted the Blair government to make them better off in the future.

The most striking electoral change was that Labour had made deep inroads into the prospering professional/managerial class and white-collar workers, formerly the backbone of the Conservative Party. A *Times* poll in March showed a thirteen-point swing to Labour since 1997 among the professional/managerial class, while support from white-collar workers was stable. These people had accepted the economic changes of Thatcher, but had abandoned Thatcherism on social issues. They wanted good public services and were willing to spend more on the poor, even if it became necessary to raise taxes. They had become liberal on gender roles, premarital sex, illegitimacy, homosexuality, marijuana, the death penalty, and immigration. Blair and Labour had won over the broad middle class—a devastating blow to the Tories.

Labour's greatest asset was the flourishing state of the economy. Gordon Brown's budget message of March 2001 displayed Labour's one shining example of success. He began by pointing with justifiable pride to the strength of the British economy: the highest economic growth in twenty years, a substantial budget surplus, more debt paid down than in the past fifty years, the lowest inflation in thirty years, the lowest unemployment since 1975, and the lowest mortgage rates in twenty years.

Brown introduced a variety of tax breaks aimed at low-income families. The Working Families' Tax Credit and the tax credit for children were increased, with an additional benefit for child care. Maternity Benefit was increased and extended, and fathers were to receive two weeks' paid leave prior to or after the birth of a child. He also introduced a £1,000 tax credit for parents of a newborn child. There was no indication whether Brown, who had recently married his live-in girlfriend, intended to take advantage of these tax breaks himself.

Brown had not abandoned his Old Labour roots, and he did not adopt the Thatcherite principle of cutting income tax in the higher brackets. Rather, he raised the level at which people paid the lowest rate, thus reducing the income tax of moderate-income workers. He took a similar approach to National Insurance contributions, which took 10 percent of the worker's income and provided 15 percent of the total public revenue. Over several years, Brown had raised the upper limit for National Insurance contributions, which brought better-paid workers into his net. He had raised the lower limit, which benefited ill-paid workers.

A secondary benefit was to encourage employers to hire more workers at the lower end of the pay scale. Brown's tax breaks, of course, affected only people who were employed; they were part of his effort "to make work pay." They were of no benefit to the unemployed, the underemployed, or the unemployable.

Some of Brown's tax cuts were in response to popular protest, reversing the Thatcherite principle of taxing consumption rather than incomes. Taxes on motor fuel and auto licenses ("the car tax"), which had sparked protests the previous autumn, were reduced; taxes on beer, wine, and liquor, which were expected to rise, remained the same. The betting tax was abolished.

Brown broke with Thatcherism in another important respect. Thatcher wanted to reduce the size, cost, and role of the state. Brown intended to increase it by providing improved and expanded state services, a concern of people with moderate to low incomes, who could not afford private schools, health insurance, or cars. He announced substantial increases for education and health and for fighting crime. In response to protests, the universal state pension was substantially increased. Brown's 2001 budget made it clear that Labour, as defined by Brown, was still a party of social democracy.

Surprisingly, the flourishing state of the economy was less of an electoral advantage than expected, since much of the new wealth had not trickled down to ordinary people. A poll taken in February showed that 32 percent of the public thought things had gotten better, 31 percent that things had gotten worse, and 34 percent that things had stayed the same. Since most voters are primarily concerned with their own circumstances, it was unsettling that only 24 percent believed that things had gotten better for them personally, while 29 percent believed that they were worse off. The most optimistic responses came from better-educated voters (readers of upscale newspapers), Londoners, and pensioners. Women were somewhat more negative than men.

Economic data confirmed the results of the polls. Under Labour, household disposable income had risen by only 1.6 percent per year, half of the increases enjoyed in the glory years of Thatcher, and a full point below the struggling years of Major. One factor was higher taxes and National Insurance contributions, which since 1997 had risen to approximately 10 percent of the Gross Domestic Product. Another was low pay settlements based on the expectation of continuing low inflation. While incomes had risen sharply for some parts of the workforce, most of new jobs were at the low end of the scale.

Other factors contributed to a sour national mood. A rainy, gloomy winter and spring led to severe flooding. Confusion reigned on the railways, and the roads were choked with traffic. Foot-and-mouth disease, which is highly infectious to cloven-hoofed animals but not a threat to people, broke out in several parts of the country. Areas with the disease were closed off, and the slaughter of infected animals began. Huge subsidies were paid to farmers, and disposal of dead animals became a health hazard and environmental disaster. Clouds of vile black smoke rose from heaps of burning carcasses.

Tourism declined sharply, especially in the rural areas that needed it most. Since foot-and-mouth disease was not uncommon and usually died out within a few months, many people thought that the reaction of the government was excessive and cost more than the disease. Despite it all, the characteristic British trait of putting up with muddle enabled people to carry on.

The Campaign

As the campaign opened, Labour's lead was almost as great as in 1997. A *Times* poll in May 2001 showed Labour at 54 percent, the Conservatives at 30 percent, and the Liberal Democrats at 13 percent. Although there was a sense of disappointment in Labour's lack of accomplishments, most voters believed that Blair deserved another term to continue work on his agenda. More than half the public believed that he would be the best choice for prime minister, while only 13 percent gave the nod to Hague. All the parties knew that the election would be decided by middle-class voters in the suburbs and smaller towns, many of whom had voted for Labour in 1997 for the first time in their lives. They could be the wild card, for their attachment to Labour was fragile.

Turnout could be important, since only 65 percent of the potential voters said they intended to vote. In 1997, many seats had gone to Labour by narrow margins, and a slight shift in turnout might make a large difference in seats. For that reason, Labour needed to energize its base among "Old Labour" voters in the still-depressed industrial cities of the Midlands and the North. Support for Labour from the working class (skilled, manual) remained virtually unchanged from 1997, but there was much grumbling from "Old Labour" leaders on the local level.

Labour's victory in 1997 had rested partially on its appeal to women. A disconcerting fact for Labour was that some of the 101 "Blair's babes" elected in 1997 did not intend to run again. They were appalled at the rude behavior of some members and fed up with being part of a "gentleman's club" that lacked adequate office space, provided no facilities for child care, and began sessions in the afternoon that sometimes continued until midnight. They had been surprised to find that the ordinary MP had little to do and served only as a rubber stamp for the government. Offsetting these disadvantages were the satisfaction of providing constituent services and the social prestige of an MP.

The opposition parties faced a bleak future. Only 19 percent of the public thought that the Conservatives would win, and 62 percent viewed William Hague as "a weak leader who will probably never become Prime Minister." Kenneth Clarke, an experienced and respected politician, was unacceptable due to his commitment to Europe and the single currency. Apart from the lack of appealing leaders, the Conservatives were in disarray on policies, and Hague was unable to stop the wrangling that had been so damaging to Major. Although people were mildly disappointed with Labour's performance and tired of Labour's hype and media manipulation, all but a loyal minority, about 30 percent, despised the Tories.

The Liberal Democrats, led by Charles Kennedy, continued to be strong in local government, where they were viewed as a capable, honest alternative to the politicians of the two major parties, but it was evident that they were getting nowhere on the national level. Kennedy, a Scot, was among the new members elected in 1983. Although Blair and Kennedy shared many ideas, Kennedy was less susceptible to Blair's blandishments than Paddy Ashdown had been. The Liberal Democrats had made gains in 1997, when some voters had seen them as a reasonable protest vote. In 2001, most voters had already decided between the two major parties. The Liberal Democrats might tip the balance in a few marginal seats.

Blair had scheduled the election for May 7, a date postponed due to the restrictions on travel imposed to control foot-and-mouth disease. When he announced the new date as June 7, Blair did not begin with the House of Commons, which constitutionally was most concerned. He wanted a photo-op that would emphasize his determination to build a better future. He made his announcement to a group of school children assembled for that purpose. People of good taste were disgusted by this "showbiz" approach to campaigning, but such methods were typical of Labour's political use of human-interest television.

Blair's colleagues and opponents adopted similar tactics, as the stale routines of modern television-oriented electioneering were again imposed on a largely indifferent and unresponsive electorate. The endorsement of Blair by Spice Girl Geri Halliwell and American teenage country–pop singer Britney Spears did little to liven up the election. One of the few instances of spontaneity took place when the bluff sailor, Deputy Prime Minister John Prescott, defended himself by punching and wrestling to the ground a heckler who had thrown an egg.

Polls showed that the main issue in the campaign was the public demand for a comprehensive, well-managed, well-funded set of public services. Blair was on solid ground when he stated: "This election is about which party can be trusted with the economy, which party will invest more in the public services, which party is capable of leading Britain into the future." He promised additional teachers, doctors, nurses, and police, plus an increase in the minimum wage. Labour even promised to reduce teenage pregnancies by 15 percent in three years; no explanation was given as to how this would be done.

Although Labour had not achieved the "radical reform" that Blair had promised in 1997, the party could argue convincingly that the groundwork had been laid by its successful economic policy. Labour's best argument was that the party deserved another term, succinctly stated on a billboard: "The work goes on."

The Conservatives had few issues, since Labour had co-opted Thatcherism and established itself as the party of consensus politics. The Conservative manifesto carped and criticized, but most of Labour's policies were not seriously challenged. Tax reductions were promised, but they were modest and did not fit with promises to increase pensions, put more police officers on the beat, and improve schools and health. The Tories could claim, with some justice, that Labour had not delivered on its promises: "The new left has used our rhetoric," Hague declaimed, "but has not delivered on our beliefs." A Conservative billboard put the argument bluntly: "You've paid the taxes, now get the services."

When all was said and done, Hague's only issue was national sovereignty and identity, which he claimed were threatened by Labour's policy toward Europe, the euro, and immigration. "We will give you back your country," he shouted. He called for tough controls on immigrants claiming asylum and stated that Britain should be "a safe haven" but not "a soft touch for bogus refugees." His emphasis on Britishness was unfairly attacked as racist, a charge reinforced by racist comments made by a Tory backbencher who was not running for reelection.

It was evident that the dominant fact about the campaign was voter apathy. The outcome was seen as a foregone conclusion: the issues were stale, people were tired of hearing Blair, Hague was a bore, and the usual tricks of campaigning no longer generated interest. When polling day arrived, people were relieved that the campaign was over.

The Vote

The results were no surprise. The turnout rate was under 60 percent, the lowest since 1918, when millions of troops were overseas. As expected, Labour won with 42 percent of the vote—not a landslide, by any measure. However, 42 percent of the vote translated into 413 seats, a loss of 6. The Conservatives polled 33 percent and garnered 166 seats, a gain of 1. The Liberal Democrats received 19 percent of the vote and won 52 seats, a gain of 6—the best ever for the party and a personal triumph for Kennedy. In Scotland, the Scottish National Party lost ground to Labour and the Liberal Democrats, and the Conservatives were again shut out.

The election strengthened those elements in Northern Ireland that were opposed to the Good Friday Agreement. The Ulster Unionists suffered a net loss of 3 seats; David Trimble survived a close call only after a recount. The Protestant hard-liners of the Democratic Unionist Party gained 2 seats. "It is a victory," one of them said, "for those who don't want to share power with gunmen." Sinn Fein gained 2 seats, while the moderate Social Democratic and Labour Party (SDLP) held even at 3. The weakening of Trimble's support was a setback for Blair, who believed that Trimble was the only leader who could make the peace agreement work.

When the polls closed and the results came in, there were no celebrations comparable to 1997. Tony Blair remained at No. 10 Downing Street and reshuffled his Cabinet. The Blair ministry had been empowered by the electorate to continue working toward the ambitious goals laid out in 1997. William Hague resigned as leader of the Conservative Party. The general verdict of the public was pronounced by *The Economist*, which declared in its story on the election: "Mr. Blair. Now it is time to produce."

CHAPTER ELEVEN

~

Major and Blair: Wrapping Up the Thatcher Revolution

Reforming Government

Although Cabinet government in the conventional sense had been declining for some time, Margaret Thatcher and her successors increased the powers and responsibilities exercised by the prime minister and the staff at No. 10 Downing Street. Thatcher and John Major had a Prime Minister's Office, a Cabinet Office of civil servants, and a small Policy Unit to consider new policies and review existing ones. Tony Blair established an American-style Chief of Staff, a Private Office staff, a Policy Unit, a Press Office, and a Strategic Communications Unit. Critics complained that "presidential" government had replaced the collective responsibility of the Cabinet.

The Cabinet Office was reorganized to make it the key administrative office of the central executive. It was responsible for management of the civil service and supervision of the departments, and it coordinated parliamentary business with the Leader of the House of Commons and the whips. Unlike Margaret Thatcher, who was obsessed with details, Blair preferred to sketch out broad goals and delegate responsibility to the Cabinet Office and relevant departments to achieve them. He gave his press secretary sweeping powers to control press officers in the departments.

He reduced the Cabinet to a virtual nullity. Thatcher and Major met with the Cabinet once a week when Parliament was in session, and both used Cabinet committees to consider important issues. Blair called Cabinet meetings rarely and made occasional use of Cabinet committees. He preferred to meet one-on-one with Cabinet members, and many of his most important decisions were made in conference with Gordon Brown or John Prescott. Frequently he bypassed the departments and appointed "special advisers" to consider particular problems. He established more than two hundred task forces and working groups. In addition to civil servants, these bodies usually included outside experts and sometimes prominent businessmen. The Cabinet Office supervised their activities.

Thatcherism brought important changes in personnel policy. Thatcher liked to bring in successful businessmen to deal with difficult management problems. Major encouraged people from the private sector to apply in open competition for high-level civil service posts. Approximately 30 percent of such posts went to "outsiders." The Blair ministry continued that practice. The civil service now seeks people with managerial training and private-sector experience rather than the generally educated gentlemen of the past who worked their way upward through the ranks.

Like Thatcher and Major, Blair attempted to introduce the principles of business management into public administration. A Cabinet Office document entitled *Performance Management: Civil Service Reform* stated that management could be improved by establishing "a well-functioning business planning system." The document aimed to "incentivise people to seek challenging responsibilities, develop their competences, and demonstrate leadership."

An important feature of Thatcherism was contracting out or market testing. Responding to the public employee unions, Blair replaced contracting out with a requirement that agencies and local governments should prepare performance plans that included targets for the delivery of services. They were to seek the best value for the money, using their own judgment. Their decisions were subject to spending controls and external audit.

Privatization

The Blair ministry was eager to continue the Thatcherite policy of privatization, but there was not much left to sell. One possibility was to sell off government buildings in Whitehall and other locations attractive to business. Some of these properties were no longer needed in the era of downsizing and contracting out. With modern communications, agencies could be moved out of high-rent areas in London to efficient, purpose-built facilities in the hinterland. The Private Finance Initiative, introduced by Major in 1994, could be used to reduce the capital budget by having private enterprise put up buildings to be leased to government agencies.

Proposals were made to sell the properties called the Crown Estate, which included office buildings and residential, agricultural, and seafront lands. These were of enormous value and would be attractive to a wide variety of private enterprises. Attempts to dispose of some of the extensive lands held by the Department of Defence to help cover the cost of new weapons encountered strong resistance. Proposals were even made to sell some of the royal palaces. Harold Macmillan's remark about selling the Georgian silver did not seem so far-fetched after all.

Major had encountered strong resistance when he proposed privatization of the Post Office. The Blair government provoked a similar response when it revived the project. Resistance came from the public employee unions, who anticipated a loss of jobs. Many people opposed privatization because they feared that small, convenient post offices would be closed. Their concern was increased when the government decided that welfare benefits would be paid at banks instead of post offices, which was expected to reduce fraud.

Always sensitive to public opinion, the Blair ministry proposed a halfway privatization, which would establish the Post Office as an independent corporation, but with the government holding all the shares. A regulator (Postcomm) would supervise postal rates and services. Eventually the Post Office was privatized under the trendy name, Consignia. It had three divisions: Royal Mail, which carried and distributed mail; Post Office, which dealt with the public; and Parcelforce Worldwide, which offered a global delivery system resembling UPS and Federal Express.

Proposals for a public–private partnership to rebuild London Underground moved forward, despite the opposition of Mayor Ken Livingstone and the people. The government compromised by proposing that operation of the trains continue to be under Transport for London, but the tracks, signaling, and tunnels, where the needs were greatest, would be privatized.

With Railtrack fresh in mind, Livingstone declared that Londoners would have to be "brain dead" to accept the proposal. He brought in Robert Kiley, an American who had rescued the New York City subway, to do the same for the Tube. Kiley, an outspoken critic of privatization, declared that only a massive infusion of government money could accomplish the purpose. In April 2001, London filed a lawsuit in the High Court to block the proposal.

Questions of public safety were raised by establishment of a public–private partnership with a consortium that purchased 46 percent of the National Air Traffic Service (NATS). Outside capital was needed to modernize the air-control system at Heathrow and other airports. One MP remarked the NATS could end up being "the Railtrack of the skies." He was right. A year later

NATS was bankrupt, and the entire concept of public–private partnerships was being reconsidered.

Another project that floundered was the Channel Tunnel, which opened for regular service in November 1994. Delays in planning the link with London meant that travelers still had to ride on the old, slow railroad tracks between Waterloo Station and the tunnel. In 1998, the government unveiled plans for a public–private partnership with Railtrack to build a sixty-eight-mile high-speed rail link. In 2001, Railtrack stated that its many other problems would further delay completion of the link. It was then announced that Bechtel, an American construction firm, would receive the contract to do the project.

The Channel Tunnel itself faced financial and technical difficulties. In November 1996, a fire broke out in the tunnel when a heavy truck carrying a load of plastic caught fire and filled the tunnel with poisonous smoke. Other trucks also caught fire, and the evacuation procedures did not function well. It appeared that the tunnel would be closed for several months, or perhaps longer. It would take much longer than that to restore public confidence.

Another privatization gone sour was Rover, which had been a headache for Thatcher and its subsequent owners. Rover had come under the ownership of the German carmaker BMW and was still losing money. In March 2000, BMW announced that it would dispose of Rover and shut down the plant, which was Britain's largest auto factory and employed nine thousand workers. Blair, who had obtained a subsidy package from the European Union to keep the plant open, was furious. BMW eventually bailed out to a consortium of investors for the symbolic sum of £10.

The National Health Service

Implementation of Thatcher's reform of the National Health Service (NHS), like so many other Thatcher reforms, fell to Major. The National Health and Community Care Act (1990) relieved the district health authorities from management of the NHS. Instead, they became purchasing agencies, contracting with doctors and hospitals for health care.

Family doctors in large practices were eligible to receive funds directly from the NHS ("fund-holding"), which they used to purchase services from medical specialists or hospitals. Hospitals were encouraged to become free-standing corporations (trusts), receiving payment for their services either from fund-holding doctors or the district health authorities.

More than half the doctors in the NHS became fund-holders. The "internal market" based on fund-holding doctors and trust hospitals was intended to bring competition into health care. An Audit Commission report stated that fund-holding had been beneficial in establishing better communications between doctors and specialists and in encouraging restraint in prescribing. The commission added that the majority of doctors "do not appear to be especially good at management."

Approximately 90 percent of the hospitals became trusts. It is likely that trust hospitals keep tighter control of their costs, and they may have become more "user friendly" to satisfy doctors and patients. The Major government required doctors and hospitals to invite competitive bids from private firms to provide clinical and maintenance needs, thus creating potentially large opportunities for private enterprise within the NHS.

Some NHS doctors organized specialized groups that contracted to provide extra medical services as needed, which enabled hospitals to maintain a smaller permanent staff. One hospital invited bids to provide up to six hundred heart operations per year. There was a temptation for hospitals to add to their income by increasing the number of private beds. In 1997, the realities of the internal market began to intrude, as some hospitals closed because they were losing money.

Under Labour, satisfaction with the NHS continued to decline, and Brown's first two budgets did not provide enough funds to make a dent in its needs. The NHS could not cope with the flu epidemics of 1998–1999 and 1999–2000. There were not enough hospital beds, and long-standing appointments for operations were canceled to find beds for the elderly, who were most at risk. Spot checks of hospitals revealed some instances of appalling sanitary conditions. A survey showed wide variations in the death rates in hospitals.

Facing severe public criticism, Blair recognized that immediate action was needed to restore public trust. In his March 2000 budget, Brown substantially increased health spending, and in his Spending Review in July, he carried those increases into the next three years.

Labour preserved Thatcher's separation of purchasers and providers, but replaced competitive bidding with long-term contracts among doctors, specialists, and hospitals. Additional funding was provided to preserve hospitals that faced closure under the existing system.

Some Labour MPs resented the intrusion of private firms into the NHS and wanted all services provided "in house." In NHS hospitals, 58 percent of laundry services, 42 percent of cleaning services, and 29 percent of catering services were contracted out to the private sector. Alan Milburn, the health secretary, received an ovation at the Labour Party conference, when he announced that hospitals would no longer be required to seek bids from private firms for ancillary services.

In 2000, the Blair government presented a ten-year plan to revamp the NHS. Blair promised to add 2,000 doctors, 7,500 specialists, 6,500 health-care professionals, 7,000 beds, and 20,000 nurses. Nurses would be authorized to administer routine medical services, including writing prescriptions. Inducements were offered to encourage doctors to practice exclusively at the NHS, a proposal vigorously opposed by the British Medical Association. In 2001, with an election approaching and the public finances flush, Labour announced an ambitious program of hospital building, the creation of "fast-track" surgical centers for nonemergency operations, and a crash program to train additional nurses.

The most important changes under Labour concerned primary care doctors, who were put into Primary Care Trusts of about fifty physicians (similar to American HMOs) serving about one hundred thousand people. Their duties were extended to include hospital care (formerly the preserve of specialists), community care for the elderly, and provision of treatments in their offices. Fund-holding doctors disappeared.

The Primary Care Trusts received fixed budgets for medical services and prescriptions and made long-term contracts with hospitals. More use would be made of nurses for minor ailments and in care of the elderly. Recognizing wide disparities of health care, the government established Health Care Action Zones in deprived areas to coordinate efforts on the local level to improve health. A Commission for Health Improvement was established to review the quality of service and suggest changes.

Schools

Thatcher's educational reforms gave schools the opportunity to opt out of local control and manage their own affairs, supported by grants from the Treasury. The Major ministry moved the process along by the Education Act of 1993, which established the Funding Agency for Schools to distribute funds to grant-maintained schools. The agency also provided funds for the building of new schools, which were expected to be grant maintained. Grant-maintained schools were allowed to select 50 percent of their pupils by test scores and interviews. Some were permitted to specialize in subjects such as languages or music for talented students.

Most of the schools that opted out of local control were prestigious schools with high academic standards; by opting out they were able to continue selective admissions and maintain their quality. Although the measure was presented as "parental choice," in many instances it was the school that did the choosing. Some critics claimed that the interview provided an opportunity to introduce social class into the admissions process. The schools that remained under local control were permitted to select only 20 percent of their pupils, so they were at a competitive disadvantage for bright students. One result of school choice was "sink schools," which collected children unwanted by other schools.

The opportunity to opt out of the local education authority was not popular. Polling showed that most parents did not want selective schools; they wanted a selective stream within truly comprehensive schools. Out of twenty-four thousand schools, it appeared that no more than one thousand would become grant-maintained, despite the attractive inducements offered by the government.

One reason was the collapse of the Conservative Party on the local level, where Liberal and Labour councils discouraged opt outs. Another was local loyalty, as the general public rallied in support of their schools. In some places, it was thought that local support would be more reliable than opting out, because funding of a grant-maintained school might be threatened by a budget crisis or by a Labour government.

The Thatcherite education reform included a national curriculum that would standardize instructional content throughout the nation, making possible national examinations that would provide "league tables" (comparative data) on student performance. Information would also be published on levels of truancy and the number of hours of instruction. Schools that ranked low would be put on the spot to improve attendance and performance.

John Patten, who became secretary of state for education in 1992, had the task of implementing the national curriculum and the examinations based on it. In the struggle for space, history was a loser. The time allocated to history was cut by more than 20 percent to leave more time for English, mathematics, and science. Among the casualties of curriculum reform was British history, which was made optional for the General Certificate of Secondary Education (GCSE). The effect of curricular change was seen in 1996, when the number of students taking history for the GCSE was down 5.3 percent.

In 1993, Patten attempted to implement national testing, but he met determined resistance from the teachers. Apart from the extra work involved, the teachers were reluctant to have the performance of their students (and themselves) made a matter of public attention and compared with the examination results of other schools. The National Union of Teachers (NUT) advised its members to boycott the tests. Patten announced that if the boycott continued, he would contract out the grading. When agreement was finally reached with the teachers, national testing with league tables began.

The next year an office for the supervision of schools (Ofsted) was established to maintain academic standards and take over schools that failed to pass muster. Chris Woodhead became the chief inspector of schools. Woodhead blamed theories of progressive education for the decline in student performance. He urged more emphasis on discipline and subject matter instead of "child-centred education," "discovery learning," "inter-active instruction," "problem-solving," and education "relevant" to the interests of the child. "Children," he said, "needed to learn the kinds of things that they would need to know when they became adults, not whatever interested them at the moment."

In 1996, the results of the first tests were revealed. The nation was shocked to find that roughly 40 percent of the pupils who took the eleven-plus exam fell below the standards in English and math. Although complete league table ratings of schools were not published, Woodhead cited thirty outstanding state-supported schools and another one hundred that had improved their test results significantly. He promised a rigorous attack on poor teaching, including naming the best and worst teachers at each school. He stated that at least fifteen thousand teachers should be summarily dismissed.

With some justification, critics claimed that league tables distorted the educational mission of schools. Schools tried to attract the brightest pupils and get rid of poor ones. Teachers concentrated on preparing pupils for quantifiable tests rather than assisting them to develop their individual potentials. Sports, music, and other desirable extracurricular activities were sacrificed in the effort to raise league table rankings.

Ofsted was concerned at the large number of expulsions, which had soared since the introduction of league tables. Expulsions rose 300 percent from 1992 to 1993, and suspensions or other disciplinary exclusions rose by 800 percent. Of those expelled or suspended, 90 percent were boys from troubled homes. Ofsted reported that Afro-Caribbean boys were falling behind in school and that "colour-blind" policies did not work with them. Expulsions of black pupils were six times those of white students. Ofsted complained that schools were expelling problem students to keep their ranking up, rather than working with them.

In 1997, Woodhead declared that his next step was improved teacher training. He advocated getting away from "child-centred" teaching where children worked in groups. He wanted "whole class" teaching, where the teacher stands in front of the class as an authority figure. This method was introduced into teacher-training programs in September 1997. A new teacher-training curriculum was developed to define what students should learn at each level of instruction.

People were shocked when the headmaster of a school in London was stabbed as he tried to stop a fight between boys of his school and another school. The incident drew attention to unruliness in schools, which teachers complained made it impossible to teach. Teachers at a school in Yorkshire, where a male pupil assaulted a woman teacher, voted to strike unless 60 disruptive pupils in an enrollment of 620 were expelled.

Education Secretary Gillian Shephard advocated a return to corporal punishment, which had been banned by the European Union. Although Major rebuked her, when her proposal came before the House of Commons, ninety Tory backbenchers defied the ministry and voted for it. They argued that caning was preferable to expulsion and more effective.

A persistent cause of dispute was religious education, mandated as part of the national curriculum by the Education Act of 1988. The act stated that the national curriculum should "reflect the fact that the religious traditions of Great Britain are, in the main, Christian while taking account of the other principal religions represented."

The study of Christianity was defended as important for strengthening moral values and understanding the national culture. It was taken for granted that religion would be taught in a neutral but favorable manner, without efforts to promote or debunk it. A brief period of daily worship was also included in the religious education requirement.

When Patten insisted that local school authorities maintain the required programs of religious education and daily worship, one head teacher remarked: "Religious education is becoming a political football booted around the back-to-basics park. The Government should clean up its own act before expecting schools to promote religious and moral values that the Cabinet conspicuously lack."

The first draft of the religious education syllabus stated that, in addition to Christianity, students by the age of sixteen should have covered Buddhism, Hinduism, Islam, Judaism, and Sikhism. The Church of England and other Christian denominations argued that Britain was a Christian country, and for that reason, most of the time for religious education should be devoted to Christianity, even for non-Christian students. Furthermore, it would be difficult for religious education teachers to be knowledgeable about all those religions.

Large immigrant populations from India, Pakistan, Bangladesh, the Middle East, and Africa meant that in some cities other religions had strong claims to attention in the schools. Eventually, it was decided that half the time would be given to Christianity and half to the other great world religions, with some freedom for teachers to make adjustments in schools with large numbers of immigrant children.

This solution did not satisfy Britain's large Muslim community. In 1996, a school in Birmingham agreed to establish separate classes for Muslim students taught by a qualified Muslim teacher. This step led to pressure from Muslim groups elsewhere for separate religious education, a principle that they were quite willing to extend to Christians, Hindus, and other denominations. In 1998, the Labour government agreed to give public funding to two Muslim schools at the same level as Protestant, Catholic, and Jewish schools.

When Labour came to office, the appointment of David Blunkett as secretary of education and employment was widely approved within the Labour Party. Blunkett, a member of Labour's left wing was born blind. He survived a Dickensian boarding school and came out an angry young man. He joined the Labour Party, and by the age of twenty-two, he was a member of the Sheffield council. Eventually he became its leader. Growing up deprived in Sheffield gave him an awareness of the problems of inner-city schools and an intense desire to do something about them. He won praise for his ability to make progress, despite the financial stringencies of the first two years.

Blunkett got rid of some of the Thatcherite reforms. The grant-maintained schools were abolished and returned to funding by the local authorities on the same basis as church schools. Although the party's rank and file were still devoted to comprehensive schools, New Labour accepted selection on the basis of academic ability or special talents, leaving the decision to the local authorities.

The Blairs sent their son to a selective state-supported church school, despite criticism from within the Labour Party and cries of "hypocrisy" from the Tories. When Labour-controlled councils proposed to abolish the remaining 161 grammar schools, Blair stated emphatically that he would resist that idea. Labour's long war against the grammar schools had ended.

Blunkett's rigor showed how much New Labour differed from the old. He preserved the Thatcherite emphasis on conventional learning, high standards of performance, and firm classroom discipline. He kept the national curriculum, national tests, comparative reports of school performance, and tough enforcement by Ofsted. Emphasis was given to numeracy and literacy, as the keys to learning. Schools that fell short of expectations would be identified ("naming and shaming"), and steps would be taken to improve them.

Blunkett continued the Thatcherite policy of demanding accountability in return for increased funding. Head teachers were given more authority, which they were expected to use to overcome the resistance of the teachers unions and local education authorities. Performance-related pay was a threat to teachers, who resented being held accountable for the performance of students, many of whom were from deprived homes. In 1997, thirteen hundred boys were expelled from school as disruptive or even dangerous. While avoiding "selection," a bogeyman in the Labour Party, a substitute was found in streaming, specialized schools, and other devices.

The National Union of Teachers was shocked when Blunkett continued Woodhead in his office as chief inspector of schools. The NUT demanded the dismissal of Woodhead, dismantling of Ofsted, abolition of grammar schools, an end to league tables, and a return to comprehensive schools. Teachers complained of large class sizes and excessive workloads. "We are giving Labour a year," said one union leader. "If we cannot get agreement from the new government we will do it ourselves and ballot to boycott all this unnecessary nonsense."

In 1998, significant improvements in the test results of primary pupils were reported. Teachers dropped their former opposition to inspection and testing and admitted that the pressure of national league tables had contributed to improved pupil performance. The largest gains took place in the top 10 percent of the pupils, while performance of the lowest 10 percent declined. An unfortunate consequence was that concerned parents avoided sending their children to "sink schools," which made them even worse.

Blunkett was a strong advocate of the "welfare to work" program and active in establishing the kinds of training programs that would be needed. He proposed Education Action Zones in deprived areas, where the government and local authorities would work together to provide schooling designed for at-risk children. Business, local education authorities, and parents would operate them cooperatively. "Sure Start" programs (similar to American Head Start) were established in areas where children needed the most help. After-school homework and clubs for study and healthful recreation were established. They provided safe and encouraging after-school facilities for children whose parents had to work late.

In January 2001, the money began to flow, and Blunkett announced the largest program of school building in fifty years. The next month he declared that efforts to improve literacy and numeracy in elementary schools had succeeded and that the thrust of a second Labour government would be to improve secondary education. His goal was "diversity" within a comprehensive system. He proposed new kinds of secondary schools that would foster individual talents and address weaknesses. Blunkett promised extra support for schools in the most disadvantaged areas and proposed financial inducements to encourage young people to go into teaching. "We have today," he declared, "moved beyond the old arguments, to create a school system for the twenty-first century."

Another problem receiving attention was the increasing disparity between the school performance of girls and boys. At all but the top schools, girls out-performed boys, sometimes by wide margins. Many boys in their teens, when glands and peer pressure are powerful, rejected scholarship as "unmanly" and turned to "laddism" (rough dress and manners and hanging out on the streets with "the lads") as a way to assert their masculinity. Modern popular culture, with its violence, use of drugs and alcohol, hedonism, and *carpe diem* attitude, was thought to exert a stronger negative influence on boys than on girls. This was especially true of working-class boys in areas of high unemployment, where good role models did not exist. "The yob culture," as it was called, was attractive to boys who lacked adequate preparation for school and faced unemployment when they left it.

In December 2000, the government introduced a Special Education Needs and Disabilities bill that required inclusion, with few exceptions, of students with learning and behavioral problems in mainstream classes. Additional funding was provided for special-needs teachers. Some educators believed that well-run schools should be able to deal with problems that arose and that all students would benefit. Others argued that more inclusion would lead to more expulsions. The teachers unions were opposed. The question was: Has Labour's crusade for social inclusion gone too far?

Universities

In 1979, one young adult in eight attended a university; now it is one in three. The number of part-time students is almost equal to full-time. A notable feature of the 1970s and 1980s was the great increase in the number of women in higher education. From 1971 to 1993, the number of women enrolled increased by 250 percent. In 1971 male students outnumbered women 2 to 1; by 1993, men and women were approximately equal. Science courses attract twice as many men as women; the ratio is almost exactly reversed in literature and arts courses. In the social sciences, the enrollments of men and women are about the same. The superior performance of girls in school carried into the universities. In 2001, more women gained honors degrees than men, and the trend was expected to continue.

When Major took office, Kenneth Clarke became secretary of state for education and science. With characteristic Thatcherite disdain for local government, Clarke removed the polytechnics from local funding and control. The Polytechnics and Colleges Funding Council was established to provide grants from the Treasury and to establish standards of expenditure and performance to which the polytechnics were required to adhere. In 1993, the funding of universities and polytechnics was combined and placed under the Higher Education Funding Council.

Over the previous thirty years, the polytechnics had grown to surpass the universities in enrollments. Their faculties, students, and curricula had changed to resemble universities, but they were less expensive and had lower admission requirements. Clarke decided that the polytechnics, which previously had emphasized career-oriented programs, should become universities, and so they did.

Academics were astonished to see a rash of new and unfamiliar names in the formerly narrow world of academia. In 1960, Britain had 24 universities; in 1996, with the transformation of the polytechnics, there were 105. This arbitrary and rapid transformation raised questions, not only of cost, but also of academic standards and the employability of graduates.

In 1993, Clarke became chancellor of the Exchequer, where he viewed universities from a different perspective. He announced that enrollments would be frozen, grants for operating funds would remain roughly the same, and capital expenditures would be slashed to the bone. In 1995, public funding for the universities and colleges was cut 2.5 percent.

The next year, Clarke called for a 7 percent cut in public funding and a 31 percent cut in capital spending. He anticipated another "efficiency gain" of 10 percent in 1997. Maintenance grants for students were being phased out, and a program of student loans was established to help students pay their living expenses. Some students began taking part-time jobs, a practice common in the United States but unusual in Britain.

In 1996, Major appointed Sir Ron (later Lord) Dearing to lead a committee to report after the election on the problem of the increasing cost of higher education. The Dearing Report (July 1997) proposed that students pay £1,000 per year, but they should be offered a loan that would not have to be repaid until they graduated and were gainfully employed. Blair knew that ending free tuition would have political repercussions, but there was no alternative, and tuition charges were imposed.

Blunkett had little sympathy with complainers, for typically Labour regarded universities as bastions of privilege, and free tuition and maintenance as indefensible handouts to the offspring of the middle class. He made it clear that the free lunch had ended. Blair suggested that the universities seek to find additional money from private sources. One example was Bill Gates, who gave a generous contribution to Cambridge to develop advanced studies in technical subjects.

The universities had no choice but to introduce tuition charges. Early in 1997, the university vice-chancellors warned students seeking admission in

1998 to prepare to pay entrance fees up to £1,000, with abatements based on need. They proposed loans to students for tuition, with twenty years to repay. The more prestigious universities joined to market themselves as world-class institutions charging higher fees than the rest. Despite tuition charges, university enrollments have held up well, because it is clear to students and their parents that the best jobs in Blair's Britain require a university education.

Oxford and Cambridge were regarded by Labour as the heart of academic elitism. *The Economist* (November 29, 1997) noted that only 7 percent of British students attended private schools, but they were awarded about 50 percent of the places at Oxbridge colleges. Oxford and Cambridge received state support higher than other universities to maintain their collegiate structures. Blunkett informed them that "top-up" funding for their colleges would be discontinued and that they would receive funding at the same level as the other universities.

To preserve their tutorial system of individual instruction, the Oxbridge colleges considered charging students additional fees, until the government stepped in and blocked the idea. Oxford, following a precedent set earlier with Thatcher, showed its indignation by refusing to give Blair an honorary degree.

The Police and Crime

"Law and Order" was a theme that resonated among the Conservative rank and file, and John Major continued the Margaret Thatcher's tough approach. Increasingly, the police were challenged by crime that was more than local bad behavior, including organized crime on the national and international level, the drug trade, gangs, political terrorism, and assemblies of hooligans from all over the country at sporting events. Recorded crimes had more than doubled since 1979. Many people felt unsafe, and the demand for tougher law enforcement intensified.

A new element in crime was the increasing use of firearms, as drug gangs fought to control their turf. In 1983, there were eight thousand such incidents; in 1994, there were almost fourteen thousand. In 1996, a shocking killing of schoolchildren in Scotland brought a powerful public reaction against private ownership of handguns.

Swept by emotion stimulated by television appearances of the families of the slain children, Parliament responded with legislation outlawing handguns except .22 caliber kept securely in gun clubs. Conservative backbenchers, responding to gun dealers and owners, claimed that the legislation went too far. The Major ministry had offended another of its special-interest constituencies.

Despite Blair's promise to be "tough on crime and the causes of crime," crime rose by 3.8 percent in 1999, including a 16 percent increase in violent crime. In a striking reversal of its traditional character, the United Kingdom had the highest incidence of violent crime and burglaries of any country in the European Union. The homicide rate was low, but rising.

Labour's home secretary, Jack Straw, promised a vigorous attack on professional criminals. He stated that one hundred thousand professional criminals committed half of all crimes and promised to close "the revolving door" that allowed them to serve short sentences and return to society, only to commit more crimes. He proposed drug testing of people charged with crimes and elimination of trial by jury in kinds of cases where juries were reluctant to convict notorious offenders (later rejected by the House of Lords). Another anticrime proposal that posed a threat to civil liberties would require anyone who used coded e-mail to give the key to the government.

Straw's tough approach to crime seemed to have little effect. A Home Office report in January 2001 stated that violent crimes had increased by 16 percent over the previous year, setting a new record. Robberies were up sharply, and murder and assault showed a slight increase. The largest increases were in London and the declining industrial areas of greater Manchester, Merseyside, and the west Midlands. Many more crimes went unreported. Teenagers perpetrated much of this crime. "The increase is due to crimes where both victims and their assailants are youngsters," one chief constable said.

Firm law enforcement was difficult for police in crime-ridden, low-income, racially mixed inner-city areas, where endemic problems contributed to negative attitudes among the police toward the people they were expected to serve. When the police cracked down with "stop and search" techniques, they were accused of racism; when they looked the other way, they were charged with neglect.

The situation was highlighted by the acquittal in 1996 of three white youths for killing Stephen Lawrence, a black eighteen-year-old who was waiting for a bus. Charges were made that the police investigation was perfunctory and that prosecution had been put off indefinitely.

Responding to complaints, Straw announced an inquiry into the case led by Sir William Macpherson, a retired judge. At the time of the killing, the Crown Prosecution Service had not brought charges, claiming a lack of evidence. The charge was made that the London Metropolitan Police were riddled with "institutional racism," which led them to fail to investigate properly, a charge that the police denied.

During the inquiry, which took place in 1998, the police apologized for a poor investigation, but said that racism had nothing to do with it. In January

1999, the Police Complaints Commission cleared the officers of the charge of racism.

In February 1999, Macpherson issued his report, which was remarkably similar to the Scarman Report of 1981. Macpherson found that the London police were "riven with pernicious and institutionalized racism," which he defined as "the collective failure of an institution to provide appropriate professional service to people because of their colour, culture, or ethnic origin." The report emphasized the resentment of young Asians and blacks at what they considered unfair treatment. More and better-trained police officers were recommended, and Brown's increased financial support for the Home Office was a step in that direction. Labour responded by strengthening the Race Relations Act to require public bodies to "promote equality and good race relations." Chief constables were made liable for racial discrimination by police officers under their command.

Drug use and the drug business were important factors in the increase in crime. Despite the toughest drug laws in Western Europe, drug use was widespread in Britain, especially among the young. Polls showed that 80 percent of the population wanted to decriminalize marijuana. A new drug, ecstasy, was associated with a vibrant dance culture in nightclubs and bars.

When a blue-ribbon commission recommended relaxing drug laws, Straw replied that the best way to fight drugs was tougher enforcement of existing laws. Home Office figures showed that two-thirds of all convicted criminals tested positive for drugs. Straw proposed special drug courts to hear drug cases and steer addicts into treatment.

He experienced the drug problem personally, when an attractive female reporter inveigled his son into obtaining marijuana. The appeal of the most widely used drug of all, alcohol, was highlighted when Blair's sixteen-year-old son was found "drunk and incapable" in Leicester Square after celebrating completion of his school exams.

A crime problem that assumed increasing importance was the role of London as a center of terrorist groups. London was ideal for terrorists: they enjoyed British freedom; they could conceal themselves among fellow countrymen; London had excellent communications with the Middle East and central Asia; and London was well equipped for laundering and making large transfers of money. Osama Bin Laden, among others, used London as a center for his financial dealings. Foreign governments in many parts of the world complained about the refuge that terrorists enjoyed.

The Blair government took steps to deal with the problem by extending the Prevention of Terrorism Act, which applied only to terrorism related to Northern Ireland. The new law made it illegal to plan a terrorist act in

Britain, even if intentions were to carry it out in another country. Fundraising and other forms of support for terrorism were also made illegal.

The Queen and the Royal Family

During the Major ministry, the role and dignity of the monarchy were threatened as a result of the personal problems of the royal family. Almost everyone agreed that Queen Elizabeth II carried out her role splendidly. Her husband, Prince Philip, Duke of Edinburgh, faithfully accompanied her on her appointed rounds, although he was occasionally chastised in the press for his stern pronouncements on social problems. The queen's sister, Princess Margaret, was divorced, as was the queen's daughter, Princess Anne. The queen's son, Andrew, Duke of York, and his uninhibited duchess (Sarah Ferguson) decided to end their marriage after months of lurid coverage in the tabloids.

The most sensational occurrence was the breakdown of the marriage of the Prince of Wales and his wife, the Princess Diana, whose chilly relationship had long been known. They were divorced in 1996. Her tragic death in an automobile accident led to an outburst of public mourning and a state funeral, in which Blair played a prominent part. In 2000, the government opened a public memorial walk and children's playground in her memory. Plans for a memorial fountain in Hyde Park were not completed until 2002.

These embarrassments led to meritocratic and populist questions about the utility and cost of the monarchy. Part of this cost was paid out of the Civil List, the public funds that support the royal family. Additional public funding was provided within departmental budgets, which picked up the cost of the royal palaces, yacht, train, and planes. Estimates of the queen's private wealth vary widely, but there can be no doubt that she is one of the world's wealthiest women.

Polls showed that most people thought that the cost of the monarchy should be reduced, and too many members of the royal family were being supported at public expense. They felt that the queen should pay taxes on her private income. To add to the queen's troubles, in 1992 a disastrous fire inflicted much damage on Windsor Castle, bringing demands that she pay for repairs from her own private funds. To help cover the cost of restoration, Buckingham Palace was opened to the public for part of the year.

Queen Elizabeth II placed great confidence in John Major, whose pleasant personality was in sharp contrast to the abrasive and opinionated Margaret Thatcher. She agreed to the Civil List Act of 1992, which provided public support only for the queen, the Duke of Edinburgh, and the aged Queen Mother. However, an inflation factor of 7.5 percent was included, and the queen gained an additional £30 million over the next few years, since inflation was low.

Prince Charles receives the income of the Duchy of Cornwall, properties located mainly in the west of England, which is considered sufficient. The queen supports other members of the royal family out of her private income. Queen Elizabeth II agreed to begin paying income taxes on her private income, as did Prince Charles on his income from the Duchy of Cornwall. In 2001, the queen agreed to pay National Insurance contributions for her employees.

In 1991 Thatcherism reached the monarchy, when the queen was given a block grant to manage the royal palaces. She cut costs by 25 percent over five years. In 1996, it was decided that the same principle should apply to royal travel other than the yacht, and block grants were provided for the royal airplanes and the royal train. In 1997, the royal yacht *Britannia* made its final voyage, carrying Prince Charles to Hong Kong for ceremonies accompanying the turnover of the colony to the People's Republic of China. When the ceremonies were finished, Prince Charles and the royal governor came aboard and sailed away into the imperial sunset.

Seeking support from "the patriotic vote," the Major ministry proposed that *Britannia* be replaced by a new yacht built in a British shipyard, a project that was well received by Tory nationalists. The ministry found that it had stepped on another banana skin. Labour had not been consulted and withheld its approval. Prince Charles was annoyed because he did not think a yacht was a good idea, given the sensitive state of the monarchy. And the queen was upset at finding herself the object of political controversy. The yacht was never built, and the royal family has learned to live without one.

Blair worked with the queen to continue Major's reforms. The cost of the monarchy was further reduced and regularized. In 1997, the Labour government established the Civil List at £7.9 million per year, with an additional £500,000 for the expenses of the Duke of Edinburgh and another £500,000 for the expenses of the Queen Mother. Other Civil List costs were for salaries, food, wine, garden parties, cars, and the like. Thatcherism penetrated further into the mysteries of monarchy in 1998, when expenditures for palaces and travel were brought under the Audit Office, and proposals were made for a similar audit of the Civil List.

In 2001 the first annual accounts of Civil List expenditures were published. They showed that the queen was the nation's most successful Thatcherite, for her expenditures had fallen by more than half since 1991. The largest expenses were salaries, but significant amounts were spent for garden parties, food and kitchens, housekeeping, and royal processions. The costs of legal advice and fine wines were rising, although there seemed to be no connection between the two.

To reduce the salaries bill, plans were announced to overhaul the royal household, eliminating such honorific posts as lord chamberlain, master of the horse, ladies of the bedchamber, grand almoner, keeper of the royal stamp collection, and swan warden. Since most holders of those offices were Conservatives of high social status, Labour welcomed such changes, as did the bulk of the population, who, in the age of popular democracy, had little sympathy for blue bloods.

After the death of Princess Diana, a new Prince Charles began to emerge: more open, relaxed, and accessible. Obviously, he had taken to heart the criticism that the monarchy was too remote from the people. He got along well with his sons, hired a media adviser, and benefited from his good relationship with Blair. The disruptions that have plagued the royal family seem to be dying down. Handsome Prince William began to replace his mother as the celebrity darling of checkout-counter magazines. The "magic of monarchy" is still alive and well in Britain.

The Church of England

One of the historic institutions of authority and respect in England is the Church of England. Church attendance has declined greatly in recent years and the pronouncements of the clergy on current issues are often dismissed as irrelevant or silly, but a segment of the British public, especially in small towns and rural areas, is deeply attached to the Church. In 2000, church attendance in all denominations was 7.7 percent of the population. Only 2 percent attended the Church of England regularly.

Promotional efforts to persuade people to come to church on Easter Sunday have not been successful. However, one-fourth of all British babies are baptized in the Church of England. The Church was not happy when Prince Charles, recognizing the diversity of religion in Britain, suggested that the monarch be called "Defender of Faith" instead of "Defender of the Faith."

The clergy have become elderly, mainly as a result of a sharp decline in ordinations. Another factor in the aging of the clergy is the considerable number of retired business and professional people who wish to pursue a new career of service in the Church. Most of the parishioners who attend regularly are also of the older generation. These days few young people are being ordained, and attendance among that age group is low.

In addition to an aging clergy, the Church is the custodian of thirteen thousand aged buildings classified as grade-one, 40 percent of all grade-one buildings in the United Kingdom. Many of them are parish churches in small villages that have difficulty maintaining them. Others are splendid Victorian churches in decaying urban centers. In the City of London, the magnificent churches designed by Sir Christopher Wren are poorly attended on Sundays, but they are used during the week for lunchtime lectures and concerts attended by visitors and the people who work in the shops and offices.

Even the Church found it necessary to engage in a bit of Thatcherism. The Bishop of London recommended that twenty-four of the City's thirty-six churches be desanctified and put to other uses, such as libraries or meeting rooms. The Archbishops of Canterbury and York announced a sweeping review of the structure of the Church, including consolidation of its ten thousand parishes. They stated that the income of the clergy could be kept at a decent level only by reducing the number of clergymen.

In 1994, after years of debate, the Church of England ordained its first women priests, although women had been filling lesser posts in the clergy for some time. The main force behind the change was the women's movement, but there was broad agreement among lay members of both genders that the step was overdue.

Women's role as caretakers has rapidly expanded from motherhood, teaching, and nursing into professional roles as doctors, lawyers, and accountants. Serving as priests in the Church seemed to be a logical extension of that process. It was opposed mainly by Anglo-Catholics, both for theological reasons and because it put another barrier in the way of reunion with the Church of Rome. When the first ordained women took up their duties, there was almost universal agreement among parishioners that they wondered what all the fuss was about.

~

CHAPTER TWELVE

Assessment: What Was the Thatcher Revolution?

In 1979, facing electoral defeat, Prime Minister James Callaghan remarked to one of his advisers: "You know there are times, perhaps once every thirty years, there is a sea change in politics. It then does not matter what you say or do. There is a shift in what the public wants and what it approves. I suspect there is now such a sea change—and it is for Mrs. Thatcher."

Labour had swept into power in 1945 on a tidal wave of public determination to change the unsatisfactory institutions and conditions of the prewar period. Callaghan recognized that the institutional and social framework established by Labour from 1945 to 1951 had fallen apart on his watch. A sea change had surged forward in the 1970s, and Margaret Thatcher was the leader who would carry it into effect.

The Thatcher Revolution was based on a set of ideas intended to result in action. These ideas came from a variety of sources, but they were fused into an agenda (not a doctrine) by the will and instincts of one person—Margaret Thatcher. The foundation of Thatcherism was an emphasis on individual freedom, opportunity, and responsibility. Thatcherism posited a market economy, strong families, and sturdy patriotism. Despite the compromises and inconsistencies inevitable in the political process, the Thatcher Revolution grew out of ideas.

Thatcher's purpose was to restore vigor to a nation in decline. She believed that British individualism had been eroded by socialism and the welfare state, which had made too many of her countrymen passive bystanders rather than self-motivated actors engaged in making lives for themselves.

British businessmen did not show the entrepreneurial spirit that was needed. She deplored the breakdown of the family, which in many instances she thought was encouraged by the welfare system. And she saw glaring failures in local government, schools, health care, and law enforcement, and she moved aggressively to remedy those problems, in most cases by using the power of the state to reform the institutions that she thought were failing the British people.

To what extent was the Thatcher Revolution a result of strong personal leadership? To what extent was it a series of improvised, ad hoc responses to circumstances as they arose? Of course, it was both. But Thatcher was determined to overcome circumstances with leadership. Hers was a confrontational leadership style, fueled by a sense of purpose and a fierce determination to deal vigorously with the ills of Britain as she saw them.

In the process, Thatcher clashed headlong with powerful institutions, beginning with the nationalized industries and trade unions, but moving on to the civil service, local governments, schools and universities, the National Health Service, many prominent figures in the Conservative Party, and political-intellectual elites resentful of the shopkeeper's daughter who extolled the Victorian virtues of self-reliance, work, thrift, strong families, and national vigor.

The Thatcher Revolution was launched during an economic crisis made worse by an institutional framework that had long failed to function well. Harold Wilson, Edward Heath, and James Callaghan had all recognized the faults in the system, but Thatcher was the leader with the courage and convictions to act. She also had the opportunity, for few politicians are willing to engage in fundamental reform until dire necessity—as in the breakdown of 1979—compels them to do so.

Her first priority was the economy. She acted to reduce the government's contribution to the crisis by establishing fiscal and monetary stability. Her main objective was to open the economy to entrepreneurship and market forces. She did so by breaking down the barriers—taxation, exchange controls, regulations, nationalized industries, trade union power—that she thought stifled enterprise. Her opening of the British economy bore fruit in economic growth and inward investment. Her policies succeeded until overwhelmed by mistakes for which she was ultimately responsible: a boom resulting from the ill-judged tax and monetary policies of Nigel Lawson, followed by the disaster of the Exchange Rate Mechanism (ERM).

When Thatcher turned to reform the welfare state, she encountered resistance. The British people did not share her individualist views. They were willing to accept reforms that were economically beneficial, but they cherished the security provided by free education (unless they chose private schools), the National Health Service (unless they chose private medicine), pensions for retirement and disability (preferably supplemented by personal savings and private pensions), and a wide range of free or low-cost amenities such as parks, libraries, museums, and recreational facilities. They were skeptical of Thatcher's insistence that her reforms of the welfare state would make the system work better.

The essential Thatcher Revolution took place during the ministries of Margaret Thatcher, but it did not end with her fall in November 1990. Thatcherism became the core principle of British public policy under her successors. John Major and Tony Blair were concerned with working out the details—where the devil lurks, as they discovered.

Thatcher pushed personal leadership to its limits, and eventually paid the price. Major and Blair were cautious leaders: Major because his majority was small, and he wanted to stay in office; Blair because his majority was large, and he did not want defections before the next election. Major could not afford to make enemies, and Blair wanted to be everybody's friend.

The Thatcher Revolution brought fundamental changes to British political parties, as they responded to a changing electorate. Thatcher rid the Conservative Party of Tory paternalism; Blair rid Labour of socialism and trade union power. Both parties accepted a strong state, the free-market economy, and a large public sector. The two major parties had to appeal to an electorate where former party loyalties had been homogenized into a broad, moderate center. The Liberal Democratic Party was marginalized to a party of local government.

Thatcher saw no need to reform the constitutional framework of the United Kingdom, which provided a strong central government for the four nationalities that comprised it. Movements for devolution revived in Scotland and Wales, but eighteen years of Conservative dominance forced advocates to wait for a better opportunity.

In Northern Ireland, Thatcher's efforts were concentrated on reducing terrorism, which blocked any reasonable resolution of communal differences. Major moved the process along, seeking a political accommodation between unionists and nationalists. Blair drifted into devolution for Scotland and Wales and completed the peace process in Northern Ireland that Major had begun.

Blair evaded the most pressing constitutional issue, reform of Parliament, by accepting a patch job on the House of Lords and ignoring proposals to reform the electoral system for the House of Commons. Efforts of all three ministries to improve local government have produced inconclusive results.

Thatcher was determined to show the world that Britain was no longer a nation in decline, but was a significant player in the global community. Major and Blair followed her example. All three prime ministers realized that a global role required partnership with the United States, since the European Union had no foreign policy, apart from trade.

When she came into office, Thatcher viewed the Soviet Union as a military threat and an obstacle to the dynamic new world that was emerging. When the opportunity arose, she joined with Mikhail Gorbachev and Ronald Reagan in an effort to reduce tensions between the Soviet Union and the West. Relations with China and the Union of South Africa had a similar purpose. She and her successors proved surprisingly willing to use military force when provoked.

Thatcher knew that membership in the European Union was necessary for access to Britain's most important market, but she resisted the march toward political unity. Major inherited a party that was divided on Britain's relations with Europe, which contributed mightily to the miseries he experienced during his tenure in No. 10 Downing Street. Blair escaped Major's struggles over monetary union by evading the issue in his first ministry.

Under Major and Blair the shortcomings of the Thatcher Revolution became clear. The Thatcher economic policies did not lead to the burst of entrepreneurship that she anticipated. Development of the economy was highly uneven, with financial services doing well and manufacturing sluggish, despite large numbers of unemployed people available to work in factories. When the crisis of the recession and "Black Wednesday" had passed, the Major and Blair ministries adopted tight fiscal and monetary policies that stifled public investment in infrastructure, education, health, and other requirements of an advanced country.

The greatest failure of the Thatcher Revolution was unemployment, poverty, and the waste of human resources that these entailed. Thatcherism brought a period of strong economic growth, but it did not raise all boats. Some people cannot be helped, but more could have been done to lift people out of the mire. Not enough attention was given to regional differences. Predictably, in a democracy, the parts of the country with the most people and wealth get the most attention despite greater needs elsewhere. Leadership is needed to offset this tendency.

The Thatcher Revolution can now be pronounced complete. Britain enters the twenty-first century with its institutions reformed in the direction of individual freedom and responsibility, the United Kingdom is fractured but unbroken, and most of its corporate character is still intact. Margaret

Thatcher failed to instill her aggressive individualism into the body politic. The British people prize freedom, but they also have a strong sense of community. They look to government to provide a wide range of public services and a safety net for those times when help is needed. A sheltered harbor within the European Union looks attractive to many.

Since the Victorian Age, Britain has gone through periods of reform followed by consolidation. Each period of reform and consolidation led eventually to another. Jim Callaghan suggested that a sea change takes place every thirty years. Is another taking shape, beneath the surface, ready to emerge by the end of this decade? The answer of history must be: "Wait and see, but expect to be surprised."

~

Bibliographical Note

The factual scaffolding for this book was derived primarily from that useful work of reference, the *Annual Register: A Record of World Events* (London: Cartermill, 1979–1999). Unfortunately, the last issue (1998) appeared in 1999. Reference works for the years 1999–2001 were *Whitaker's Almanack*, published annually by the Stationery Office, and *Facts on File*. Useful works of reference are *Encyclopedia of Modern Britain*, ed. Fred M. Leventhal (New York: Peter Lang, 2000), and *Twentieth-Century British Political Facts: 1900–2000* by David Butler and Gareth Butler (8th ed., New York: St. Martin's, 2000). The main periodicals used were the *Times* (London), the *Sunday Times* (London), the *New York Times*, *The Economist*, and the Internet edition of the BBC News.

A general survey of postwar Britain is David Childs, *Britain since 1945: A Political History* (5th ed., New York: Routledge, 2000). Two good studies of modern British government are Dennis Kavanagh, *British Politics: Continuity and Change* (4th ed., Oxford: Oxford University Press, 2000) and Ian Budge et al., *The New British Politics* (2nd ed., London: Longman, 2000). Stimulating discussions of recent British politics are found in Stuart Weir and David Beetham, *Political Power and Democratic Control in Britain: The Democratic Audit of the United Kingdom* (London: Routledge, 1999); Ian Budge et al., *The New British Politics* (2nd ed., 2000); Bill Jones and Dennis Kavanagh, *Politics: U.K.* (4th ed., New York: Prentice Hall, 2000); Jones and Lynton Robins, *Debates in British Politics Today* (Manchester: Manchester University Press, 2000); and Patrick Dunleavy et al., *Developments in British Politics 6* (2000). All have good, up-to-date bibliographies and some list Internet sites.

The Conservative Century: The Conservative Party since 1900, ed. Anthony Seldon and Stuart Ball (Oxford: Oxford University Press, 1994), puts Thatcherism in perspective. The Conservative Party, ed. Philip Norton (New York: Prentice Hall, 1996), has a similar purpose. Contemporary British Conservatism, ed. Steve Ludlam and Martin Smith (New York: St. Martin's, 1996) offers a stimulating collection of essays.

Andrew Thorpe, A History of the British Labour Party (2nd ed., Houndmills, U.K.: Basingstoke, 2001), is a good starting-point book. The Labour Party: A Centenary History is a multiauthor work edited by Brian Brivati and Richard Heffernan (New York: St. Martin's, 2000). Labour's First Century, ed. Duncan Tanner, Pat Thane, and Nick Tiratsoo (Cambridge: Cambridge University Press, 2000), presents stimulating chapters on Labour ideas as they related to policy.

The transformation of the Labour Party is covered in Eric Shaw, The Labour Party since 1945: Old Labour, New Labour (Cambridge, Mass.: Blackwell, 1996). New Labour: The Progressive Future? ed. Stuart White (New York: Palgrave, 2001), considers Labour in the light of "Third Way" ideas. See also Steven Fielding, The Labour Party since 1951 (Manchester: Manchester University Press, 1997). The electoral history of "New Labour" is covered in The Rise of New Labour: Party Policies and Voter Choices by Anthony F. Heath, Roger M. Jowell, and John K. Curtice (Oxford: Oxford University Press, 2001).

David Butler with Dennis Kavanagh has published studies of the British general elections of 1979, 1983, 1987, 1992, 1997, and 2001. See also David Butler and Gareth Butler, Twentieth-Century British Political Facts: 1900–2000 (8th ed., 2000), cited earlier.

Margaret Thatcher's memoirs entitled The Downing Street Years (London: HarperCollins, 1993) and The Path to Power (London: HarperCollins, 1995) were important sources for the earlier chapters, not only for Lady Thatcher's own perspective on her life and political career, but as storehouses of factual information. They are well indexed, with useful appendixes providing a chronology and lists of officeholders.

Memoirs of other participants also were useful. Sir Geoffrey Howe, Conflict of Loyalty (London: Macmillan, 1994) tells the story of Thatcher's chancellor of the Exchequer and foreign secretary. Nigel Lawson, The View from No. 11 (New York: Doubleday, 1993) is a full account of the Thatcher ministry written by her brilliant, willful chancellor of the Exchequer. Interesting autobiographies are Nicholas Ridley, "My Style of Government": The Thatcher Years (London: Hutchinson, 1991) and Norman Fowler, Ministers Decide: A Personal Memoir of the Thatcher Years (London: Chapmans, 1991). Relevant to the Thatcher and Major ministries is Michael Heseltine: Life in the Jungle (London:

Hodder & Stoughton, 2000), an autobiography. A good biography is *Michael Heseltine: A Biography* (London: Hamish Hamilton, 1997) by Michael Crick.

John Major offers valuable insights into the Thatcher government, as well as a detailed account of his own, in *John Major: The Autobiography* (New York: HarperCollins, 1999). Other biographical accounts of Major's ministry are Norman Lamont, *In Office* (London: Little, Brown, 1999); and Sarah Hogg and Jonathan Hill, *Too Close to Call: Power and Politics—John Major in No. 10* (London: Little, Brown, 1995). Anthony Seldon, *Major: A Political Life* (London: Weidenfeld & Nicolson, 1997), is a detailed biography.

An informed assessment of the Thatcher ministry with valuable economic data is Peter Riddell, *The Thatcher Era and Its Legacy* (2nd ed., Oxford: B. Blackwell, 1991). See also Anthony Seldon and Daniel Collings, *Britain under Thatcher* (New York: Longman, 1999), Shirley R. Letwin, *The Anatomy of Thatcherism* (New Brunswick, N.J.: Transaction, 1993), and Andrew Gamble, *The Free Economy and the Strong State: The Politics of Thatcherism* (2nd ed., London: Palgrave Macmillan, 1994). A book offering an alternative view of Thatcherism is Will Hutton, *The State We're In* (rev. ed., London: Random House, 1996).

An assessment of the Major ministry is offered in Peter Dorey, *The Major Premiership* (New York: St. Martin's, 1999). Hywel Williams, *Guilty Men: Conservative Decline and Fall, 1992–1997* (London: Aurum Press, 1998), is a devastating indictment of the Major ministry with many shrewd insights.

John Rentoul, *Tony Blair: Prime Minister* (London: Little, Brown, 2001), is an outstanding biography. Valuable studies of the Blair ministry are found in *New Labour in Government*, ed. Steve Ludlam and Martin J. Smith (New York: St. Martin's, 2001), and *New Labour in Power*, ed. David Coates and Peter Lawler (Manchester: Manchester University Press, 2000). Richard Heffernan, *New Labour and Thatcherism: Political Change in Britain* (New York: St. Martin's, 2000), shows the continuity of New Labour with Thatcherism.

Vernon Bogdanor, *The Monarchy and the Constitution* (Oxford: Clarendon Press, 1995), takes a broad historical view of a continuing constitutional question. A valuable study is Helen Thompson, *The British Conservative Government and the European Exchange Mechanism, 1979–1994* (London: Pinter, 1996). On foreign policy, see Paul Sharp, *Thatcher's Diplomacy: The Revival of British Foreign Policy* (New York: St. Martin's, 1997), and Percy Cradock, *In Pursuit of British Interests: Reflections on Foreign Policy under Margaret Thatcher and John Major* (London: John Murray, 1997).

The earlier chapters of this book benefited greatly from the publications of the Institute of Contemporary British History, published by Blackwell.

Regrettably, there are no plans to update the series. The volumes used for this book are James Barber, *The Prime Minister since 1945* (Oxford: Blackwell, 1991); Dennis Kavanagh and Peter Morris, *Consensus Politics from Attlee to Major* (2nd ed., Oxford: Blackwell, 1994); Peter Dorey, *British Politics since 1945* (Oxford: Blackwell, 1995); Eric Shaw, *The Labour Party since 1945: Old Labour, New Labour* (Oxford: Blackwell, 1996); David Butler, *British General Elections since 1945* (2nd ed., Oxford: Blackwell, 1995); Robert M. Worcester, *British Public Opinion: A Guide to the History and Methodology of Political Opinion Polling* (Oxford: Blackwell, 1991); Kevin Theakston, *The Civil Service since 1945* (Oxford: Blackwell, 1995); Michael Dockrill, *British Defence since 1945* (Oxford: Blackwell, 1988); Alec Cairncross, *The British Economy since 1945: Economic Policy and Performance* (Oxford: Blackwell, 1995); Howard Glennerster, *British Social Policy since 1945* (2nd ed., Oxford: Blackwell, 2000); and Robert Taylor, *The Trade Union Question in British Politics: Government and Unions since 1945* (Oxford: Blackwell, 1993). My figures on unemployment are based on Appendix 5: Table A5.1 of this book. Figures concerning inflation (the retail price index) and earnings are based on Appendix 5: Table A5.6.

Other useful volumes from this series are Zig Layton-Henry, *The Politics of Immigration: Immigration, "Race," and "Race" Relations in Post-war Britain* (Oxford: Blackwell, 1992); Stephen George, *Britain and European Integration since 1945* (Oxford: Blackwell, 1995); and Paul Arthur and Keith Jeffery, *Northern Ireland since 1968* (2nd ed., Oxford: Blackwell, 1996).

Index

~

About the Author

Earl A. Reitan was born in Grove City, Minnesota, in 1925. He received his B.A. degree from Concordia College, Moorhead, Minn. (1948) and his Ph.D. degree in history from the University of Illinois (1954). Since 1954, he has been a professor of history (now emeritus) at Illinois State University, Normal, Ill.

His academic specialty is eighteenth-century Britain. His first book was *George III: Tyrant or Constitutional Monarch?* (Boston: D.C. Heath, 1965). He published a series of articles in scholarly journals on the political importance of the Civil List, 1689–1804, and the role of Edmund Burke in administrative reform, 1779–1783. He edited *The Best of the Gentleman's Magazine, 1731–1754* (Lewiston, N.Y.: Mellen, 1987). He is the author of *Politics, War, and Empire: The Rise of Britain to a World Power, 1688–1792* (Arlington Heights, Ill.: Harlan Davidson, 1994).

He is co-author and general editor of *English Heritage* (3rd ed., Arlington Heights, Ill.: Harlan Davidson, 1999), a textbook on English history, for which he wrote the chapters on nineteenth- and twentieth-century Britain. His book entitled *Tory Radicalism: Margaret Thatcher, John Major, and the Transformation of Modern Britain, 1979–1997* (Lanham, Md.: Rowman & Littlefield) was published in 1997. *The Thatcher Revolution: Margaret Thatcher, John Major, Tony Blair, and the Transformation of Modern Britain, 1979–2001* is a revised and extended version of *Tory Radicalism*.

He has told the story of his family and his early years in *Crossing the Bridge: Growing up Norwegian-American in Depression and War, 1925–1946* (Red

Wing, Minn.: Lone Oak Press, 1999). He is a veteran of World War II. *Riflemen: On the Cutting Edge of World War II* (Bennington, Vt.: Merriam Press, 2001) is based on his experiences in Italy and France, supplemented by archival research, relevant unit histories, and the memories of his comrades.

His wife, Carol, is an executive with the Collaborative Solutions Institute located in Bloomington, Illinois. They have two children: Julia, who lives in San Francisco, and Thomas, Chagrin Falls, Ohio. They have two grandchildren, William Andrew and Mary Veronica of Chagrin Falls.